T0313685

Rails through the Wiregrass

Rails through the
Wiregrass

A HISTORY OF THE
GEORGIA & FLORIDA
RAILROAD

H. Roger Grant

NORTHERN
ILLINOIS
UNIVERSITY
PRESS

DeKalb, IL

© 2006 by Northern Illinois University Press

Published by the Northern Illinois University Press, DeKalb, Illinois   60115

Library of Congress Cataloging-in-Publication Data

Grant, H. Roger, 1943–

Rails through the wiregrass : a history of the Georgia & Florida railroad / H. Roger Grant.

    p. cm.

Includes bibliographical references and index.

ISBN-13: 978-0-87580-365-4 (clothbound : alk. paper)

ISBN-10: 0-87580-365-2 (clothbound : alk. paper)

1. Georgia and Florida Railroad Co.—History. I. Title.

TF25.G464G73 2007

385.09758′8—dc22

2006010695

To Keith L. Bryant, Jr.

Contents

Preface

Writing a book-length account of the Georgia & Florida Railroad Company (G&F) has been a challenge. Although I have conducted in-depth studies of the Chicago & North Western, Chicago Great Western, Erie Lackawanna, and Wabash railroads, I have never before examined a carrier in the South. I needed to learn more about railroading in the region, but unfortunately, professional historians have largely ignored the subject, especially happenings in the twentieth century. The existing literature is limited. Scholars have even failed to examine some of the largest roads, including the Seaboard Air Line and the Southern Railway. Of course, no one has bothered to consider the G&F, the "God Forgotten," and only a few modest enthusiast-oriented publications about the carrier have appeared. The focus has mostly been on motive power and other pieces of rolling stock. When the G&F is mentioned, the company is often characterized in negative terms, being labeled a "wheezier of a road" or "a railroad mistake."

Some observers might argue that the G&F already has enjoyed its "fifteen minutes of fame." In two landmark railfan books the company receives due notice; Archie Robertson includes a photograph of a G&F passenger train taken at Moultrie, Georgia, in his widely praised *Slow Train to Yesterday: A Last Glance at the Local* (Boston: Houghton Mifflin, 1945), and Lucius Beebe, in his immensely popular *Mixed Train Daily: A Book of Short-Line Railroads* (New York: Dutton, 1947) (with 300 photographs by Charles M. Clegg, Jr.), features several images of the G&F in the "Classic Short Lines of the Old South" section. One beautifully crafted picture captures No. 5 at the Swainsboro, Georgia, station a few years before passenger service ended.

The tendency to ignore railroads in the South has been shortsighted. The region possesses a colorful and significant transport past not limited to the formative years of railroading or the era of the Civil War. The founder of the G&F, John Skelton Williams, who played an instrumental role in creating regional giant Seaboard Air Line, is as important as such strong-willed contemporary railroad leaders as Edwin Hawley, A. B. Stickney and Arthur E. Stilwell. Before the merger mania of the 1960s there were a dozen or so major roads in the Southlands and individually or collectively they deserve closer scrutiny. As the twenty-first century evolves, the two dominant carriers east of the Mississippi River, CSX and Norfolk Southern, are both headquartered in southern cities: Jacksonville, Florida, and Norfolk, Virginia, respectively. These giant corporations also have not been examined in any thoughtful way.

An understanding of the G&F unquestionably enhances knowledge of railroading in the most neglected region of the nation. Even though the company made a remarkable contribution to public betterment, it was a hard-luck road. Indeed, its financial difficulties make the G&F unusual, largely because it spent much of its corporate life in the hands of court-appointed receivers. Between the time that Williams and his associates officially launched the road in 1906 and its purchase by the Southern Railway fifty-seven years later, the G&F stood alone, independent of receivers, for only nineteen years. No other Class 1 carrier experienced a greater tenure under court control. Although other railroads endured long-term money woes, the G&F struggled longer and perhaps harder just to survive.

The G&F demonstrated an interesting quirkiness as a railway. It became the only carrier that for decades belonged to both the Association of American Railroads (for Class 1 roads) and the American Short Line Railroad Association. It is likely that management sought to exploit membership in these two trade organizations, but the company could hardly afford the luxury of these expenditures. Such a commitment suggests that the G&F really did not know whether it was a "big" or a "little" railroad. Arguably, though, the firm showed characteristics of both.

There is the temptation to call the G&F the "Little Engine That Could," but that would not be wholly correct. The G&F was much more the "Little Engine That Tried." In the process of explaining that perspective, I have sought to explore several themes. Of considerable importance were the company's enduring efforts to develop its service territory. By 1930 what the railroad repeatedly called "The G.& F. Land of Opportunity" stretched between Greenwood, South Carolina, and Madison, Florida, served by slightly more than 500 miles of track. The G&F did more than any other entity to encourage production of "bright" or "flue-cured" tobacco in the "Wiregrass Region" of south Georgia and north Florida, an area covered historically by large stands of trees and a dense undergrowth of distinctive grass. The relationship between the railroad and the federal bankruptcy court, too, is worthy of attention, and a distinctive part of the G&F story. As with my previous company histories, I remain intrigued by the human side of railroading. The G&F saga offers numerous insights into the roles of groups and individuals, ranging from labor to colorful, innovative employees and a not-so-reputable federal bankruptcy judge. As a southern road the G&F was deeply involved in something different from what I have encountered with carriers elsewhere, namely racial segregation. This meant "Jim Crow" depot waiting rooms, toilet facilities and passenger cars. It also involved limited advancement opportunities for people of color. Yet unlike most railroads outside the South the G&F employed African-American firemen, commonly called "fireboys," at times a demeaning racial slur. Nevertheless, blacks in engine service and many more who worked as track laborers, shop helpers, or freight handlers or who toiled in other low-level positions generally achieved social status and some economic independence in their home communities or neighborhoods.

I have told family members, colleagues, friends, and anyone who will listen that my labors on the G&F have been the most fascinating and, at times, most difficult work that I have encountered as a transportation historian. My only regret is that I am unlikely to find another railroad with so many intriguing dimensions.

Acknowledgments

I have been fortunate in receiving a variety of support in writing this history of the Georgia & Florida Railroad Company (G&F). Financial assistance is always appreciated. In 2004 the Mercantile Library of St. Louis, Missouri, awarded me a generous research fellowship. Then during Spring Semester 2005 when I served as the Maxwell C. Weiner Distinguished Visiting Professor in the Humanities at the University of Missouri—Rolla, this position included a handsome professional development stipend, permitting me to complete much of my research and writing.

But funding alone is hardly enough. Several former employees and friends of the G&F shared with me their memories and materials. Since this was frequently information that was lacking in archival holdings, I gained insights and data about important aspects of the railroad and the territory it once served. I am enormously indebted to Augusta, Georgia, residents Pete Belvin and Frank Napier for their assistance, encouragement and kindness.

I am also appreciative of the patience and knowledge of archivists and librarians at several institutions. Specifically, I owe much to the personnel of the Alderman Memorial Library, University of Virginia, Charlottesville; Curtis Laws Wilson Library, University of Missouri—Rolla; Digital Library and Archives, Virginia Tech University, Blacksburg; Georgia State Archives, Morrow; John W. Barriger III National Railroad Library of the St. Louis Mercantile Library; John W. Hargrett Rare Book and Manuscript Library, University of Georgia Libraries, Athens; Lowndes County Historical Society, Valdosta, Georgia; National Archives and Records Administration, College Park, Maryland; Norfolk Southern Corporation, Atlanta, Georgia; R. M. Cooper Library, Clemson University; Railroad Museum of Pennsylvania, Strasburg; Railway & Locomotive Historical Society Archives, Sacramento, California; and W. S. Hoole Special Collections Library, University of Alabama, Tuscaloosa.

I also wish to thank these individuals: the late James A. Bistline, Alexandria, Virginia; Lloyd W. Brown, Jr., Lexington, South Carolina; James Hagen, Wilmington, North Carolina; Cornelius W. Hauck, Cincinnati, Ohio; Larry Goolsby, Kensington, Maryland; Donald R. Hensley, Jr., Waynesburg, Pennsylvania; Richard ("Dick") L. Hillman, Marietta, Georgia; J. Parker

Lamb, Austin, Texas; Albert M. ("Al") Langley, North Augusta, South Carolina; Arthur Lloyd, Portola Valley, California; Charles McDiarmid, Augusta, Georgia; Edward Metz, Crawford, Nebraska; La Forest ("Tree") Meyer, Augusta, Georgia; John ("Jack") E. Parker, Aiken, South Carolina; Russell Tedder, North Little Rock, Arkansas; C. T. Trowell, Douglas, Georgia; Albert Weber, Fort Myers, Florida; and Tom Wilcockson, Woodstock, Illinois.

As with several previous book manuscripts, my long-time friend and former colleague at the University of Akron, Keith L. Bryant, Jr., gave a draft of this work a careful reading. Keith identified shortcomings, and hopefully they have been rectified.

Robert ("Bob") H. Hanson, an accomplished historian of railroads in the South, not only provided me with a wide variety of primary source materials and illustrations, but he painstakingly read a version of the manuscript. Moreover, Bob answered a host of questions about railroads in Georgia, especially shortlines, and he shared with me his meticulously compiled work, "The Railroads of Georgia, 1833–2000."

There would be no book without my wife, Martha Farrington Grant. She has always encouraged me to continue with my railroad interests; indeed, she suggested that I find a scholarly project in the South (and not too far from Clemson). And our daughter, Julia Dinsmore Grant, proposed the title for this work. In a sense the G&F has been a family affair.

Railroad Company Abbreviations

A&B	Atlantic & Birmingham Railroad
A&F	Augusta & Florida Railway
A&GSL	Atlantic & Gulf Short Line Railroad
AB&A	Atlanta, Birmingham & Atlantic Railroad
AB&C	Atlanta, Birmingham & Coast Railroad
ACL	Atlantic Coast Line Railroad
AG&S	Augusta, Gibson & Sandersville Railroad
AP&L	Americus, Preston & Lumpkin Railroad
AS	Augusta Southern Railroad
AUS	Augusta Union Station Company
C&O	Chesapeake & Ohio Railway
C&WC	Charleston & Western Carolina Railroad
CC&A	Charlotte, Columbia & Augusta Railroad
CofG	Central of Georgia Railway
DA&G	Douglas, Augusta & Gulf Railway
FC&P	Florida Central & Peninsular Railroad
FM&G	Florida, Midland & Georgia Railroad
G&A	Georgia & Alabama Railway
G&F	Georgia & Florida Railway/Railroad

G&FRy	Georgia & Florida Railway (second company)
G&FT	Georgia & Florida Terminal Company
GM&N	Gulf, Mobile & Northern Railroad
GS&F	Georgia Southern & Florida Railway
L&N	Louisville & Nashville Railroad
M&SW	Millen & South-western Railroad
MR	Midland Railway of Georgia
MS	Millen & Southern Railway
MS&MtV	Midville, Swainsboro & Mt. Vernon Railroad
MS&RB	Midville, Swainsboro & Red Bluff Railway
N&S	Nashville & Sparks Railroad
NOM&C	New Orleans, Mobile & Chicago Railway
NS	Norfolk Southern Corporation
OP&V	Ocilla, Pinebloom & Valdosta Railroad
P&N	Piedmont & Northern Railway
S&S	Savannah & Statesboro Railway
S&T	Sandersville & Tennille Railroad
SA&N	Savannah, Augusta & Northern Railway
SAL	Seaboard Air Line Railway
SA-L	Stillmore Air Line Railroad
SN	Statesboro Northern Railway
TFM&G	The Florida, Midland & Georgia Railroad
VS	Valdosta Southern Railway
VSR	Valdosta Southern Railroad
W&MtV	Wadley & Mt. Vernon Railroad
W&MtVE	Wadley & Mt. Vernon Extension Railroad
WSR	Wadley Southern Railway

Rails through the Wiregrass

CHAPTER ONE

Before the G&F

Southern Rails

At the dawn of the Railway Age the iron horse made a spectacular entry in the American South. In December 1830 the South Carolina Canal and Rail Road Company began regularly scheduled service for a few miles in the vicinity of Charleston and quickly extended operations westward. Three years later the company completed what was then the longest railroad in the world, a line that stretched from Charleston to Hamburg, South Carolina, situated on the east bank of the navigable and strategic Savannah River, allowing business interests in Charleston to divert some of the mostly agricultural traffic that was destined for Savannah. This pioneer railroad grew and on the eve of the Civil War operated a network of 242 miles of track and a fleet of sixty-two steam locomotives, more than any other southern road. By 1860, however, regions outside Dixie had dramatically embraced the railroad, helping to shift the direction and mode of commerce between the states of New England, the Middle Atlantic, the Old Northwest and the Upper Mississippi Valley. Still, southerners enjoyed access to hundreds of miles of iron rails. Virginia (including the future West Virginia) boasted more than 1,800 miles, Georgia claimed the second largest network with about 1,400 miles, and South Carolina had nearly 1,000 miles.[1]

By the outbreak of the Civil War, then, some Georgians found that the iron horse had shattered their isolation or at least made travel and shipping faster and more convenient. Such carriers as the Central Railroad & Banking Company of Georgia (the state's first chartered road), the Georgia Railroad (the state's oldest operating road), the Muscogee Railroad, the Southwestern Railroad and the Western & Atlantic Railroad had helped to usher in the new age of transportation. No longer did citizens depend so heavily on the navigable inland rivers. Yet for some time, traffic remained active on the Altamaha, Chattahoochee, Flint, Oconee, Ocmulgee and, of course, Savannah rivers, even though periods of high and low water might preclude waterborne commerce. As late as 1908 navigation on the Altamaha River and its principal tributaries covered approximately 480 miles, namely 131 miles from the mouth on the Atlantic Ocean to the junction of the Oconee and Ocmulgee rivers, 147 miles along the Oconee to Milledgeville, and 202 miles via the Ocmulgee to Macon. (Occasionally shallow-draft steamboats with their small, high-pressure engines had moved on the Oconee above Milledgeville to the Athens area but only during periods of high water.)[2]

Undeniably the Civil War caused a dramatic setback for southern railroads, including companies that served Georgia. There was the unprecedented wear and tear on track and rolling stock and toward war's end, General William Tecumseh Sherman's destructive and long-remembered "March to the Sea" that left some carriers "in tatters for miles." Then there was the general economic malaise. The war brought about the widespread collapse of the traditional southern plantation culture. Investors and corporations lost virtually all their money in Confederate bonds and currency, and the overall credit of nearly every enterprise, including locally based railroads, was badly strained. As a result, much of Dixie, including the future service territory of the Georgia & Florida Railroad (G&F), became an economic backwater. During the Gilded Age most "smart" money flowed into northern and western commercial, manufacturing, and transportation projects. To make matters worse for railroads in the South, the sudden and deadly Panic of 1873, which triggered several years of deep depression, threw approximately two-thirds of the region's railway mileage into the hands of court-appointed receivers.[3]

Nevertheless, the financial difficulties experienced by Georgians and other southerners during the post-war period did not either stop a host of railroad proposals or end construction. Many new or expanded carriers sold securities, laid track, acquired rolling stock, and hired employees. The motivation of their backers was often to exploit some natural resource, usually timber and naval stores (turpentine, tar, pitch, and rosins), or to haul agricultural products, primarily cotton. In an 1890 prospectus for the Middle Georgia & Atlantic Railway (later the Central of Georgia Railway), which proposed a 240-mile line between Atlanta and Savannah, promoters told potential investors that "after an examination of the country through which the Middle Georgia and Atlantic Railway is chartered to run, the first thing will occur to one passing over the line is, that it seems incredible, such a country, endowed by nature with all that is requisite to make a railroad possible, should have been left so long without good transportation facilities."[4]

The writer of the Middle Georgia & Atlantic Railway prospectus, however, ignored the negative. By the latter part of the nineteenth century large sections of Georgia, especially the northeast, had become a hotbed for political radicalism that culminated in the Populist Party crusade of the 1890s, spearheaded by the demagogic Tom Watson of Thomson. Farmers felt the sting of dropping cotton prices that between 1875 and 1894 fell from 14.1 cents to 4.6 cents per pound (eight cents per pound was considered the break-even price), prompting thousands to flock to the largely self-help Farmers' Alliance and later to the aggressive People's Party. This political

organization's famed Omaha Platform, which demanded government ownership of railroads and other socialistic programs, gave pause to promoters and
investors alike, as did popular populist epithets of "railroad tyrants," "silver con-
spiracy," and "the grasp of the gigantic, cold-blooded money trust."[5]

Even though the People's Party in Georgia did not fizzle out immediately
following defeat of the Democratic-Populist fusion presidential tickets of
1896 (Williams Jennings Bryan and Arthur Sewall and Bryan and Watson),
the state generally turned more pro-business. After 1898 a succession of
staunchly conservative governors held power. It would not be until 1906
that the progressive movement, initially supported by Watson and fellow
hard-line reformers, gained state-wide clout with the gubernatorial election
of Hoke Smith. Resembling earlier populists, the Smith regime, which controlled Georgia between 1907 and 1911, focused on perceived railroad shortcomings and went so far as to embrace public ownership. During Smith's
first term Georgians experienced the greatest number of major reform measures, including a stronger railroad commission. Indeed, the effectiveness of
this regulatory body prompted other southern states to copy this popular
Smith triumph.[6]

It would be in this interlude between active populism and the progressive
experience in Georgia that financiers felt more comfortable about investing
in local railroad projects. Even though the state's agrarians continued to be
plagued by remnants of the decades-old crop-lien system, and the percentage of farms operated by owners decreased from 55.1 in 1880 to 34.6 in
1910, the overall economy improved. Farm bankruptcies declined, farm
prices increased and stabilized, agricultural credit expanded, and land values
rose, helping to bolster the notion that attractive opportunities existed.
Especially appealing were the areas south and west of Augusta and Macon,
the "Wiregrass Region" (see Chapter 5) that seemingly cried out for better
transportation to develop its vast resources, whether timber or agriculture.
Urban growth also seemed likely, and that meant the potential for more
freight and passenger traffic. Moreover, the area was comparatively easy for
the railroad builder, except at places where waterways, swamps, and low-
lands necessitated bridges and enhanced grading.

The impact that railroads had on Georgia between 1898 and 1906 was
enormous. Hundreds of miles of new line appeared, providing the state an
impressive network of more than 7,000 miles. While the cobweb of lines
knew no geographical bounds, railroad services expanded impressively in
the Wiregrass Region. Construction had a wide-ranging impact, including
growth of a host of "railroad towns" that in 1905 precipitated lawmakers'
creating eight additional counties as part of the "New County Movement."
The demise of subsistence farming and herding and expansion of the lumber, turpentine, and other industries and commercial agriculture reflected a
reinvigorated Peach state. This growth reinforced the evangelical "New
South" or "Capitalist Eden in the American South" creed espoused by Henry

Grady, Walter Hines Page, Henry Watterson, and others that Georgia was the land of unlimited opportunities that would come about through agricultural and industrial modernization, reconciliation with the North, and racial peace.[7]

By the twentieth century Georgia had a mixture of large and small railroads, but much of the recent construction involved small private and common-carrier "tramways" or "tap roads" that appeared in the sprawling Southern Pine Barrens in the lower part of the state. These projects were hardly threatening to even the most advanced reformer; they certainly lacked any elements of being or becoming parts of a corporate "octopus." Nearly all of these pint-size pikes were poorly built and cheaply equipped, or as a Georgia newspaper editor aptly labeled them: "little spike and jerk-water roads." Nevertheless, these companies expanded the presence of the iron horse and in some instances offered promise for larger, more substantially built carriers to evolve or expand. It would be from a half-dozen of these minor railroads that a group of southern investors, spearheaded by Virginian John Skelton Williams, would use to assemble the G&F, a railroad launched in 1906 that soon stretched between Augusta, Georgia, and Madison, Florida.[8]

BUILDING BLOCKS OF THE G&F

The beginning point in the saga of the G&F involves several predecessor roads. These constituent parts were a somewhat motley assortment of predominantly Georgia shortlines that ranged in length from the 11.6-mile Nashville & Sparks Railroad (N&S), which connected the two communities of its corporate name, to the 55.6-mile Douglas, Augusta & Gulf Railway (DA&G), which stretched between Barrows Buff and Nashville. Although each carrier possessed it own history, collectively these railroads shared much in common: they were of modest length and inexpensively constructed; owned light-weight motive power and only a few pieces of often second-hand rolling stock; and had local investors and managers.[9]

These forerunners of the "new Georgia & Florida Railway system" left only a limited historical record. Following passage of the monumental and far-reaching Valuation Act of 1913, representatives of the Interstate Commerce Commission, charged with implementing the legislation, frequently commented that they could not gather the needed information about these little roads, largely because records either had not been generated or had been discarded or lost. But this caused only limited consternation among the progressive, consumer-sensitive lawmakers who created this landmark statute. When reformers sought to determine "original cost" of the national railway network, they knew that the major railroads must be thoroughly examined. That is where troubling corporate chicanery, for example issuance of "watered stock," most likely had occurred, or so they argued.[10]

Georgia & Florida Railway
Predecessor Companies

Even though the predecessor railroads of the G&F left only a scattered paper trail, including local and regional newspaper coverage, it is possible to glean some pertinent information. The scope and nature of these carriers reveal that creators of the G&F were generally blessed with existing trackage that *could* be assembled into a logical network of lines stretching from Augusta, Georgia, a vibrant manufacturing, trading, and railroad center of nearly 40,000 residents that claimed to be "the greatest cotton milling center in the South," southwestwardly to north Florida, "with the view to its possible extension on to the Gulf of Mexico," possibly to the bustling port of Tampa.[11]

As with the histories of virtually every American railroad, the process of system building occurred. Even though the G&F never became a large carrier, slightly more than 500 miles at its peak, the corporate genealogy consists of a remarkable number of once-independent and at times quaint and colorful carriers.

AUGUSTA & FLORIDA RAILWAY

The plan developed about 1905 and speedily executed by John Skelton Williams and his Richmond, Virginia, and Baltimore, Maryland, associates to form a railroad that might possess a bright future by vastly improving the linkage between Augusta, south Georgia, and north Florida, thereby eliminating "circuitous and broken journeys, obstructive and discouraging alike to commerce and travel," involved the Augusta & Florida Railway (A&F). By 1906 this 29.9-mile road ran between Keysville, Georgia, on the north and Midville, Georgia, on the south, thus allowing for interchange at its northern terminus with the Augusta Southern Railroad (AS), nee Augusta, Gibson & Sandersville Railroad (see Chapter 3), a rehabilitated former narrow-gauge line, and at its southern terminus with the Central of Georgia Railway (CofG), whose main stem linked Savannah and Atlanta. (Midville claimed to be the "greatest lumber shipping point along the Central.") At Midville the A&F also connected with what would become a controlled property, the Atlantic & Gulf Short Line Railroad (A&GSL), a sixteen-mile carrier that much earlier had opened under the banner of the Midville, Swainsboro & Red Bluff Railway (MS&RB) southward from Midville to Swainsboro, seat of Emanuel County. In fact, the railroad trade press reported that "It [A&F] is practically an extension of the Midville, Swainsboro & Red Bluff."[12]

The A&F experienced a short corporate life. On November 16, 1904, the company received its Georgia charter and nearly three years later the G&F absorbed the railroad, although the corporate shell remained until October 12, 1910. Apparently, local capitalists, spearheaded by Allen W. Jones, "[the railroad's] leading promoter" and a Savannah investor-speculator, created the A&F with the announced intent to "build a line from Augusta to Midville, Ga., 60 miles." In late 1904 construction began on the lightly graded right-of-way northward from Midville through the somewhat undulating and mostly cleared countryside toward Keysville. By February 1905 along the southern portion of the newly graded line "the work of laying ties is going on in a rush." In early April a railroad official told the *Swainsboro Forest-Blade* that "we have about 10 or 12 miles ready for the track and plenty of material to complete the work with." By late summer of 1905 trackmen had installed the last untreated ties and light steel rails to Keysville, allowing for connecting freight and passenger service to Augusta via the AS that began on September 18. Completion meant that recently harvested cotton "from one of the richest cotton sections in Georgia" could move conveniently to the Augusta marketplace. With the opening of the A&F, shippers had to worry less about the region's endemic bad public roads.[13]

As so frequently occurred with construction, commercial activities accelerated at trackside. Although the newly built A&F was a small enterprise, its promoters still found opportunities to either create or expand the communities of Gough, Oatts, Rosier, and St. Clair. In September 1905 the *Augusta Chronicle* told readers that "already town lots are being laid off and stores erected" and optimistically believed that "the wholesale and a large part of the retail trade of this rich and unexploited section will now be secured by Augusta merchants, whereas it formally went altogether to Savannah." For Augustans the A&F was a potentially valuable asset; urban rivalry in Georgia was far from dead.[14]

Until the A&F entered the orbit of the G&F, the railroad operated in a typical shortline fashion. Its motive power was modest, yet adequate for its needs: an older 4-4-0 American-type locomotive and a 4-6-0 Ten Wheeler, which in 1905 the company had purchased from the Baldwin Locomotive Works. The remaining rolling stock included a coach and "combine," the latter a combination coach and baggage car, and both featured separate sections for white and "colored" travelers. A daily-except-Sunday mixed train (freight and passenger) and a triweekly local freight train met the road's transportation requirements.[15]

Even before the G&F became formally involved with the A&F, management understandably wanted to extend beyond tiny Keysville. In August 1905, prior to the driving of the last spike, the A&F approached the Southern Railway (SR), which had earlier acquired the AS, for trackage rights between Keysville and Augusta. The SR, however, resisted, prompting the A&F to announce that it intended to build directly to Augusta, a distance of about thirty miles. But unlike the initial construction, the proposed extension would involve coping with the steep terrain that surrounded Augusta and the Savannah River valley.[16]

ATLANTIC & GULF SHORT LINE RAILROAD

The expansive nature of the A&F can be related directly to its corporate relationship with the A&GSL. By the time the A&F contemplated how best to reach Augusta, the company had taken control of the A&GSL; the official lease arrangement occurred on November 22, 1905. Five years earlier the

A&GSL itself had gone through a reorganization, and in the process it had dropped its quaint Midville, Swainsboro & Red Bluff Railway moniker.[17]

Much of the history of the MS&RB is obscure. The 16.7-mile common carrier had begun its official corporate life in 1887 as the Midville, Swainsboro & Mt. Vernon Railroad (MS&MtV), although a year later its owner, Jesse Thompson, an Augusta lumberman "largely interested in lumber business throughout the state," received a Georgia charter for the MS&RB. It appears, however, that physically much, if not all, of the MS&RB predates 1887. Apparently in the late 1870s a crudely constructed tram or logging railroad opened on a superficial grade between Midville and the Summertown area, about six miles to the south. Later this primitive pike reached the "George Wiggins Place," a mile or so north of the Modoc community in Emanuel County, and it entered Swainsboro in 1887, the year of the MS&MtV incorporation.[18]

The overall construction strategy of the MS&MV can only be surmised by its corporate name. Presumably, the destination was the village of Mt. Vernon, seat of Montgomery County with a population of only several hundred, or the navigable Oconee River that flowed a few miles to the north, but these locations were never reached. In time, the MS&RB arrived in Swainsboro and within a few years this southern terminus offered a connecting link with another lightly built shortline, the thirty-three-mile Stillmore Air-Line Railway (SA-L). In July 1893 the SA-L ran its first trains between Swainsboro and Collins, Georgia, the latter to the southeast and located on the Georgia & Alabama Railway (Seaboard Air Line). These railroads, albeit small, stimulated Swainsboro, prompting a neighboring newspaper, the *True Citizen* of Waynesboro, to proclaim: "Swainsboro is none of your little one horse towns. She's a young city—up-to-date and first-class in every particular."[19]

The MS&RB developed into the quintessential Southern shortline. "The equipment was of the pioneer type—a small wood-burning engine, fitted with an odd shaped spark arrester to prevent . . . forest [fires] . . ., a combination passenger coach, [and] such freight cars as the traffic justified." Employees were recruited locally and they included men of color who likely worked as track laborers, freight handlers, or firemen. When compared to the trunk roads of the region, pay was substantially less for whites and still less for blacks. The Swainsboro newspaper noted, for example, that "Mr. J. F. Underwood has resigned his position as engineer on the M.S. & R.B. . . . [and] will go south in a few days, where he has made arrangements to accept a more lucrative position," a hardly surprising happening. For much of its existence, the MS&RB dispatched two daily-except-Sunday mixed trains between Midville and Swainsboro. The published timetable indicated that each movement took an hour and fifteen minutes to make a through run, with scheduled stops at Summertown, Wiggins, and Modoc. Perhaps sensitive to being called the "Miserable, Sorry & Rough Road," management announced publicly, "Trains always on time. No Delay." Not only were these unlikely truths, but the unballasted track with its forty- and fifty-six-pound (to the yard) steel rail spiked to locally harvested crossties and at times resting on a spongy grade surely did not make for a smooth, comfortable ride.[20]

The transportation-starved citizens of the greater Emanuel County area accepted the MS&RB for what it was. Indeed, in 1904 an area newspaper praised the carrier for being "one of the best and safest short lines of railway in Georgia." About the same time a Columbia University–trained botanist, who studied plant life in the Southeast and traveled a variety of shortlines in order to conduct his field research, noted in his diary, "M.S. & R.B. RR much better than Sylvania RR [fifteen-mile road between Sylvania and Rocky Ford, Georgia]. Makes about 20 m. an hour."[21]

Once the hard times that had been ongoing for decades showed signs of dissipating, a feeling developed among patrons that the MS&RB might become the nucleus for a longer railroad, reaching perhaps Augusta or some other strategic railroad center. Early in the century rumors circulated that the property would be pushed to the southwest, ultimately to the boom town of Soperton, the soon-to-be seat of newly formed Treutlen County. At this point a connection could be made with the expanding Macon, Dublin & Savannah Railroad, officially "The Vidalia Route" but jokingly dubbed "Mud, Dirt & Sand" by residents. Something would surely happen to make the MS&RB more of a local asset.[22]

Although the MS&RB and the successor A&GSL never reached Soperton, union with the Augusta & Florida brightened the transportation picture for residents of Emanuel County and vicinity. It appears that Jesse Thompson, who owned the Midville-Swainsboro line and presumably had an interest in the Midville-Keysville property, and Allen Jones of the A&F believed that a longer, largely north-south route could be formed, a precursor of what the G&F would accomplish. Speculation appeared, too, that Thompson and Jones might join with George Brinson, developer of the SA-L, creating a "mini-system" with additional strategic interchange points. Newspaper reports also noted that the A&F had surveyed a line between Midville and Garfield and also to Summit, Georgia, designed to create an interchange with the Millen & South-western Railroad (M&SW), a fifty-three-mile road that connected Millen and Vidalia. Whatever the speculation, the local citizenry was hopeful about prospects for more and better railroads. "The territory is too fine and too much has already been done in that direction for the work to be left incomplete."[23]

MILLEN & SOUTH-WESTERN RAILROAD

The Millen & South-western Railroad became a major component of the G&F. By the end of the 1890s this important Georgia shortline stretched more than fifty miles through pine woods and farm land between Millen, seat of Jenkins County (a county created in 1905, but then in Screven

County), and Vidalia, seat of Toombs County (also formed in 1905 and formerly located in Montgomery County). As with most carriers that the G&F absorbed, the M&SW consisted of predecessor firms. The earliest unit dated from 1889 with formation of the Rogers & Summit Railroad, intended to be mostly a lumber-hauler. Its backers sought to link Rogers, located on the CofG, with Stillmore, a distance of nearly thirty-two miles to the southwest; the following year they succeeded with their track-building endeavors. Soon, however, the owners, mostly area lumbermen, faced financial difficulties and quickly reorganized the property as the Millen & Southern Railway (M&S). As part of this restructuring, the larger, more important Millen, which was strategically situated at the junction of the Augusta line and the main Savannah-Macon stem of the CofG, replaced Rogers as the northern terminus, leading to the relocation of approximately ten miles of line in the vicinity of Thrift, Georgia. Apparently the original road was lightly built. By 1895 only half the mileage had steel rails, and rail weight varied from forty to fifty pounds, indeed true-to-type. Still, in 1894, the worst year of the depression of the 1890s, the little carrier generated net earnings of slightly more than $26,000 and seemed to be financially durable.[24]

Nevertheless, the M&S failed in any sense to become a money machine. The continued hard times forced another reorganization, and on October 28, 1897, under a foreclosure sale of October 5, the M&S gave way to the Millen & Southwestern Railroad. Now owned by the local Durden family, the railroad improved the roadbed, track, and rolling stock and built a small shop facility near Millen. As a consequence, residents received better, more dependable service. By the dawn of the twentieth century, the M&SW operated three daily mixed trains over the Millen-Stillmore line, making convenient travel connections for Atlanta, Augusta, Macon, and Savannah through Millen and Stillmore.[25]

Moreover, the M&SW showed an interest in expanding. As the century began, rumors spread that the company planned to push fifty miles or so northward to Augusta, largely paralleling the CofG, and also expected to build to the south or southwest, perhaps to Vidalia or even beyond. Although the railroad never extended past Millen, construction did occur in a southwestwardly direction. In the later part of 1903 work began on this twenty-one-mile extension from Stillmore through Selma (and connection with the just completed fourteen-mile Garbutt & Donovan Short Line Railway, a poorly built common carrier) and Normantown to Vidalia. The routing seemed wise; "the line will penetrate a splendid section of Georgia. . . . All along the way there are said to be large lumber mills, with an output of many tons of material yearly; the turpentine industry is also worked there, and there is, in addition, much cotton produced in that vicinity." Not inconsequentially, Vidalia, the newly established southern terminal, was a town on the move. "Vidalia . . . is rapidly becoming a city of no inconsiderable proportions," observed the *Atlanta Constitution*, "various industries like cotton oil mills, compresses, etc., being already located there."[26]

By 1905 a lengthened M&SW fared well and in the process received kudos from the public. "No wonder, though, that this road is prosperous, for a more clever and accommodating set of officials and employees cannot be found," opined the *Swainsboro Forest-Blade*. The company's daily freight train was busy, "and you hardly ever see one shorter than twelve or fifteen loaded cars and many times thirty to forty." Moreover, the quality of passenger operations improved noticeably on what was self-proclaimed as "The Short Cut Route." Since the line did not serve directly Monte, Georgia, location of the company's headquarters, trains needed to back into town from Monte Junction, a distance of about two miles. But early in 1905 the M&SW put on a "special" shuttle that ran over the stub "which meets all passenger trains on the main line." More significantly, the M&SW offered "Three First-Class Passenger Trains—Daily," including No. 1, the "Twilight Limited," that left Millen at 4:45 a.m. and arrived in Stillmore at 6:05 a.m. and in Vidalia at 7:00 a.m., allowing for a connection with all early trains to the east and west, a convenience for travelers and an aid for dispatching U.S. mail. Although the "Twilight Limited" was hardly a ballast scorcher, the train's average speed of slightly more than twenty-three miles per hour made it far more attractive than travel over the poor-quality local dirt roads in a buggy or wagon behind a team of horses or mules or in the occasional pioneer automobile. "The Millen and Southwestern railroad has the most complete and accommodating schedule to be found on any line of road—long or short, in this part of the country," concluded an observer in a burst of hyperbole. And these trains "give the traveling people an opportunity to attend to business anywhere along the line of this road without having to lose but very little time waiting for [connecting] trains."[27]

DOUGLAS, AUGUSTA & GULF RAILWAY

Although the M&SW evolved into a respectable shortline, the crown jewel of the gestating G&F, at least strategically, was the fifty-six-mile Douglas, Augusta & Gulf Railway. Before the G&F made its corporate debut, the DA&G, this core carrier, took control of a portion of another lumber hauler, the Ocilla & Valdosta Railroad (O&V), forming a small, integrated network in south Georgia. Specifically, the DA&G purchased nearly thirty miles of the recently completed O&V that operated over the one-time tramway of the Southern Pine Company between Broxton and Hazlehurst, seat of Jeff Davis County, leaving the O&V with about twenty-five miles between Ocilla and Broxton that in 1907 another lumber road, the Broxton, Hazlehurst & Douglas (soon the Fitzgerald, Ocilla & Broxton), absorbed.[28]

As suggested with acquisition of the O&V trackage, the genealogy of the DA&G reveals a rich heritage. The original component was a short carrier with a long name, the Wadley & Mt. Vernon Extension Railroad (W&MtVE),

explainable because its backers already operated another shortline with a similar moniker, the Wadley & Mt. Vernon Railroad (W&MtV). Chartered in 1901 and constructed in 1901–1902, the W&MtVE linked Douglas, Georgia, the rapidly developing seat of Coffee County, which was quickly becoming more than a "stop in the road," with Broxton, an established lumber and trade center. In 1904 a visitor succinctly described Broxton: "a typical wiregrass sawmill town of several hundred inhabitants. Several brick stores there." After completion of the line on August 30, 1902, two mixed trains, using a coach purchased from the Atlantic & Birmingham Railroad (A&B), operated daily over the nine miles that sliced through pine barrens having been "heavily lumbered and turpentined." The trip took about thirty minutes. Arrival of the iron horse delighted residents of the former "inland" and growing Broxton, which by 1910 claimed a population of 1,040. "The train makes very good time, . . . making close connections with the A&B from Waycross [Georgia]. Only three cents a mile is charged for fare and the freight rates are reasonable."[29]

Although Douglas had already received railroad service, first in 1895 from a twenty-mile, short-lived logging road, the Douglas & McDonald Railroad (Douglas to Axon, Georgia), and then three years later from the Waycross Air Line Railroad (future core of the Atlantic Coast Line, nee Atlantic & Birmingham and Atlanta, Birmingham & Atlantic railroads), citizens of this "Queen City of the Wiregrass" were excited about the appearance of the W&MtVE. "We are anxious to have a road so that our Broxton friends may come to see us often," wrote the editor of the *Douglas Breeze* in a piece titled, "On to Broxton." "And we can go out among them, help them cuss and discuss politics, enroll their names as subscribers and find out about their needs in the job printing line."[30]

Soon after the W&MtVE reached Broxton, the company added mileage. Construction crews pushed further northward to a hamlet on the Ocmulgee River, completing in March 1904 their labors after an annoyingly long delay in obtaining rail. This new end of track stopped at strategic Barrow's Bluff, that unlike what its name suggested, was on "a big bend [of the Ocmulgee], but bluff not over 10 ft. high & therefore subject to overflow." Thus the company could boast of being a twenty-mile road with an important outlet at Douglas via the A&B and access at Barrow's Bluff to water navigation.[31]

Extension of the W&MtVE delighted Coffee Countians. The little road provided new travel opportunities. Special trains, for example, handled crowds that flocked to "Bishop Bayfield's camp meeting at Barrow's Bluff." Citizens took pride in the road's new locomotive, likely an American 4-4-0, that came from the machine shop of the nearby Gillon Company in Waycross. Most of all, residents believed that steamboat connections to the Georgia coast at Darien for Brunswick and Savannah would allow freight charges to drop, some even dramatically. And, again, the railroad might well become part of a longer, stronger rail network.[32]

Promoters of the W&MtVE sought more than a line between Douglas and Barrow's Bluff. These individuals, who included lumbermen Captain T. J. James, Sr. of Wadley, Georgia; T. W. Garbutt, also of Wadley; Captain J. W. Miller of Macon, Georgia; and W. W. McDonald of Douglas, intended to link the W&MtVE with their already established W&MtV. In 1889 the latter firm opened as a twenty-nine-mile private logging road between Wadley, a Jefferson County community strategically situated on the CofG, and Ricksville, Georgia. Within a year it became a common carrier, and early in the twentieth century reached Rockledge, forty miles southwest of Wadley. Backers of the W&MtV hoped to push further southwestward, perhaps ultimately extending to Fitzgerald (after 1907 in Ben Hill County), an evolving rail hub of south-central Georgia. In the process of expansion, the W&MtVE and W&MtV roads would be physically united, presumably by bridging the Ocmulgee River at Barrow's Bluff. If the W&MtV ultimately stretched between Wadley and Fitzgerald, the W&MtVE would likely become an appendage of the main stem, connecting somewhere northeast of Fitzgerald. There was even a proposal to go further northward, terminating at either of the twin communities of Helena or McRae, Georgia, the former being located on the SAL and SR and the latter on the SR. Talk also occurred of these affiliated properties reaching Augusta, probably through construction, purchases, and leases, a scheme paralleling what promoters of the G&F would eventually accomplish. Moreover, newspaper reports suggested that the W&MtVE, locally dubbed the "James Road," would likely go southward to the Lowndes County capital of Valdosta, by way of the Berrien County community of Milltown (later Lakeland).[33]

The fate of the W&MtV turned out much differently than what was initially discussed. In 1906 the property consolidated with the SA-L to form the eighty-nine-mile Wadley Southern Railway (WSR), a financial transaction that pleased Capt. James and his colleagues. This new company never entered the orbit of the G&F, serving instead as a feeder for its ultimate buyer, CofG, and expansion came to an end. Following World War I the WSR became a chronic money loser and in the late 1920s the abandonment process began.[34]

Before the DA&G acquired the W&MtVE in 1905, construction occurred south of Douglas. This new trackage, which connected Douglas with Nashville, the lively seat of Berrien County, involved two separate undertakings, namely purchasing in 1905 the Ocilla, Pinebloom & Valdosta Railroad (OP&V) between Pinebloom (Willacoochee Crossing) and Nashville, and building a connecting link from Douglas to Pinebloom-Willacoochee.[35]

At the start of the 20th century the initial segment of the Douglas and Nashville trackage came into being, handiwork of the OP&V, a private logging road that operated extensively in Berrien and Coffee counties. The firm's principal line, which dated from the 1890s, extended fifty-eight miles between Lax in southwestern Coffee County and Garrant's, southwest of

Pinebloom in Berrien county. As with most tram operations, trackage expanded and contracted as stands of lumber were worked, and for the OP&V that meant a maximum size of about seventy miles. Although the OP&V did not receive its official charter as a common carrier until March 22, 1905, two years earlier the company had begun operating regularly on twenty miles of cheaply built track structure between Nashville and Willacoochee Crossing. Significantly, the road provided a mixed train for the convenience of the public and the enhancement of revenues. According to the *Nashville Herald* there was a daily accommodation that departed Willacoochee Crossing (near Pinebloom) at 11:40 a.m., arriving in Nashville at 1:05 p.m. and returning at 5:10 p.m., and provided connections with passenger trains on the Albany-Waycross route of the Atlantic Coast Line (ACL).[36]

The ownership of the OP&V was in the hands of the Gray family. The president was Captain Ben B. Gray, who also headed the Gray Lumber Company, based in Pinebloom. In the spring 1904, Gray and the owners of the W&MtVE struck a deal that involved linking their two properties. The OP&V would push northward from a point known as Leliaton, adjoining Pinebloom and a station on the ACL three miles from Willacoochee, to the Satilla River, a stream that flowed southeastward through Coffee County. The W&MtVE would also build to the river. As with most shortlines of the region, the project involved "all home capital in construction and equipment." About the same time the OP&V decided to build into Willacoochee from Willacoochee Crossing, installing a short spur and soon thereafter constructing a depot. An "enthusiastic" mass meeting of Willacoochee residents had prompted Captain Gray to commit to these much-applauded betterments.[37]

During the summer of 1904 gangs of workers engaged by both the OP&V and W&MtVE labored furiously to connect Leliaton and Douglas. "On to Willacoochee is the slogan now," proclaimed the *Douglas Breeze* in August. "The crossing of the Wadley & Mt. Vernon over the track of the Atlantic & Birmingham [Waycross Air Line], about 200 yards west of the latter's depot, was perfected last Thursday morning. . . . The work of track laying will be pushed to the Satilla as fast as possible." Added the *Breeze*, "On the other side of the river Capt. Ben Gray is at work, and, although he has one mile more than the builders on this side had, he expects to be ready to meet the Douglas end track layers without delay. So it's on to 'Coochee.'"[38]

The only troubling problem that affected construction south of Douglas involved labor. In order to keep costs low, the W&MtVE hired convicts from Coffee County. But soon state prison authorities ruled that these men could not be leased to the railroad, and so they returned to assignments of building and maintaining public roads. The need to find replacement workers slowed the process of installing the track structure and the Satilla River bridge.[39]

By fall rail services had begun. Trains ran between Barrow's Bluff and Nashville, with "daily double" round-trip service between Broxton and Pinebloom and single daily service between Pinebloom and Nashville. This scheduling surely pleased patrons north of Pinebloom but it annoyed residents to the south. "We want two trains," proclaimed the *Nashville Herald,* "and believe Mr. Gray will give them to us if he can possibly do so." Within months Nashvillians got their wish. Soon, too, the OP&V and W&MtVE contracted with the Southern Express Company for package service.[40]

Owners of the OP&V and W&MtVE wanted more than just a railroad between Barrow's Bluff and Nashville. As 1905 began, representatives of the two companies agreed to work together on future expansion, a step that on March 7, 1906, led to formal merger. Not long thereafter Ben Gray sold his interest in the Nashville to Satilla River line, receiving approximately $150,000 in cash and stock in the DA&G, the new name that in January 1905 directors had approved for the W&MtVE. During 1905 discussions by DA&G-OP&V management centered on extending to some point beyond the Ocmulgee River, likely following plans mentioned earlier when the W&MtVE and W&MtV contemplated growth. Also pondered was reaching the Gulf of Mexico by way of Adel, Georgia. Yet before the enlarged DA&G could build in any direction, the G&F had gained control.[41]

Prior to the DA&G losing its corporate identity on August 12, 1907, the railroad resembled most shortlines. The company operated with vintage equipment that rumbled slowly over poor track. Nevertheless crews were usually courteous and accommodating, whether "spotting" a freight car on a private siding or stopping a mixed train at a rural road crossing to receive or discharge a rider. The DA&G's timecard, which became effective on June 10, 1905, showed daily double service between Broxton and Nashville and three daily movements between Broxton and Douglas. The short Barrows Bluff to Broxton segment, however, had the least service, featuring one daily-except-Sunday southbound train and curiously only a Tuesday and Saturday northbound run.[42]

As with both big and little roads, the DA&G repeatedly ballyhooed its passenger services, running church, picnic, and other specials. In an unusual public promotion, William Touchton, the road's General Freight and Passenger Agent, in January 1905 offered a free annual pass "to the person guessing the exact number of passengers carried between Douglas and Broxton during the month of August, 1904." Touchton told potential entrants that "Remember, it is free and you may be the lucky one. Just to give you an idea I wish to say we carried 1,896 passenger between Douglas and Broxton during July 1904." Unfortunately, the local press failed to publish a follow-up story on the correct number and winner's name.[43]

Although the number of trains dispatched by the DA&G, including occasional "extras," generally met public need, the overall quality of service was often found to be wanting, at least when compared with the M&SW, a similarly sized carrier. The leading complaints involved speed and schedule reliability. "Trains on the Douglas, Augusta & Gulf run so slowly," snarled a local editor, "that a man can walk in the opposite direction and keep up with them." Citizens of Nashville fussed about the poor quality of the road's facilities. "There is [sic] absolutely no depot facilities here," observed the *Nashville Herald* in September 1905. "If a lady has occasion to board a train here at night now and during the winter she has to stand out in the cold, or sit down on a suit case, box or cross tie." The community felt shortchanged; more than a year before Captain Gray had promised to erect a "large and convenient depot." The DA&G, however, continued to ignore the problem. Nearly a year later the newspaper wrote in disgust: "Nashville is putting up with very poor railroad facilities, in the hope of a great improvement before long. We just can't stand the present program much longer, and we trust we are not expected to do so." Then the railroad responded, but hardly in a way that pleased residents. "The Douglas, Augusta & Gulf erected a cow shelter in the rear of the Peoples-Bullard block, and the passenger trains stop there now instead of at Dr. Edie's barn and horse lot. Seems that every move the railroad makes just makes matters worse."[44]

NASHVILLE & SPARKS RAILROAD

While a love-hate relationship developed in Nashville toward the DA&G, local residents appeared more satisfied with what many considered to be their hometown carrier, the Nashville & Sparks Railroad (N&S). This diminutive road ran for nearly a dozen miles in a mostly westward fashion from Nashville to Sparks in Berrien County (after 1919 Cook County), where the line connected with the 394-mile Georgia Southern & Florida Railway (GS&F), the "Suwanee River Route" or as some called it, "Go Slow & Flag." This strategic trunk carrier, affiliated with the sprawling Southern Railway system, linked Macon, by way of Valdosta, with Jacksonville and Palatka, Florida.[45]

Chartered on April 12, 1900, the N&S opened for business eleven months later, providing three daily round trips with mixed-train service. A fleet of two small 4-4-0s and two coaches, subsequently increased to three locomotives and three coaches, made these runs possible. Later the road dispatched four daily movements each way, "making close connection at Sparks with all trains on the G.S.& F. Ry." Also, after early 1905, a morning accommodation provided a convenient connection with the regularly scheduled northbound OP&V run. It would not be until April 1906, however, that the N&S and the DA&G, successor to the OP&V, forged a direct physical link. When this tie-in finally occurred, the DA&G-N&S operated several "through" trains between Broxton, Douglas, Nashville, and Sparks, much to the delight of patrons.[46]

It would be the N&S much more than the OP&V that gave Nashville, already the county seat, a significant economic lift. By 1904 the *Nashville Herald* bragged that the community "is not the old village it used to be. We now have about 1,000 people. . . . We have four large brick blocks, a large modern brick ginnery in course of erection; bonds have been voted for a large brick school building." Other developments followed. In spring 1906 the Nashville Land Company conducted a large and apparently successful town-lot auction. As part of the firm's promotional efforts, it crowed that "Nashville is outgrowing all towns in this section of the State. Ours is not a temporary boom. We have no saw mills to move away and kill our boom. Nashville was the last county seat town in this section of the State to get railroads. Real estate values have doubled in the last twelve months." For potential buyers who were not fully convinced by these statements, on sale day the company enticed bidders by giving away ten building lots.[47]

Even though Sparks had enjoyed access to the steamcar civilization since the late 1880s, construction of the N&S also stimulated the local economy. The population rose from 307 in 1890 to 693 a decade later. About the time that the Nashville Land Company boomed sales of town lots there, a similar occurrence took place in Sparks. In August 1906 real-estate developers held a well-attended town-lot auction and barbecue. Sales were brisk and "five beeves and a half dozen mutton were barbecued," presumably enjoyed by the attendees, some of whom traveled by special train from Nashville. Growth continued and in 1910 Sparks claimed 842 residents. The town appeared destined for a bright future.[48]

Backed by Georgia capital, including interests tied to the Massee-Felton Lumber Company of Macon, the N&S developed a close relationship with the GS&F. In an unusual arrangement, the N&S had title to only the lightly graded right-of-way, bridges, ties, and fixtures. The GS&F, on the other hand, owned the rails, angle bars, and switch paraphernalia and, at a modest annual charge, leased them to the N&S. This agreement worked, allowing for the quick and relatively inexpensive construction of the N&S.[49]

Throughout its brief history, the little N&S prospered, providing much of the freight and passenger service for Nashville. During the period December 1, 1900, to March 31, 1906, which covered most of its corporate life, the road generated $143,194 in operating revenues and only $77,291 in operating expenses. Between 1902 and 1905 the company paid out nearly $10,000 in dividends to its several shareholders, who had committed about $30,000 to the line; in April 1904 investors received a tidy cash dividend of eight percent. At the time of its takeover by the G&F, the N&S lacked either long- or short-term indebtedness.[50]

The overall financial success of the N&S did not go unnoticed. Captain Gray, who owned the OP&V, had his eyes on the property. Apparently about 1905 he offered to buy the N&S, but its owners ignored his overture. Annoyed by his inability to win control of the N&S, Gray sought a charter to extend the OP&V to Adel, the twin city of Sparks to the south, and rumored to become part of the seventy-seven-mile South Georgia & West Coast Railway (which included the West Coast Railway) that by 1904 had linked Adel and Perry, Florida, an important lumber and turpentine center.

Perhaps Gray had no such intentions, but rather used "this application for a charter from Nashville to Adel . . . [as] a bluff to scare the N&S Railroad . . . into a deal looking to the consolidation or sale of that road." The G&F and not the OP&V, though, would shortly gain control.[51]

VALDOSTA SOUTHERN RAILWAY

The southern end of the future G&F once flew the corporate banner of the Valdosta Southern Railway (VS). When officially acquired by the G&F on August 1, 1907, this property stretched 27.2 miles between Valdosta, a rising manufacturing and trading center of nearly 6,000 people and seat of Lowndes County, and Madison, Florida, a Sea Island cotton marketing hub and capital of Madison County with a stable population of several thousand.[52]

The VS possessed a history as complicated as any G&F predecessor. The origins of the company date from the mid-1880s when the Florida Midland & Georgia Railroad (FM&G) came into being. Backers proposed connecting Valdosta with Deadman's Bay (Steinhatchee area), located on the Gulf coast of Florida, a distance of more than 100 miles. Yet the best that they could do was to construct about fifteen miles south from Valdosta to the Georgia-Florida state line near Starling's Ferry on the Withlacoochee River. Apparently interests associated with J & P Coats Company, a major maker of spool thread, were behind the FM&G, explaining why residents called the property the "Spool Cotton Road." This manufacturing firm depended heavily on the high-quality Sea Island cotton for producing thread and related products.[53]

Although J & P Coats continued to operate in Florida, the FM&G failed during the early days of the depression of the 1890s. When the little road tumbled into receivership on May 19, 1893, the federal court assumed temporary charge. Then in July 1894 a public sale occurred and Colonel J. M. Wilkinson, a prominent area businessman, led an investment group that took control. The Wilkinson property became The Florida Midland & Georgia Railroad (TFM&G), but quickly changed the corporate name to the Valdosta Southern Railway. As part of the railroad activities of Wilkinson and his associates, they gained ownership of the recently built Withlacoochee Railroad (WR) that operated on approximately thirteen miles of poorly fashioned line northward from Madison to the Withlacoochee River. Its history, though, is virtually unknown. "The records reviewed did not indicate whether the Withlacoochee Railway Company was controlled by any individual or corporation on August 9, 1895, the date of its demise," noted a federal valuation examiner. Thus in 1895 the VS included both the former TFM&G and the WR.[54]

But the VS did not amount to much. Apparently, the overall quality of the combined properties was dreadful, necessitating major reconstruction. The process, however, was painfully slow with the initial work on the ten-mile section between Valdosta and the sawmill village of Clyattville,

Georgia. By 1898 reconstruction had reached Pinetta, Florida, and two years later, Hanson, Florida, making for a twenty-mile operation. Then in the spring of 1901 the former WR line into Madison reopened, making a connection with the Seaboard Air Line (SAL). On July 1, 1901, the first train of the renewed VS steamed over the forty-pound steel rails into the Madison station, heralding advent of the reborn VS. Soon two daily-except-Sunday mixed trains operated each way between the terminals, service made possible by a pair of 4-4-0 locomotives, one built in 1883 by Baldwin and the other listed as a McDonough-constructed engine of 1896; a combination passenger, baggage, and mail car; and a standard wooden coach. On Sundays the VS dispatched a mixed train that made a single round trip.[55]

Even with considerable betterments, the VS hardly became a stellar property. Columbus Smith, editor of the *New Enterprise*, the weekly Madison newspaper, repeatedly blasted the railroad for slow, undependable service. "The trains come into Madison with a disregard for schedule time that would be funny if it wasn't aggravating." In September 1902 a traveler noted: "Left on V.S. Ry. at 9:43 a.m. Mixed train like on many of the 1-horse roads of S. Ga. No mile-posts along RR, or any kind of signs." Complaints to state regulators, instigated by the *New Enterprise*, failed to produce noticeable improvements.[56]

Still the VS provided a useful transportation service for the counties of Lowndes and Madison. Although the road hauled general freight and handled passengers, express, and mail, it was primarily a lumber carrier. The VS served several important sawmills, including operations of Fender Lumber Company in Valdosta and West Yellow Pine Lumber Company near Olympia, Georgia, about four miles south of Clyattville. The latter community was the quintessential mill town of the piney woods. "About 50 houses at Olympia," noted a visitor in 1902, "and a sawmill on spur track about 1/2 m. away." The VS had a close relationship with West Yellow Pine Lumber; company logging trains operated over the VS for the two miles between Olympia Junction and Pinetta Junction, providing a source of additional income.[57]

Even if the VS was a "1-horse" road, its presence enhanced the lives of local inhabitants. As with virtually every common carrier, the VS operated "specials" at the drop of a hat and offered attractive excursion rates, often in conjunction with a connecting railroad. In 1903 the company gave "very low rates" for the "Big colored K. of P. [Knights of Pythias] picnic at Olympia, May 22nd. 50 cents round trip." That same month the VS advertised: "Grand annual excursion to Tampa via Valdosta Southern and Atlantic Coast Line. $4.00 for the round trip, tickets limited to May 30th."[58]

As might be imagined, the VS was not particularly profitable. Revenue on a per-mile basis, for example, was far less than that of the M&SW and N&S. During the final year of its corporate life the VS generated gross freight and passenger revenues of $38,555 and claimed net earnings of $13,459. Still, resembling other shortlines that joined the G&F, the VS operated in the black. The six roads the new owners acquired did not languish in, or teeter on the edge of, bankruptcy. Moreover, reflecting on these properties, John Skelton Williams, the driving force behind the G&F, noted that "their construction has in every case been followed by the immediate development of the territories invaded, despite the fact that they have been isolated links, connecting simply with east and west lines, and with poor and roundabout connections for the North."[59]

THE RAILROAD SCENE

If organizers of the G&F had not fused the six predecessor shortlines, a union of some sort still might have occurred. Already an expanded carrier, the DA&G, likely would have been involved, largely because of its size and location. Indeed, the company would become the centerpiece for expansion. Captain Gray of the OP&V, for one, publicly contemplated a south Georgia and north Florida network. Such a road might have been extended northward, reaching Atlanta, Augusta or Macon, and southward to the Gulf of Mexico, perhaps Tampa or St. Petersburg. Gray and other railroad owners and promoters surely sensed that the regional railway map had not fully jelled. An argument could have been made that the transportation needs of the south Georgia–north Florida area had not been completely met. Significantly, by 1906–1907 the final burst of new construction was in full swing, although in places interrupted or halted by the brief, yet severe, Panic of 1907. As years passed, however, new projects became more limited in scope and far less numerous. What was occurring in Georgia and Florida after 1900 was part of a much larger national construction pattern. Between 1901 and 1905 more than 40,000 miles of track had been added to the country's steam railway network and another 16,563 miles were placed in service during 1906 and 1907.[60]

What ultimately took place in the Wiregrass Region was that the jumble of shortlines, often constructed in the late nineteenth and early twentieth centuries, did not usually find new corporate homes as parts of expanding systems, although the more valuable properties commonly came under control of trunk carriers. In the case of the G&F, the company would make its debut by following the practice of merging existing railroads and enhancing their value through installing connecting links. The chief instigator, John Skelton Williams, who earlier had used such a strategy with stunning success with the SAL, believed it possible, even by 1906, to replicate his earlier triumph. The saga of the G&F was about to begin.[61]

CHAPTER TWO

The G&F Emerges, 1906–1910

John Skelton Williams

"**A**n institution," insisted American philosopher Ralph Waldo Emerson, "is the lengthened shadow of one man." Had Emerson lived in the South early in the twentieth century, he could have had the Georgia & Florida Railway (G&F) in mind as the institution and John Skelton Williams as the man. It was Williams, more than any other individual, who brought the G&F to life. And, arguably, Williams became the personification of this largely Georgia carrier much as Henry Flagler stood for the Florida East Coast, James J. Hill for the Great Northern, A. B. Stickney for the Chicago Great Western, and Arthur E. Stilwell for both the Kansas City, Pittsburg & Gulf (Kansas City Southern) and the Kansas City, Mexico & Orient.

Described as a "vigorous, physically well proportioned male" who stood at somewhat over six feet in height, and by age fifty weighed approximately 225 pounds and projected a "military bearing which is not traceable to military training," John Skelton Williams came from a prominent Virginia family. His great-great grandfather, Edmund Randolph, a "founding father" of the Republic, served George Washington as his first Attorney General and later as his second Secretary of State. Another ancestor, Bartholomew Dandridge, brother of Martha Washington, participated in the momentous Virginia Convention of 1775.

Born on July 6, 1865, in Powhatan County, Virginia, one of eight children of John Langbourne and Maria Skelton Williams, the young Williams received his education in the private schools of Richmond and briefly studied law at the University of Virginia, his father's alma mater. In 1886, at age twenty-one, Williams officially joined the family firm of John L. Williams & Sons, a Richmond-based banking house, although as early as 1879 he had clerked for his father. It would be the Williams company, which included his father and younger brothers R. Lancaster and Langbourne M., active in promoting and financing public utilities in the South, that drew him into the regional transportation business. At age thirty Williams married Lila Lefebre Isaacs, who also claimed a prominent Virginia lineage, and they became parents of two sons, John, Jr. and Hubert.[1]

Williams did not stand out as an unusual business leader. Contemporary anecdotal evidence reveals that he was bright, hard-working, principled, honest, and loyal to colleagues. The always nattily attired Williams expressed a deep commitment to the Episcopalian faith; showed enthusiasm for the southern or Jeffersonian-Jacksonian wing of the Democratic Party; and dedicated himself to the business of finance and railroads, focusing on forging a modern, prosperous South. After his sudden death on November 14, 1926, the *Banker's Magazine* commented briefly on his nature, characterizing him as "highly efficient but unnecessarily harsh." Evidence also suggests that Williams could be pompous, thin-skinned, short-tempered, and even vindictive. And resembling so many of his peers in the South, he was an ardent racist, having an exceedingly negative view of people of color.[2]

In 1895, the year of his marriage, this young, albeit experienced Richmond investment banker entered the world of railroading amidst a national depression. Unlike some fellow executives who worked their way from errand boy to president, Williams started out in the top position. The company was the Georgia & Alabama Railway (G&A), a 457-mile road connecting Savannah, Georgia, with Montgomery, Alabama, much of which had been the bankrupt Savannah, Americus & Montgomery Railway, described before Williams's involvement as being "in a hopeless state of insolvency." Working with a close business associate, John William Middendorf, a prominent Baltimore, Maryland, banker and lead partner in Middendorf, Oliver & Company (later Middendorf, Williams & Company), Williams skillfully brought the G&A to profitability. Success with the G&A led Williams and his associates to take controlling interest in the roads that comprised the "old Seaboard Air-Line properties," and on February 1, 1899, Williams became president of this 955-mile-long mostly Virginia and North Carolina carrier. A few months later, he took command of the Florida Central & Peninsular Railroad (FC&P) that the Williams-Middendorf group had recently acquired. This 960-mile-long company served the Florida cities of Jacksonville, Orlando, and Tampa and stretched westward into the Florida panhandle and northward to Columbia, South Carolina. Then the partners created the "new" Seaboard Airline Railroad (SAL). Williams later noted that he "conceived and developed [a] plan for the formation of the greater Seaboard Air Line System," taking the throttle in 1900 and helping to fashion a leading southern trunk road. The SAL scheme was strikingly simple. By fusing the several properties, most importantly the G&A, the old Seaboard Air-Line and the FC&P, and building strategic links, including a ninety-one-mile segment between the old Seaboard Air-Line at Chersaw, South Carolina, and the FC&P at Cayce (outside Columbia), South Carolina, an integrated network of 2,603 miles came into being by mid-1901. Yet this approach to railroad building was hardly unique. A few years earlier, albeit on a smaller scale, businessman Jere Baxter, for example, used existing trackage and construction to create his approximately 300-mile Tennessee Central Railroad.[3]

John Skelton Williams (left), the force behind the creation of the G&F, stands by his friend and associate William Gibbs McAdoo, in Williams's Richmond office. The occasion is possibly Williams's appointment in 1913 by Woodrow Wilson to the Treasury Department. (John Skelton Williams Papers [#10040], Special Collections, University of Virginia Library)

It was a proud John Skelton Williams who headed the SAL. The railroad was a regional giant that served five Southern states, holding great promise for investors, employees, and patrons. At the time of the official dedication in 1900, Williams, ever the ardent Virginian and southerner, wholeheartedly endorsed the observation that the SAL was a "Southern system, created by Southern enterprise and Southern money against the machinations of Wall Street, manned by Southern men, devoted to the upbringing of Southern cities [and] the prosperity of Southern states."[4]

Williams and his associates had accomplished more than a business victory for the South: the expanded SAL revealed progressive qualities. These men sensed the importance of "system building," realizing that long-haul freight and passenger operations would be essential for stability and profitability. Somewhat earlier such forward thinking had led to creation of the Southern Railway System (SR) and then to formation of the Atlantic Coast Line (ACL), the region's other two dominant railroads.[5]

But unfortunately for Williams, the SAL triumph mostly turned to dross. Although the Williams group had seemingly mastered the complexities of railroad finance, the company faced fiscal embarrassment when the sudden Panic of 1903 made it difficult to sell construction bonds for the extension being built between Atlanta, Georgia, and Birmingham, Alabama. In order to "save" the new SAL, Williams borrowed $2.5 million from a leading financier, Thomas Fortune Ryan. By 1903 this self-made multimillionaire, who earlier had reaped a personal bonanza with the Metropolitan Street Railway Company in New York City, had extensive railroad holdings, including investments in the SAL and several predecessor firms. In order to protect his sizeable position in the SAL, Ryan formed a seven-member voting trust. Although Williams personally participated, Ryan and his allies wielded real control, and in 1904 they "ruthlessly" ousted the Richmond banker from the presidency. The Ryan faction liked neither how the new SAL had been fashioned nor Williams himself. As might be expected, Williams and his supporters, who retained considerable clout because of their stock holdings and connections with some powerful investors, immediately began a long, difficult battle to regain control. In the midst of this bitter SAL dispute Williams brought the G&F into being.[6]

During the Williams-Ryan conflict, Williams repeatedly argued that he represented the small investor or "little fellow" and that Ryan was a predatory Yankee plunger, even though Ryan, like Williams, had been raised in Virginia (in rural Nelson County). Williams also viewed himself as defender of southern business interests, and much to his satisfaction the regional press generally saw him in that role and proclaimed his greatness. "Mr. Williams is a man of the people," opined the editor of the Swainsboro, Georgia, *Forest-Blade*. "He is a Southerner who hails from Richmond, Va., and barring Samuel Spencer [of the SR] is the greatest railroad genius ever reared in the South, if not the entire country." Of course, the latter was so much hyperbole, but Williams nevertheless exhibited considerable business acumen, and his plans for creating the G&F seemed grounded in economic reality.[7]

THE G&F SCHEME

John Skelton Williams and his associates in Richmond and Baltimore possessed a good grasp of business conditions in the South and understood the nature of railroad service, including its weaknesses. These men had been closely involved in the predecessors of the new SAL and then the assembly, development, and promotion of the expanded property. The Williams group sensed two significant aspects of the region, most notably involving the Wiregrass Region of Georgia: first, the area was a land of considerable agricultural, business, and manufacturing promise; and second, railroad facilities were inadequate, at least on a north-south axis. As these promoters told prospective investors in a special advertisement that appeared in the 1906 issue of *Poor's Manual of the Railroads of the United States* and subsequently was reprinted in circular form, "the Georgia & Florida Railway will bisect the rich and rapidly developing territory lying between Macon, Georgia, on the west and Savannah on the east, which, *for a distance of more than 150 miles at its widest part, is without a north and south railroad,* and conspicuous for its need of railroad facilities, although already producing a large amount of tonnage, which, with adequate means of transportation, must rapidly increase."[8]

During the carrier's gestation period, Williams expected the Wiregrass Region to become a rich part of the nation. In both his private and public comments, the theme always remained the same: the South, especially Georgia, was the right place to invest. "The very great resources of the south and the excellent opportunities of wealth have in the last few years been attracting more and more the earnest attention of capital in the north and abroad," he told the *Baltimore News* in January 1909, "and the growth and development of this section in the last fifteen years are unprecedented."[9]

There may have been more to his enthusiasm for the G&F proposal than the likelihood of a business triumph. In 1907 John William Middendorf told Williams that he could advance his cause in the ongoing battle for control of the SAL by succeeding with this new railroad venture. "The consummation of the Georgia & Florida scheme is going to be highly beneficial to us and eventually will help you more than anything that can be done at present." Surely investors would look kindly upon Williams and his partners if they could turn several rather woebegone shortlines into a thriving interstate carrier. Indeed, Dow, Jones & Company, publisher of the *Wall Street Journal,* anticipated success. "A striking feature about this railroad is that it will run through a section of Georgia much in need of north and south trunk-line facilities," observed the firm in 1907, "and it will cross at right angles all the principal railroads in that section of the State, namely, the Southern Railway, the Atlantic Coast Line, the Seaboard Air Line, the Central of Georgia, and the Georgia Southern & Florida Railway."[10]

When Williams and his colleagues forged the idea for the G&F is not precisely known; likely it was at some point in 1905, not long after the blow-up at the SAL. Although remaining personally involved in SAL affairs, it is probable that Williams thought that he could replicate the earlier SAL triumph. While perhaps never intending to create another SAL, Williams might accomplish what he earlier had done with the G&A (that road's moniker surely inspired the naming of the G&F), forming a viable intermediate size carrier that could profitably exploit both local and through traffic. At this time, too, Georgia was the scene of considerable railroad excitement, prompting the *Manufacturer's Record* to editorialize that "the activity prevailing in Georgia with reference to new railroad construction is a matter of considerable comment in railroad circles, as well as among financiers who are interested in transportation development."[11]

As had been customary in previous ventures, Williams was not about to build blindly. In late 1905 he employed the services of John Scott, an accomplished railroad consultant from New York City and formerly president and general manager of the Cincinnati, New Orleans & Texas Pacific (Queen & Crescent) system; president of the Colorado Midland Railway, and comptroller for the receivers of the Northern Pacific Railroad. In two reports, the first submitted on January 26, 1906, and the second on January 11, 1907, after the G&F project was well along, Scott endorsed the Williams scheme. As he told his employer in his first assessment, "The lines from the North to the East coast of Florida are all prosperous and there is every reason to believe that such a line as that projected from Augusta, which will eventually reach a point on the West coast of Florida, will be equally successful." Added Scott: "I consider the projectors of the new line have been fortunate in finding so many undeveloped existing lines which with quite small new mileage (91 miles) can be put together and be merged into a system (with branches) of 345 miles in length." He concluded: "The main points are: *I. That the scheme is good. II. That the cost is reasonable. III. That traffic results are not overstated. IV. That the financial plan is conservative.*" In his second report Scott remained optimistic: "Nearly all new roads are built in an entirely new territory, wherein development must be made from the very first start, and, naturally the earnings of such roads increase slowly, as they have to grow up with the country. *Here, there is a partly developed section which has largely passed through the early stages and is now ripe for substantial growth.*"[12]

With what Scott considered to be convincing evidence that the G&F would become a viable railroad, Williams and his associates set out to buy and rehabilitate the core shortlines and construct connecting trackage. This undertaking would involve acquisition of all or parts of seven railroads and construction of eighty-seven miles of line. Their efforts took an amazingly short time to complete; indeed, much transpired in 1906 alone, including the official incorporation by the State of Georgia on July 7, 1906.[13]

Arranging financing was an early priority. Although optimism prevailed, challenges developed. On the positive side the Williams-Middendorf banking associations meant that there existed access to pools of capital. Not only did the two firms have their own investment funds but they had connections with financial institutions in other major centers, both domestic and foreign, especially through the closely connected International Trust Company, based in Baltimore, Maryland. Before the Panic of 1907, which produced a credit stringency much more severe than the Panic of 1903 and raised havoc in the banking industry, funding was readily available for an array of transportation projects, including smaller steam railways. But the panic understandably caused concerns. The more important railroad endeavors, though, found financial support once the hard times lifted, although significantly some electric interurban railway projects had to be abandoned midway in construction and were never completed.[14]

The Williams-Middendorf group also anticipated raising some funds from communities that badly wanted the G&F. The railroad was hardly building ahead of settlement, and in these places public-spirited individuals and government officials might purchase securities or provide direct cash incentives. The former arrangement generated an undisclosed yet important amount of funding, while the latter, as it turned out, proved disappointing. Only two towns actually gave aid, Douglas and Swainsboro, the former providing $10,000 and the latter $20,000.[15]

There was the expectation that G&F backers would not only benefit from their investments in a money-making G&F, but also would profit handsomely from the construction and rehabilitation phase. The building of a railway almost always was carried on by a separate contracting company and interested parties commonly organized such a concern. In this case, the Williams-Middendorf group incorporated in Virginia a satellite firm, the Augusta Construction Company (ACC). And even before the G&F received its charter from the State of Georgia, another ancillary property, the Georgia and Florida Construction Company (G&FCC), "the syndicate," was launched to buy the several shortlines and to begin line survey work and reconstruction. Later the G&FCC took control of the ACC. With any construction affiliate, an opportunity existed for its investors to make generous returns from the sale of bonds, which usually were acquired at an attractively discounted price, and preferred and common stock that the railroad awarded for building and equipping the property. Also the construction company would pay bankers' commissions, and ultimately this meant $162,000 for the promoters.[16]

ASSEMBLING THE G&F

With a business plan in mind, Williams moved rapidly to acquire the individual properties that would constitute what he commonly called the "Augusta and Florida proposition." Once this task had been accomplished, connecting links built, and improvements made, other destinations might be seriously contemplated, including the mostly widely discussed: Columbia, South Carolina, Savannah, Georgia, and Tampa, Florida, but also Athens, Georgia, and Carrabelle, Florida. If the Gulf of Mexico could be reached, the G&F would surely exploit a dramatically altered mariner's map that the Panama Canal, then under construction, created.[17]

No business transaction is flawlessly executed, yet Williams and his associates apparently avoided major problems with the purchase of the railroads they sought. Although details of all these negotiations are not known,

Williams's personal correspondence fails to reveal any great difficulties. In a letter to Middendorf, dated February 2, 1906, Williams explained his endeavors and reported positive results:

> I had a very satisfactory day in Atlanta yesterday. I paid [Frank R.] Durden $2,500 and got a renewal of the option on the Millen & Southwestern for 30 days. Felton turned up with his Brother and attorney and I closed for the Nashville and Sparks Railroad, paying him $20,000. I also closed an agreement with [Col. J. M.] Wilkinson for the purchase of the Valdosta Southern Railroad at a net cost of about $232,000. I also entered into a contract with [J. A. J.] Henderson for the purchase of either 30 miles or 55 miles of the Ocilla & Valdosta Railroad, we to determine within 30 days which we will take, and I paid him $10,000 on account of the purchase. If we buy only the 30 miles from Hazlehurst to Broxton, the price will be $130,000. If we take the additional 25 miles from Broxton to Ocilla, the price will be $285,000 net, which is a reduction of $15,000 from his option price.
>
> McLean and Allen Jones are to be in Baltimore Monday morning in order that we may close for the Douglas, Augusta & Gulf and the Augusta & Florida.[18]

Ultimately, the syndicate raised the necessary capital from both domestic and international sources and transferred the securities to the ACC. By the time the G&F opened for through service, the ACC received paper valued at $14,397,000, of which $5,650,000 was in first mortgage, five percent bonds; $3.5 million preferred stock, and $5,247,500 common stock. The parent corporation, however, assumed directly the first mortgage, five percent bonds of the Millen & South-western Railroad (M&SW) that had a par value of $212,000.[19]

During the period 1906–1908 the Williams railroad focused its efforts on developing the southern end of the gestating Augusta-Madison main line. A critical link involved connecting Nashville, former southern terminus of the Douglas, Augusta & Gulf Railway (DA&G) and the eastern end of the Nashville & Sparks, with Valdosta, northern point on the Valdosta Southern Railway. In late May 1906, the *Valdosta Times* reported that "the line from here [Valdosta] to Nashville, which surveyors are now going over, will be built as speedily as possible." This newspaper assessment, however, proved too optimistic. Construction on this 27.4-mile segment, characterized as being "straight as an arrow" and the first to be undertaken by the ACC, started on March 22, 1908, and finished about seven months later after crews worked south from Nashville and north from Valdosta.[20]

But the *Times* was not guilty of flawed journalism. Because of the need to finalize finance and construction plans, officials decided to allow the separate railroad units to operate under their old banners and mostly independent of each other until October 1, 1907. Furthermore, no building began because of the negative impact of the Panic of 1907. "The management of the Company thought it wisest to proceed slowly with the construction of new lines," commented Williams, "and with the purchase of materials and equipment in order to secure the full benefit of the radical declines which were taking place in the prices of all materials entering into railroad construction, and in the cost of labor."[21]

The completed trackage between Nashville and Valdosta, which resulted in "two of the brightest stars in the group of south Georgia's cities [being] bound by a band of steel," was a logical first building step. The line opened up a largely rail-starved area and gave rise to what evolved into an important community, Ray's Mill (later Ray City), and several other shipping points, including Bemiss, a station that honored Major E. L. Bemiss, president of the ACC and second vice president of the G&F. Significantly, the G&F was able to initiate service directly between Broxton, Douglas, and Valdosta, beginning about October 1, 1908. Although it was unlikely that many passengers rode the entire distance, freight could now easily travel from the Ocmulgee River to Madison and hence on the SAL to Florida destinations, including Jacksonville. But it was more likely that freight moved through Valdosta, connecting with the Georgia Southern & Florida (a SR property) and the ACL for coastal points. Passengers, too, more likely switched carriers in Valdosta.[22]

The second piece of new construction involved the 9.6-mile segment between Douglas and Garrant (later renamed West Green), Georgia. The syndicate concluded that operating trains between Douglas and Hazlehurst via the existing Broxton trackage was a bad idea. By extending northeast from Douglas, the company saved mileage and could benefit from a considerably better engineered right-of-way. At Garrant, the G&F met the former Ocilla & Valdosa (O&V); earlier management had acquired from J. A. J. Henderson, head of the O&V, nearly thirty miles that stretched between Broxton and Hazlehurst, leaving him with the remainder of his line between Broxton and Ocilla that another shortline carrier, the short-lived Fitzgerald, Ocilla & Broxton Railroad, soon absorbed. In late October 1908, track laying began and at times progressed at the rate of half a mile a day. On December 1, 1908, this new piece of main line opened for regularly scheduled traffic and the G&F retired the Garrant-Broxton segment.[23]

The Douglas-Hazlehurst section involved more than building the "Garrant Cut-off." The old O&V line could not be easily rehabilitated, and so for approximately twenty miles the ACC built a closely paralleling new roadbed and installed "heavy [seventy-pound] rail," making for a more modern railway between these two important county seats. As with previous construction endeavors, the railroad reported that "there is no point where a steam shovel could be put to work," adding that "all of the work is very light, calling . . . only for teams, plows and scrapers and a working force." The soil was soft and there were no outcroppings of rock.[24]

Next the G&F decided to span the gap between Hazlehurst and Vidalia, southern terminus of the M&SW that the syndicate now owned. Although this twenty-eight-mile segment ran over comparatively level countryside, about seven miles northeast of Hazlehurst the line encountered the navigable, wide, and flood-prone Altamaha River. In order to serve bridge builders, the ACC first constructed the section between Hazlehurst and the stream's south bank. Somewhat later, during the summer of 1909, gangs completed the line between Vidalia and the river. "Mr. M. A. Elkins, of Macon landed a force of 65 horses and mules, 85 people and wagons and scrapers and such tools as are used in modern railroad building," announced the Swainsboro newspaper in February 1909, and the work accelerated. The G&F, of course, could not establish service between Hazlehurst and Vidalia until the bridge was ready.[25]

The Altamaha River bridge, though, developed steadily. The ACC received bids on September 30, 1908, and a month later the company formally contracted with the American Bridge Company, the nation's foremost bridge-fabricating firm, to construct what became the signature structure on the G&F. And it was an impressive engineering feat. The 539-foot main bridge consisted of two through-pin-connecting truss spans, one through-riveted truss span, one Scherzer draw section, and one deck-plate girder span. These bulky components rested on a half-dozen six-foot thick concrete piers. The ninety-foot lift draw span became the showpiece, capable of being raised or lowered by the bridge tender in only two minutes to accommodate boat traffic. This amazing, moveable section demonstrated the wizardry of William Scherzer, whose 1893 patent led to establishment of the Scherzer Rolling Lift Company. In the latter part of 1909 workers completed this impressive $139,904 project, and on November 15, 1909, the first train steamed over the Altamaha River.[26]

The G&F made additional improvements between Madison and Vidalia. Southwest of Douglas on the former DA&G workers constructed 5.4 miles of right-of-way, known as the Willachoochee Cut-off. The result was a better engineered line between Bannockburn and Oberry in Atkinson and Berrien counties that eliminated a heavy grade and reduced considerable track curvature. When opened in 1908, the G&F saved about a mile in actual distance on the main line, and this betterment permitted the company to abandon 2.3 miles of existing trackage.[27]

Although "contemplated in our original plans," it took until June 15, 1911, before a somewhat more modest improvement was finished. In the general vicinity of the Willachoochee Cut-off, construction crews installed a nearly two-mile spur between Sparks, western terminus of the former Nashville & Sparks Railroad, and Adel, the future seat of Cook County. The G&F wanted a direct connection in Adel with the seventy-seven-mile largely lumber-hauling South Georgia & West Coast Railroad that extended to Quitman, Georgia, and Perry, Florida. Announced Williams: "it is believed [this trackage] will result in a considerable interchange of business between these two roads."[28]

Another short extension appeared on the south end of the gestating G&F. A refinement to the track configuration in Madison allowed for connections

Unquestionably the signature structure of the G&F was the massive bridge over the navigable Altamaha River, Georgia's largest stream, northeast of Hazlehurst. An employee of the Bureau of Valuation, a unit of the Interstate Commerce Commission, took this view from the north end of the bridge, revealing both the shack used by the lift-span operator and the ninety-foot lift span itself. (National Archives)

with both the SAL and the Madison Southern Railway, "now being built through a valuable body of timber to Perry, Florida." By 1909 the latter company operated a freight-only standard gauge line of nearly seven miles between Madison and Waco, Florida, and Williams believed that an agreement for interchange business "would prove of considerable revenue to the Georgia & Florida Railway." Although the Madison newspaper editor expected that the road "will open up a fine country south of Madison and will prove a blessing to residents of the country along its route," this little pike faltered, closing down shortly after World War I.[29]

Throughout the early years of the G&F Williams and his associates felt pressures for additional appendages. The proposal that constituted the greatest mileage involved a line between Dublin, seat of Laurens County southeast of Macon, southward through McRae, seat of Telfair County, to Barrow's Bluff and a connection with the Broxton branch to Douglas. "A railroad from the Ocmulgee river to Dublin via McRae, would run through some of the best country in Georgia and would connect Dublin and McRae, two of the best towns in the state with the Georgia and Florida road," editorialized the *Dublin Courier-Dispatch* in November 1908. Although supporters argued that this fifty-five-mile extension "could be very cheaply built," the expense of bridging the navigable Ocmulgee River surely scuttled the project. Although G&F officials considered a Dublin line, the scheme remained wholly in the good-idea or "hot-air" category.[30]

Not only were there abundant hot-air plans proposed, but the railroad map of south Georgia and north Florida continued to change. With existing trackage there was a continuum of "revision" or improvement projects, and the G&F activities were no exception. The objective, of course, was to rehabilitate existing trackage. After 1907 "several hundred negroes and white men" installed modern seventy-pound steel, lengthened sidings, replaced rotted crossties, and filled, renewed, or replaced trestles, including the installation of a fifty-five-foot truss span across the Withlacoochee River on the "Valdosta Southern Division." In late spring 1908 a Douglas newspaper noted that "two thousand new cross-ties have just been put down on the line of the G&F between Broxton and Barrow's Bluff, the bridges rebuilt and the dangerous places filled in." These replacement ties consisted either of untreated, albeit durable cypress or southern yellow pine. Workers also built or remodeled depots, section houses, water tanks, coal chutes, and other support facilities. As with Willacoochee Cut-off, various grades and excessive track curvatures were reduced or eliminated, mostly on the "Douglas, Augusta & Gulf Division."[31]

During the early years of the G&F crews also engaged in betterment projects north of Vidalia. In 1908, for example, the company erected a 50,000-gallon water tank and a large coaling chute at Midville and installed a replacement 1,400-foot wooden trestle over the Ogeechee River. But management turned to the northern section only after most of the "south-end" had been rehabilitated.[32]

Resembling typical construction arrangements, the ACC worked with a variety of subcontractors. When building lines, for example, the ACC usually awarded contracts for three- or five-mile stretches. For what was often unskilled, manual labor, some firms either hired local residents or acquired prisoners who had been "rented" to area sawmill operators. Lumbermen leased these convicts for about $200 annually from the state of Georgia on a long-term basis and were required to pay a rental fee and to provide room and board. The lumber business fluctuated, however, and during slack periods a railroad contractor could assume the costs of these prisoners. "They [sawmill operators]," explained ACC President Bemiss, "are very anxious to find some work to put them to."[33]

Whether they employed free or convict labor, some contractors apparently possessed poor-quality machinery. Early on the chief engineer reported that adding fill had been more expensive per cubic yard than anticipated. "This work has been done with very deficient equipment which has made the cost larger than it otherwise would be." With the exception of bridge building, most grading and other tasks were fortunately neither difficult nor exceedingly costly.[34]

While there existed a clear picture of what to do south of Vidalia, considerable discussion ensued about the precise route between Vidalia and Augusta. Ownership of the M&SW gave the G&F a link between Vidalia and Millen and access over the Central of Georgia Railway (CofG) to Augusta. But being a tenant on the fifty-three-mile line between Millen and Augusta did not please management for several reasons: the CofG charged a substantial annual rent; CofG dispatchers failed to give G&F trains priority status, in fact frequently delaying movements; and there was no opportunity to develop online customers. Initially the G&F thought that the preferred way to reach Augusta would be to build approximately eighteen miles from at or near Summit, a station on the Vidalia-Millen line, generally northward to Midville, use the former Augusta & Florida Railway to St. Clair, six miles south of Keysville, and then construct thirty-two miles of line from that community directly to Augusta.[35]

By early 1909, however, the Board of Directors decided on another way to reach Augusta. The railroad would build between Normantown, about seven miles north of Vidalia on the former M&SW, and Swainsboro, where the G&F rails would connect with the forty-eight-mile "Swainsboro and Keysville Division," the former Atlantic & Gulf Short Line Railroad that previously had owned the eighteen-mile segment between Swainsboro and Midville. Although this route involved nearly twenty miles of construction, management believed that it was far superior to a Summit-Midville project. "By the adoption of this new route for the connecting line," observed Williams, "the actual distance from Augusta, Ga., to Madison, Fla., will be reduced by about five miles, and the new 19.5 mile extension will be constructed across a more satisfactory country, from a revenue standpoint, than the section through which it was originally proposed . . . between Summit and Midville." Indeed, the editor of the *Forest-Blade* in Swainsboro earlier had echoed Williams. "Besides being a cheaper route it would unquestionably be a more paying one. It is a splendid farming country. . ., one of the very best in Georgia, and besides this feature if the road be built from Midville to Summit it will parallel the Savannah, Augusta and Northern all the way."[36]

Moreover, the G&F expected that Swainsboro would contribute to this project, an expectation that materialized. Local boosters were delighted with this opportunity to enhance rail connections. "Swainsboro is elated over the certainty of a through line. The Georgia & Florida can well expect good treatment at the hands of the citizens of Swainsboro." The community raised a modest $10,000 in cash aid and successfully pressured landowners to donate much of the right-of-way. The arguments were persuasive:

> We appeal to the people along the line to give the rights of way, not alone from a Swainsboro standpoint, but for their own good and for the good of the county as well. In other words a main line of road the entire breadth of the county would add $2,000.00 in taxes every year. . . .
>
> Let no man feel that the right of way is a burden on him. He will get back double the damages to him in the form of a reduction in freight rates and increased property valuation in a few years. . . . And you may rest assured that if the right of way can't be secured from here to Normantown, it can be secured elsewhere, for others are wanting the road.[37]

Residents of Swainsboro and portions of Emanuel County realized that the Normantown project offered their last best hope for improved rail transport; they were not happy with their present situation. The Wadley Southern Railway, controlled by the CofG, offered modest service and at the time the G&F scheduled only one train between Swainsboro and Keysville, connecting with the evening passenger run of the Augusta Southern Railroad (AS) to Augusta.[38]

· But change came. In February 1909 surveys began for the Normantown-Swainsboro extension. Then in August work commenced on what was to be the last major line project until the late 1920s when the company built between Augusta and Greenwood, South Carolina. "Construction work on the Georgia & Florida Railway is now being rushed here," reported a delighted Swainsboro *Forest-Blade* on September 23, 1909. "A large force of hands is now actively engaged at work here, and a steam shovel is also being used for all it is worth. The section of hands located here will grade for a distance of seven miles, where it will join the other sections." By November laborers had finished their efforts.[39]

The final part of the main line involved the segment to Augusta. Although the G&F took over the thirty-mile Augusta & Florida Railway between Midville and Keysville, technically the railroad did not own all of this shortline. The Williams group did not buy outright the portion between St. Clair and Keysville, because "it . . . would not be necessary for the use of the consolidated company when the link from St. Clair to Augusta . . . should be finished, but until this link into Augusta is finished, this five and a half miles from St. Clair to Keysville is being operated by the Georgia and Florida Railway under an operating agreement by which the Georgia and Florida Railway receives all of the earnings of the line and is responsible for all of its operating charges." But the costs and difficulties of building the "St. Clair-Augusta survey" and the opportunity to secure attractive rights over the AS between Keysville and Augusta ended talk of new trackage and prompted the G&F to acquire the St. Clair to Keysville segment, thus making it a permanent part of the Augusta-Madison main line. At the time of the lease announcement an Augusta newspaper noted "a trackage right having been secured over the Augusta Southern from Keysville, which will be practically the same as the Georgia and Florida owning the track."[40]

Once the Keysville-Madison main line was completed, members of the Board of Directors officially thanked officers of the G&F and the ACC for a job well done: "This work has been prosecuted uninterruptedly throughout a period of financial depression that embarrassed many of the strongest; and . . . it is evident from other sources that the work of construction and revision has been efficiently, economically and faithfully prosecuted and concluded." The official resolution passed by the Board read: "BE IT RESOLVED that the stockholders do hereby express their lively appreciation of what has been accomplished, . . . of the zeal that did not flag, and of the honest work that now furnishes us such an excellent property."[41]

There were other changes to the original plans: an omission and an addition. In its first published prospectus the company contemplated a line from the Summit area on the M&SW southeastward to the trading center of Statesboro, seat of Bulloch County, a distance of about twenty-five miles. Seeking this growing community of 1,200 residents was hardly astonishing. "In the decades that followed the turn of the century, a wild and unrealistic series of railroad schemes rained down in Bulloch County, each begetting a new wave of euphoria in an ongoing flood of expectations," observed historian Wilber Caldwell. "At the end of all of this, only one railroad laid any track [Savannah, Augusta and Northern Railway (SA&N)]."[42]

Backers of the Savannah, Augusta & Northern Railway, Statesboro's new outlet, had big plans. They originally contemplated a 420-mile railroad that would link Savannah with Chattanooga, Tennessee, and a branch between Washington, Georgia, and Augusta. But they became more realistic, scaling back their objective to Athens, making for a road of approximately 160 miles. In June 1907 construction began with high hopes. "The fact that the firm of W. J. Oliver & Co., the largest contractors in the United States, have [*sic*] signed the contract for its construction means that it is a go," concluded the *Statesboro News*. Within two years the road extended from Statesboro to an interchange with the G&F at Stevens Crossing (south of Midville) and also connected with the former M&SW at Garfield. Although grading and bridge work progressed northward toward Louisville, nineteen miles beyond Stevens Crossing, the company never became more than a shortline of forty miles, and quickly failed. In November 1911 the Savannah & Statesboro Railway (S&S), a thirty-three-mile carrier affiliated with the SAL, leased the SA&N (in 1903 the S&S had considered extending to Garfield), and in 1915 the Midland Railway acquired the property. Finally in 1924, the original SA&N segment, reorganized as the Statesboro Northern Railway, came under G&F control (see Chapter 3).[43]

Williams and his associates followed carefully the gestation of the SA&N. Although its appearance largely precluded any construction by the G&F on its own, the coming of the SA&N and the existence of the S&S offered an opportunity for the G&F to reach Savannah. The whole affair was complex. In 1908 Cecil Gabbett, a civil engineer, former general manager of the Georgia & Alabama Railway and then a lumberman who lived in Savannah, urged the G&F to buy the SA&N and also to take the S&S. "In order that the Receivers of the Seaboard would have more than one bid for the majority stock of the S. & S., held by them, I might get up some parties at Statesboro to submit a bid for that road's stock—it being understood, of course, that the G. & F. would get it at cost, if they took over the S. A. & N," he explained to John William Middendorf. "If the S. A. & N. fails to build, as it now seems likely, I would like to see the G. & F. get both roads." The Williams group, though, did nothing, although members knew that the SA&N could become a friendly connection and potentially a good feeder. Who knew what the morrow would bring for these two shortlines? After all, the G&F had an established record of acquiring small roads that it wanted.[44]

Resources went instead to a more promising proposition, acquisition of the Sparks-Western Railway (S-W). Indeed, this property became an important and enduring feeder. It was chartered on September 8, 1908, by local interests, and rumors flew that the project would be an electric interurban. Backers, however, quickly denied these reports and the soon-to-be steam road rapidly pushed westward from Sparks, western terminus of the former Nashville & Sparks. The S-W first reached Ellenton, ten miles, and by 1910 arrived at Pineboro, another five miles, and then terminated at Kingwood, near Moultrie, the bustling seat of Colquitt County and a developing railroad junction. When finished the S-W met the Atlanta, Birmingham & Atlantic Railway (AB&A) about one and one-half miles east of Moultrie, and the company obtained trackage rights into the Colquitt County capital. (For decades the G&F contemplated reaching Moultrie but it never built further.)[45]

In the latter part of 1910 involvement of the G&F with the S-W became public. Newspaper accounts of the Board of Directors meeting held in Valdosta on November 10 revealed that "the Sparks and Western [sic] road . . . was recently acquired by the Georgia and Florida." And more press coverage followed: on February 27, 1911, the G&F officially took control "so the line from Sparks to Kingwood has now become an integral part of the Georgia & Florida Railway."[46]

Yet much earlier the Williams group had become involved with the S-W. On November 11, 1908, Williams told fellow board members that he had just agreed to lease about ten miles of second-hand rail to the S-W, "under which certain preferential privileges were accorded the Georgia & Florida Railway." And at the same meeting he indicated that "negotiations were in progress with the owners of the Sparks Western Railway whereby that road, upon its construction, might be operated by the Georgia & Florida Railway, under an arrangement by which the Georgia & Florida Railway should have full charge of the operations of the Road, collecting its earnings and revenues and to apply them."[47]

Two years later actual ownership of the S-W occurred. The G&F paid shareholders $100,000, specifically, $25,000 in cash that was followed by three equal annual installments. As with many shortlines, the S-W president, J. R. Barfield, was the "principal owner of the stock of that Company."[48]

DOUGLAS SHOPS

As the G&F emerged, the company made Douglas, the rapidly growing seat of Coffee County, its temporary operating headquarters. This was a sensible decision because of the town's central location in relationship to the initial wave of line construction and rehabilitation activities. Shop facilities, however, were concentrated in Millen, where the former M&SW had conducted modest repair operations. But Millen was poorly situated and the G&F never had any serious intention of extending from Millen to Augusta, which, if that had occurred, might have made the site more acceptable. At the May 15, 1908, meeting of the Board of Directors, members voted to create a five-person committee "to canvas the situation and investigate the localities proposed for shops, and to ascertain what inducements will be offered to the Company, for the location of the shops, by the several towns now asking for the location of the shops." There were several contenders: Augusta, Douglas, Hazlehurst, Valdosta, and Vidalia.[49]

It is understandable that communities aggressively sought the G&F shops. Such a facility meant a substantial, and arguably stable, payroll. When the Chicago Great Western Railway announced in 1894 that it would centralize its repair work in Oelwein, Iowa, President A. B. Stickney uttered a widely appreciated sentiment: "As an element of permanent prosperity to a village or city, railway shops are superior in value to any other manufacturing establishment, inasmuch as they continue to run as long as the railway runs, which is perpetual, for although men die, the railway, like the babbling brook, 'runs on forever.'" Early in the twentieth century, the nation had scores of railroad "shop towns" like Oelwein and these places usually prospered. Although tasks varied, railroads faced the constant need to maintain, rebuild, or even construct their rosters of labor-intensive steam locomotives, and this demanded large, skilled workforces. Other pieces of rolling stock, most commonly freight and passenger cars, also required attention.[50]

By October the race to become the G&F shop town was in full swing. Civic boosters realized that inducements were expected; railroads had long made such demands. Understandably officials received several proposals for "this ripe, mellow plum." Augusta offered thirty acres and $20,000 or $30,000 without the land; Douglas tendered 100 acres and $10,000, Hazlehurst volunteered 100 acres and $5,000, and Vidalia replicated the Hazlehurst deal. Valdosta, though, did not propose a specific amount of either real estate or cash incentives.[51]

Then in November 1908 the G&F made its decision: "Douglas gets the shops!" Not surprisingly the contest boiled down to the offers made by Augusta and Douglas. But the earlier observation that "Augusta has geographical disadvantages that will operate against her" probably had an impact. Also location in Augusta was hardly perfect; namely a piece of broken-down equipment would need to be pulled or loaded onto a flatcar to reach the north end. Douglas was better situated, being 160 miles from Augusta, ninety miles from Madison, and at the end of the Barrow's Bluff-Broxton branch, or as the *Douglas Enterprise* put it: "The road at the present time has 270 miles of road in operation [and] 170 miles of it being south of the Altamaha river." Furthermore, the G&F would compete with other railroads and industries in Augusta for skilled workers, particularly carpenters, machinists, and painters. Outsiders, too, mostly thought Douglas to be a good choice. The place thrived and its citizens "do not 'hunt possums with brass bands.'"[52]

The win delighted the citizenry of Douglas. "The prize is a big one." A local editor rightly believed that "the growth of Douglas has just begun." And he added, "In fact the root has just taken a good hold and the growth from now on will be steady and sure," an observation that repeated those earlier comments made by Stickney of the Great Western.[53]

It did not take long before crews, made up of "over 150 hands and 200 mules," began preparing the site north of Douglas. Carpenters, bricklayers, and other construction workers followed. Although not as massive as facilities found on large roads, the complex consisted of nine structures, including an 86x14-foot brick machine and erecting shop that contained four engine pits, and a 63x63-foot brick blacksmith shop. Williams happily noted that "these buildings have been constructed in a substantial manner, of brick and wood, with fireproof tile roof, securing, as far as possible, protection against fire, and they provide, in the aggregate, floor space of nearly an acre." The buildings and the accompanying track work covered about three-quarters of donated land; later the company sold the remaining real estate for non-railroad purposes. One parcel, which consisted of sixteen acres and was valued at $5,000, went to J. M. Turner, general manager of the G&F, for $1,400, although for a railroad-related function. "Mr. Turner's purpose in purchasing this [land] was to erect thereon houses for negro laborers at the shops, a need that was quite pressing." This "need" reflected the extent of "Jim Crow" segregation in the Deep South. At last, in January 1910, about seventy-five shops' employees, both white and black, skilled and unskilled, took up their assignments in a complex that cost about $70,000.[54]

Douglas hoped that the general offices would also become permanent. In April 1908 the *Augusta Chronicle* noted that G&F employees were not too happy being assigned to this community of approximately 4,000 residents. The journalistic pronouncement: "Better come home, Mr. Georgia and Florida headquarters." A Douglas editor candidly admitted that "Douglas people are accustomed to a small town and get along all right, but these railroad people want the comforts of a city as near as possible. Of course, this is impossible here." But because of work on the south end, the company did not relocate the approximately seventy office employees to the Leonard Building in downtown Augusta until October 1, 1909. "The different departments have been busy all the week packing and loading in special cars. The entire force including baggage and the office fixtures will occupy a special train, leaving this city Tuesday morning," reported the *Douglas Enterprise*. "Douglas gives these people up with much reluctance and wishes for them much pleasure and success in their new quarters. That they will be missed would be putting it mildly, for they have made numerous friends in the city who will ever hold them dear in their memory."[55]

EQUIPPING AND OPERATING THE G&F

Obviously the G&F needed more than a track structure and support facilities; it required proper rolling stock for freight, passenger, and maintenance purposes. The hodgepodge of locomotives, freight, passenger, and miscellaneous cars inherited from the predecessor firms allowed the G&F to function, but not at the levels of efficiency and economy desired. The locomotive situation was particularly troubling. "The motive power is still largely made up of small inefficient engines acquired with the original property," as Williams noted in March 1910, "all of which are in very bad physical condition." Therefore after mid-1909 the G&F began to acquire replacement rolling stock, including eleven locomotives. The Baldwin Locomotive Works built six of these engines for the company. They sported the popular 4-6-0 wheel arrangement with 28,493 pounds of tractive effort and were intended for both freight and passenger assignments. The five other locomotives, 2-6-0s, were "purchased from another system [Richmond, Fredericksburg & Potomac] that found it necessary to use a heavier type of engine, but which locomotives were sufficiently heavy and well adapted for the service to which we find it desirable to apply them."[56]

In 1909 the Baldwin Locomotive Company of Philadelphia built for the G&F No. 50, a husky 4-6-0 Ten Wheeler. This piece of motive power, with its 57-inch drivers, later would be renumbered 205, remaining mostly in freight service until its sale in 1937 to another southern carrier, the Applachicola Northern Railroad. (Railroad Museum of Pennsylvania [PHMC])

Other pieces of new rolling stock also appeared. In late 1908 the G&F arranged for a substantial number of freight cars from the South Atlantic Car & Manufacturing Company of Waycross. The order included a hundred 80,000-pound capacity box cars and thirty 60,000-pound capacity flat cars, representing an investment of $200,838. Between 1908 and 1911 the railroad added eight passenger cars from the Hicks Locomotive & Car Works of Chicago. All but two featured steam heating systems although they came equipped with cheaper oil rather than electric lights. For cost considerations the G&F did not opt for the more expensive coaches with vestibules. During this same period two combination mail and baggage cars, also constructed by Hicks, arrived on the property. The G&F spent $4,700 for the former and $4,400 for the latter. The company also paid $740 each for three cabooses from the Georgia Car & Locomotive Company of Atlanta. And that firm supplied an office car for $5,800, but unlike the passenger coaches it came with electric illumination.[57]

As of June 30, 1910, the inventory of rolling stock appeared adequate for the operation of a 332-mile carrier. The G&F owned twenty-eight locomotives, the majority of which were the small American Standard (4-4-0) type. Freight equipment, including six cabooses, totaled 609 pieces, and there were twenty-one passenger coaches, two mail-and-baggage cars, and the office car. Miscellaneous units completed the equipment roster, including twenty-one "camp cars," two steam shovels, and a pile driver, all for maintenance-of-way purposes.[58]

As the property took shape, the G&F adjusted its passenger service. Early on, the company largely replicated the schedules offered by predecessor companies. The trackage between Valdosta and Madison is representative.

Part of the early fleet of motive power included No. 17, a stately 4-4-0 locomotive built in 1883 by the Baldwin Locomotive Company and in 1909 acquired from the Cincinnati, New Orleans & Texas Pacific Railroad (CNO&TP). John Skelton Williams's close connection with John Scott, former president and general manager of the CNO&TP, may explain the purchase. This photograph, taken in Douglas, Georgia, about 1910 shows more than a young boy and G&F employees; it reveals wonderfully the individualistic nature of southern railroading. A set of antlers and an Indian with bow and arrow rest on the front of the engine, surely the handiwork of the locomotive's engineer. (Albert M. Langley, Jr. Coll.)

The schedule for the "Valdosta Southern Division of the Georgia & Florida Railway," which became effective on December 18, 1907, listed two daily mixed trains between its terminals and a single run on Sundays. These movements connected conveniently in Valdosta with other trains for Brunswick, Montgomery, and Waycross on the ACL and Macon and Jacksonville on the SR (Georgia Southern & Florida). As the several short-lines became connected, longer runs appeared over G&F rails.[59]

The most dramatic improvement came in November 1909 with the opening of the "Vidalia-Hazlehurst Extension." Happily announced the railroad: "We are now operating through trains from Augusta to Madison, using the Central of Georgia Railway's tracks from Augusta to Millen, giving the only direct through service to Southern Georgia and Florida points." This new long-distance service was enthusiastically received. When the first train steamed over the joint CofG-G&F route, hundreds of residents showed up to gawk at dignitaries and to express their pleasure. At Vidalia a brass band stood on the depot platform to entertain the assembled by playing popular tunes, including that Spanish-American War era favorite, "There's going to be a hot time in the old town tonight."[60]

Not long thereafter when the "Swainsboro-Normantown Extension" was ready and the lease made with the AS, the G&F offered what the Passenger Traffic Department immodestly billed as "Unexcelled Passenger Train Service." On August 3, 1910, the railroad distributed a circular that showed "daily double" round-trip service between Augusta Union Station and Douglas and a daily round-trip through train between Augusta and the SAL depot in Madison. The Broxton, Millen and Sparks branches each had two daily trains, although times varied for Sunday runs. Since the G&F did not operate dining cars, food stops became necessary. Take No. 4. This north-bound train left SAL's Madison depot at 7:40 a.m. and paused in Hazlehurst at 1:00 p.m. for twenty minutes so the hungry could eat quickly at an adjoining hotel. At 7:20 p.m. No. 4 reached Augusta (it was actually an hour later since the city used Eastern rather than Central time), and passengers could find food at a nearby hotel or restaurant.[61]

Even before through-line trains chugged along the G&F, the company ran a variety of extra movements. Newspapers repeatedly announced these "specials" and "excursions." On Washington's Birthday, 1910, for example, the railroad operated a special sponsored by the Augusta Chamber of Commerce and the Merchants and Manufacturers' Association. The purpose was for Augusta area businessmen to better acquaint themselves with their counterparts in online G&F communities. Augusta boosters were not going to miss any opportunities for enhancing their city's sphere of influence over the Wiregrass hinterlands. "Augusta is sure to become the trade distributing center for a large part of the territory traversed by the new road." City interests would benefit not only from the convenience of service, but also because the presence of the G&F brought about reductions in passenger fares and freight rates. As for the latter, the Swainsboro editor believed that "on first class matter it will be something like a reduction of 18 cents per hundred."[62]

Freight, of course, was the crucial business. At the time the G&F established through passenger service between Augusta and Madison, it announced "a most convenient freight train service . . . between Augusta and South Georgia and Florida points." Although the railroad by 1910 began its long crusade for crop diversification and expansion, it was hardly an agricultural carrier. "Products of Agriculture," including cotton and cotton seed, amounted to less than ten percent of tonnage. It would be "Products of Forest," namely logs, lumber, ties and naval stores, the principal commodities handled by its predecessors, that constituted more than sixty percent of tonnage. The other sizable amount (twenty-one percent) included "Manufactures," with the largest being fertilizers for the nutrient-drained soil of Wiregrass cotton fields.

The shabby nature of structures on the G&F is revealed in this ca. 1916 photograph made of the Broxton, Georgia, station by the Bureau of Valuation. It was common for the railroad to have depots with a small, passenger waiting room, containing both white and colored sections, and larger freight shed designed for storage of cotton, fertilizer, and LCL shipments. (National Archives)

The railroad, too, did a good business with package or less-than-carload (LCL) freight. With the opening of the main line a freight left at 8:00 p.m. with "package cars," a service enabling "Augusta merchants to deliver their goods the following morning." Yet although profitable, the "merchandise" category amounted to only about one percent of overall tonnage.[63]

Company officers labored to develop every possible freight revenue opportunity. Not only did H. C. McFadden, the general freight agent, and Colonel A. Pope, the traffic manager, beat the bushes for business, but Williams himself also did what he could. In September 1910 the G&F president contacted James T. Wright, who served as vice president and general manager of the Macon, Dublin & Savannah Railroad, which connected with the G&F at Vidalia, and told him: "I wish we could find a way to develop a larger interchange of business." This aggressiveness in traffic solicitation became a hallmark of the usually financially strapped G&F.[64]

By Fall 1910 Williams felt good about the financial prospects of the G&F. "Since the completion of the final connecting link and the opening of the through line between Madison and Augusta during the past summer, the business . . . has shown a gratifying increase." Yet he admitted that "it will naturally take some little time to draw a full share of competitive traffic to the new line, develop the local business and secure the consequential benefits from through service for the new short north and south route."[65]

Gross earnings mostly bore out Williams's optimism. The figure for the fiscal year that ended June 30, 1911, amounted to $704,936, an increase over the previous fiscal year's earnings of $182,697 or thirty-five percent. The June 30, 1910, gross earnings had been $131,069 or thirty-three percent better than those for the fiscal year that ended on June 30, 1909.[66]

Interested observers confirmed the good news. "On Friday last fifty-six cars of freight were handled in and out of Augusta," noted the *Douglas Enterprise* in October 1910. "The incoming cars brought cotton, cotton seed and lumber, while the outgoing ones carried merchandise of all kinds and cotton consigned to Savannah." Concluded the newspaper: "A wonderful record for business has been made by the Georgia and Florida railroad since its line was completed into Augusta just a few months ago." And there were repeated published reports about new businesses that appeared at trackside. "Messrs. G. F. Flanders and John F. Price have purchased an excellent turpentine location nine miles below Vidalia on the Georgia & Florida Railway," the editor of the *Forest-Blade* told readers in 1909, "and will open up business as soon as possible."[67]

There was every reason to expect that the developing G&F held a good future. If this "Augusta South Georgia Short Line" were to reach deep water at Tampa, Carrabelle, or some other port and could extend beyond Augusta, perhaps to Columbia, earnings would surely become stronger. In the process the overall quality of the physical plant and service also would undoubtedly improve. Maybe crack name-trains would someday race along the main line, making the G&F a darling of the South. Conceivably, too, owners of the G&F might sell out at a handsome profit to another carrier, most probably the SAL, and the new regime would further develop the property. While great expectations existed, reality, however, would be considerably different. Within a decade the G&F would be in the hands of a bankruptcy judge and rumors would abound that much of the road would be junked. The optimism that had been so pronounced prior to 1911 had mostly disappeared, and the survival of the G&F emerged as the paramount issue.

CHAPTER THREE

Established at Last, 1911–1925

Improving the G&F

J ohn Skelton Williams and his business partners had no intention of ignoring the most troubling limitations to their newly assembled Georgia & Florida Railway (G&F). The property had shortcomings, best represented by the lack of its own line into Augusta from its northern terminus at Keysville. For some time this weakness would not be overcome, largely because of the opportunity to operate over the connecting segment of the Augusta Southern Railroad (AS). The trackage-contract agreement, which became official on January 1, 1910, proved workable and convinced management that constructing a mostly parallel line could be postponed, perhaps indefinitely. Explained Williams to an investor friend in early 1911: "The arrangement under which the Georgia & Florida Railway uses the tracks of the Augusta Southern Railway from Keysville, Ga., to Augusta, Ga., about 26 miles, runs for a term of years, and it is the expectation that it will be continued so long as it may be satisfactory."[1]

Although renting (and later buying) the AS solved the most glaring deficiency, another matter required attention, namely the trackage situation in Valdosta. Although the main line from the north reached this active trading and manufacturing community of nearly 15,000 residents and from the south the former Valdosta Southern Railway extended into the city, the two lines lacked a direct physical connection. The immediate solution involved acquiring trackage rights, duplicating the plan of how to enter Augusta. In this case, G&F trains rumbled over Atlantic Coast Line (ACL) rails, but the G&F wished to end that expense. More significantly, the company sought to develop its own money-generating terminal facilities in a prime commercial locale.[2]

Solving the Valdosta problem was far less costly than building into Augusta. What the Skelton regime did was to form the Georgia & Florida Terminal Company (G&FT), which on June 27, 1910, received its official corporation papers from the State of Georgia. The wholly owned G&FT subsidiary quickly purchased about fifteen acres of urban property, mostly east of the commercial district, and constructed 1.1 miles of track that connected the G&F's detached main lines. The land offered ample room for railroad operations and online businesses; the result was wholly satisfactory. In 1911 George B. Hazlehurst, a consulting engineer from Baltimore, reported that the terminal addition "places the Georgia & Florida on a par, as to location, with either the Atlantic Coast Line or the Georgia Southern & Florida Railway [Southern Railway]." Added Hazlehurst: "This property is capable of considerable development for industrial purposes, and will in course of time add to the Company's revenue." Soon the G&F contracted to build a sixty-two by 210-foot, two-story brick warehouse that workers finished in the spring of 1912. And later the company made additional improvements, including construction of its own passenger station.[3]

Even though the G&F entered Augusta on leased trackage, the railroad nevertheless owned and developed its own local terminal facilities. As with the Valdosta betterments, the company quickly created a functional presence in Augusta's Twigg Street neighborhood. "The location of the terminal property of the Georgia & Florida Railway is excellent, being unexcelled by that of any Railway in Augusta," observed Consulting Engineer Hazlehurst following a system-wide inspection. "The ground was formerly occupied by a large steam cotton compress and its warehouses. These old brick buildings have been so remodeled as to provide good freight depots. The buildings not required by the Railway for its own use have been arranged as warehouses, and rented to commercial firms, producing some $1,800 per year revenue." Concluded Hazlehurst, "The freight yard is provided with the necessary receiving and delivery tracks, and the present facilities are amply sufficient for the Company's needs for some years to come, and are then capable of being enlarged for a considerable future growth."[4]

During these formative years, discussions regularly occurred about making the G&F even longer. Early in 1911 Williams wrote confidentially that "No plans for the extension of the Georgia & Florida Railway beyond Moultre or Madison have yet been determined upon." Yet, the owners did not believe that the company map was complete. Later in the year Williams mentioned privately that "The Georgia & Florida Railway has had several extensions under consideration, including an extension of its lines from Augusta, Ga., to Columbia, S.C., where it would connect with the three important Southern trunk line systems [ACL, Seaboard and Southern]." And he continued, "We have also been considering an extension from Augusta, northeastwardly [sic], to Athens, on the Seaboard Air Line, which if built, would make a line equally as short, if not shorter, than the existing route over the Georgia Railroad between those two important cities."[5]

Williams was not alone with such proposals and expectations. Other contemporary railroad promoters discussed projects in the region. Surely the most grandiose involved an electric interurban, the Atlanta & Carolina Railway. This "juice" road, incorporated in 1908 by largely Atlanta interests, sought to build a high-speed line between Augusta, Atlanta, and West Point,

Georgia, a distance of more than 200 miles. The scheme sputtered and then quietly disappeared, although in the summer of 1911 the *Electric Railway Journal* reported that the company "has completed grading [from] White City to Carters, a distance of about 10 miles," adding that "grading will be completed between Atlanta and Conyers by Oct. 1, and track laying will begin immediately."[6]

As for the G&F, rumors flew and public pronouncements repeatedly indicated that existing termini would not be "permanent." While this reflected the intent of Williams and his associates, unfounded, even extravagant press reports circulated. In late 1912 the *Savannah Morning News* believed that the company contemplated an extension between Douglas and Savannah, a project that this newspaper wholeheartedly endorsed. Not long thereafter an enthusiastic newspaper editor from Swainsboro penned this speculative and outlandish observation: "To build a through trunk line from Florida to the north is said to be the direct aim of the management of the road having its Northern terminus at Washington or probably New York." Added the hopeful journalist, "All this means a better outlet and inlet for our town and county." Unmistakably, railroad expansion remained a topic of great interest, indicating that the transportation needs of the Wiregrass Region and beyond had not been fully met. Every community craved a trunk line, hardly content with the services of a shortline or an appendage of a larger road.[7]

If the Williams group had wanted to add quickly and inexpensively to the "system," there were opportunities. Several owners of small logging roads offered their properties at bargain-basement prices. In May 1912, for example, Max McRae contacted the G&F president about taking over his Jacksonville, McRae & Northern Railway project. In this instance and in others, Williams politely declined. Likely Williams recognized that such pikes would contribute little to overall revenues and that any acquisitions should extend to major communities or reach strategic connections.[8]

Others, too, discussed the future of the G&F. About the time McRae wrote Williams, Richard Edmonds, editor of the *Manufacturers Record*, a Baltimore-based business publication, editorialized that the "development of Florida, in which the Seaboard has a very strong strategic position, is in its infancy. The Seaboard and the Georgia & Florida road ought to unite and get a line down the West Coast of Florida, and then the two roads would have an exceptionally strong position." Until the mid-1920s speculation about a G&F union with the SAL intermittently appeared in the trade, business, and local press as did occasional references to other possible suitors, usually the Southern Railway (SR).[9]

In 1912 the G&F took some modest action to increase mileage. Widespread reports once more circulated that the G&F planned to build its own connecting link between St. Clair and Augusta. But this time there were a few flames beneath the smoke. "A corps of civil engineers is marking out a road for the Georgia & Florida Railroad Co. from St. Claire [*sic*] to this city [Augusta] on

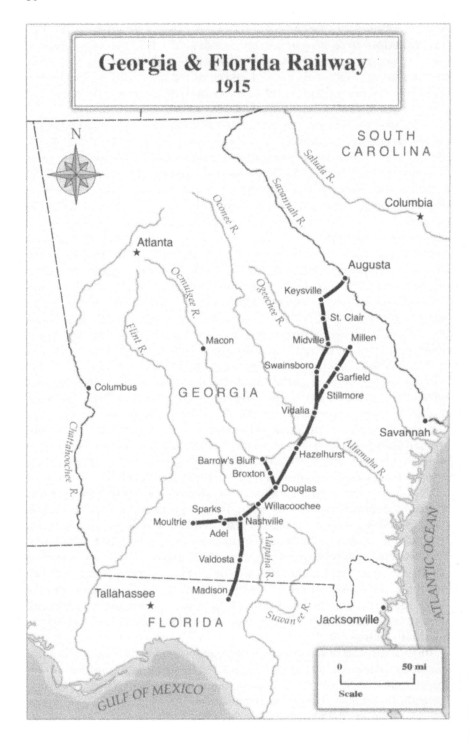

Georgia & Florida Railway
1915

an almost direct line," noted the *Wall Street Journal.* "It will carry the line near Story's Mill, across Ridge and on to Augusta, between the Central of Georgia and the Augusta Southern roads." But only surveys, likely some detailed, resulted; graders never followed.[10]

Irrespective of future growth the G&F needed to attend to its immediate equipment needs. Although the railroad inherited a hodgepodge of rolling stock and early on made some major acquisitions, including motive power, in May 1911 online newspapers reported that the "Georgia and Florida Railway has just purchased four handsome new passenger coaches from the Central Locomotive & Car Works of Chicago and one 60-foot combination baggage and mail car from the same company." Other additions were even more noteworthy. "The Georgia and Florida has also purchased two 12-section buffet and drawing room sleeping cars. . . . [The railroad] also announces the purchase of two 100-ton locomotives from the Baldwin Locomotive Works and these monster engines will supplant the lighter type . . . now in use." The press, however, ignored the mundane. In mid-1912 Williams told investors that "thirty-two flat cars were rebuilt and put back into service, and six caboose cars were built in our shops during the year." And more pieces of freight equipment were to arrive before World War I, including 100 flatcars. By September 1912 the motive power, freight, and passenger equipment roster consisted of thirty-seven coal-burning locomotives, 587 freight cars, with the largest category being flatcars (311) designed primarily for logs and lumber, seventeen coaches, seven combination baggage, express and passenger cars, two baggage units, and two sleeping cars. The company also owned office car No. 100.[11]

Even though journalists and Williams touted betterments and acquisitions, the G&F could not claim to be fully a first-class property. The greatest limitations appeared centered along the old Valdosta Southern. In late 1911 Sheriff A. D. Stanton of Madison County complained to the Florida Railroad Commission about the sad state of the railroad in his jurisdiction. In April 1912 the regulatory body reassured him that the G&F was dealing with the situation. The Commission included a letter received from the railroad's general manager, acknowledging shortcomings but indicating that improvements either had been or were being made to the physical plant.

> I noticed the Withlacoochee River trestle was badly out of line. I immediately ordered a gang there and had this trestle lined up and put in safe condition. I also found plenty of crossties between Withlacoochee River and Madison, Fla., and plenty of men to do the work on the track, if they had been property utilized. I instructed the road master on that division to discharge his foreman, which he did, and put another foreman in charge of the section, and I am pleased to report that we have had good results in improvement of our roadbed and track.

Now, in regard to ditching and widening of embankments, would advise that we have just recently purchased an improved ditching machine and it is my intention to widen the cut just south of the Withlacoochee River and fill up part of this trestle, which work will be done as early as possible.[12]

SERVING THE PUBLIC

The improvements made to the G&F during its formative years mostly satisfied the traveling and shipping public. With the additions to the locomotive and car fleets the company added trains, adjusted schedules, and cut prices. Although "daily-double" passenger service remained on the main line between Augusta and Madison, additional trains appeared between Augusta and Douglas and Hazlehurst and Madison. And night train No. 7 left Augusta two hours later, allowing for more convenient intermediate connections and faster travel time to Valdosta. The company also reduced the lower sleeping-berth rate to $1.50 between Augusta and Douglas and Valdosta and $1.25 for the upper berth. In early 1913 these actions prompted the *Swainsboro Forest-Blade* to conclude that "while the Georgia & Florida has not yet reached perfection and may never, its service now is good—better than it has ever been—and the management of it is working hard to give the public every accommodation and every advantage it can possibly give." The editor believed that "the road has been brought up to a very good standard and the trains are all modernly and comfortably equipped. Schedules are arranged excellently, and all told the service is very good."[13]

The G&F continued to push hard for greater passenger patronage. Newspaper advertisements, press releases, and printed broadsides repeatedly sought to increase ridership on regularly scheduled trains. During the summer of 1913 the company enticed heat-weary residents of the Wiregrass Region to take advantage of a reduced joint fare offered by the G&F and SR to "THE BEAUTIFUL ISLE OF PALMS," outside Charleston, South Carolina, where "the Surf Bathing is unsurpassable. The beach without an undertow. No flies, mosquitoes or other insects on the Island." At the same time, the G&F promoted travel to Asheville and nearby Waynesville, North Carolina, again in conjunction with the SR. "Cool off in the Lake of the Sky at very small cost for your health and pleasure." That same year the G&F again teamed up with the SR to offer "SPECIAL LOW RATES TO CHATTANOOGA, TENN. AND RETURN." The company sought to attract attendees from south Georgia and north Florida to the Confederate Veterans' Reunion to be held in Chattanooga from May 27 to May 29. The G&F offered a special round trip rate of $8.70 from Madison to the conclave via a connection with the SR at Hazlehurst. And in 1915 the G&F gave "Uncle Charlie Wilkinson," a civic booster from Swainsboro, a bargain rate for his party of townspeople going to Augusta, where they would spend a day at the popular Lake View Park served by the cars of the Augusta-Aiken Railway & Electric Company.

Tickets, priced at one dollar, included the fare charged by the local interurban to "This Greatest Pleasure Resort in the Southeast. Splendid Boating, Wild Animals, Excellent Swings [and] Cool Breezes that remind one of Tybee [Island, Georgia]." According to the *Swainsboro Forest-Blade,* "Uncle Charlie sets out that the train will be handled in a most careful manner, that ladies and children may go with the utmost complacency, that all unpleasantness and carousing will actually be eliminated, giving Swainsboro residents protection seldom had on such occasions."[14]

The G&F repeatedly offered special rates for online destinations. The company, for instance, advertised "picnic parties" to Mayhaw Lake near Ray's Mill (Ray City), a small resort that opened in May 1914. The attractions were varied: "A fine bathing pool supplied with fine Sulphur water, one of the best Skating Rinks in this Section. Cold drinks, hot lunches at all hours during the day and night; also a good base ball diamond open to visiting teams for match games." Somewhat later the G&F tempted the public with reduced rates on all of its trains to attend the "GREAT TOBACCO BOOSTER DAY" in Douglas. "Experts from all the tobacco belt will speak explaining to the people great benefits of tobacco culture. The speel of the auctioneer never fails to entertain. You should take advantage of this opportunity to come in contact with the industry and get valuable information on the subject."[15]

The company remained committed to special excursions. Although extra passenger trains commonly operated to Augusta and back for a wide range of events, including baseball games, circuses, and fraternal gatherings, the Passenger Department did not neglect opportunities elsewhere. For years, beginning in 1911, the railroad invited Douglas residents to attend the annual G&F employee basket picnic at Dixie Lake Park outside Sparks. "Now remember, good people, this is your invitation to join us on this big picnic, and we assure you a good enjoyable day—such as dancing, skating, bathing, ball game, and other amusements too numerous to mention." As for details, "the picnic train will leave G. & F. Depot at 8:00 A.M., leave Sparks at 6:30 P.M. Round-trip tickets, adults $1.00, children $.50." On June 27, 1916, area farmers, however, might have found more inviting the opportunity to board a special train that departed Douglas for Moultrie so that riders could attend a livestock-improvement meeting. "Everybody is urged to attend this conference," proclaimed the G&F. "It is going to be worth many times the cost and time."[16]

Just as the Passenger Department sought to fill seats on regularly scheduled and special passenger trains, company personnel, led by the traffic manager, labored to increase freight tonnage. The railroad aggressively solicited all types of traffic. In April 1913 the Swainsboro newspaper told of the recent success of G&F Commercial Agent Harry Thompson. "It [G&F] has handled much of the guano manufactured by the Swainsboro Fertilizer Co., and Mr. Thompson has succeeded in pulling their way a large amount

Special Excursion
Monday July 12th,

VIA

Georgia and Florida Ry.

to Augusta

Round Trip Fares $3.50

TRAIN LEAVES

DOUGLAS 3:15 A. M.—ARRIVES AUGUSTA 8:50 A. M.

Returning Leave Augusta. 8:10 P. M.

EVERYBODY INVITED TO AUGUSTA ON JULY 12th.
GO TO AUGUSTA AND VISIT THE CONEY
ISLAND OF THE SOUTH.

EXTRA COACHES FOR WHITE & COLORED PEOPLE.
PLENTY OF ROOM.

AMUSEMENTS FOR WHITE PEOPLE: VISIT DEANS
BRIDGE. THE CONY ISLAND OF THE SOUTH.
FOR THE COLORED PEOPLE: BIG BALL GAME BE-
TWEEN SWAINSBORO TIGERS—AUGUST WHITE SOX

For further information consult:
JOHN BANKSTON, General Agent

Georgia & Florida Railway

Prior to World War II, the G&F repeatedly offered a variety of special passenger excursions. Augusta, the largest city on the road, became a popular destination. In the Jim Crow South, the company strove to attract both white and African-American patrons, but members of each race rode separately. (Author's Coll.)

of that shipped in this county during the season." The railroad sought to maintain freight schedules, supply necessary equipment, install switches and side tracks, and "do whatever we can to do to pamper the shipper."[17]

THE FINANCIAL PICTURE

The private correspondence of John Skelton Williams reveals that he and his business associates paid careful attention to the financial condition of the G&F, and optimism prevailed. In a May 4, 1911, letter to an investor in Paris, France, Williams commented that "The Georgia & Florida Railway is developing slowly, but steadily. The gross earnings for March 1911, amounted to $68,244, an increase of $15,299 over the same month last year, the increase being approximately 30%."[18]

Public pronouncements likewise reflected overall satisfaction with the road's financial progress. In 1911 John L. Williams & Sons issued an eight-page brochure, "Concerning the Georgia and Florida Railway," in which both the road's favorable bonded debt and earnings potential were emphasized. "The total mileage *operated* by the Georgia & Florida Railway at the present time is about 350 miles; *owned* 325 miles, so that the total outstanding bonded debt on the Georgia & Florida Railway now is just *$18,000 per Mile of Road owned,* or $16,750 per mile operated. In addition to these bonds the Company has also outstanding $218,000 of Car Trust Obligations, and has guaranteed the bonds of the Georgia & Florida Terminal Co., of which the amount outstanding at the present time does not exceed $150,000." Although the G&F did not open fully until the latter part of 1910, the expected earnings per mile were estimated at $2,515 for 1911, $3,520 for 1913, and $4,600 for 1915 with gross earnings increasing from $880,250 in 1911 to $1,251,400 in 1913 and $1,610,000 in 1915. This assessment contended that "the Georgia & Florida Railway has been financed and constructed on a conservative basis," and believed that "to meet interest on its entire bonded debt it will be only necessary for the railroad to earn gross *$2,700 per mile,* if operating expenses and taxes be kept at 66 2/3% of the gross; or if the road should be operated at a 70% ratio, gross earnings of *$3,000 per mile* would suffice to meet all interest charges." Compared to other railroads in the South and all independent carriers that operated 350 or more miles, the Williams banking house anticipated this performance. Moreover, the service territory continued to grow and conditions "are favorable to economical railroad operation, such as cheap materials, timber, cross-ties, etc., satisfactory labor conditions and the low cost of living incident to the long open seasons, absence of snow and ice, economy in fuel, etc., etc." It was a rosy picture, indeed.[19]

Unfortunately, the financial scenario did not develop as supposed. Although for several years after the G&F began through operations between Augusta and Madison, management believed that "the outlook for a large business was most auspicious." Yet threatening clouds gathered, some literally in the skies. The Wiregrass Region was susceptible to thunderstorms and heavy rains and the occasional torrential downpours spawned by ocean-born storms. In August 1911 a powerful hurricane struck Georgia and South Carolina, inflicting considerable, widespread destruction. The G&F was more vulnerable than nearby roads because of its recent construction and rehabilitation projects. Water softened or washed away sections of its "green" embankments and cuts and also weakened or destroyed numerous wooden bridges. "The damage done to the Georgia & Florida Railway by this storm and the incidental washouts was large, involving serious interruption to the company's business for a considerable part of the month of August, and running into September."[20]

To exacerbate the problems, a succession of storms followed. Unfortunately for the region, the winter and spring of 1911–1912 turned out to be a time of record-setting rainfall. More costly problems with roadbeds, bridges, and train operations resulted. Furthermore, agricultural production was disrupted. "The continued wet weather greatly delayed the preparation of the land for crops, and this delay occasioned a material reduction in the use of commercial fertilizers, the transportation of which in the Spring is usually the source of important revenue." The excessive moisture led to a nearly total failure of the cantaloupe and watermelon crops and greatly reduced cotton yields. Output in Georgia fell by about forty percent. Car loadings lagged. With less money in Wiregrass communities, fewer people traveled and bought from local businesses.[21]

Not long after the August hurricane a bitter fireman's strike erupted. Throughout its corporate life, the G&F suffered from repeated labor troubles that were easily explained. The company paid poorly, often less than seventy-five percent of wages provided by neighboring Class 1 roads. Admittedly, the costs of living were generally low in most communities served by the G&F; still, these pay differentials annoyed and at times angered employees. And periodically other work-related issues entered the equation.[22]

The issue that prompted firemen to strike at 4 p.m. on September 28, 1911, centered on wages. H. O. Teat, Vice-president of the Brotherhood of Locomotive Firemen and Enginemen (BLF&E), whose office was in Atlanta, explained the position of the disgruntled G&F workers in a letter of October 3 to the *Atlanta Georgian:*

> These men have worked for small wages for the last seven years, while this road has bought different lines of road and made great improvements and is now running more than 350 miles of track and its report to the comptroller general shows thousands of dollars increase yearly. The men are only paid 40 per cent. of the engineers' pay which is nothing like standard pay. They have only asked for 50 per cent. of the engineers' wages, which is a small increase and does not bring them up anywhere to the standard rate of pay of other roads in Georgia.

I say that Mr. [John Skelton] Williams' statement is false in toto when he says the men are paid as much as other roads. The officials of this company treat the employees worse than any railroad that I know of. They are not allowed to make any complaint whatever. If they do they are discharged. . . . I am satisfied that the fair-minded citizens will not condemn the firemen, as Mr. Williams would have them do in every statement he has made.[23]

As the BLF&E official indicated, major differences existed between workers and managers. What followed would be a total walkout; "the strikers include the negroes as well as the white men." Six days into the job action the *Nashville Herald* reported that "it is said that a good deal of freight is tied up on the line and that passenger trains are also unable to run." This situation greatly annoyed the editor: "The people of Nashville are especially anxious that some kind of settlement with regards the Georgia and Florida strike be speedily made, since our mail must be brought from Sparks in an automobile and our freight hauled from Adel in wagons, bringing about extra expense upon the part of our merchants."[24]

The region's newspapers indicated that the firemen caused more than suspension of train service. Violence erupted. The aggressive acts were not committed toward personnel, but against property. Several instances of fires "believed to be of incendiary origin" damaged or destroyed bridges, including the 100-foot timber trestle over Brushy Creek between Keysville and St. Clair. Although the G&F offered a hefty $250 reward for the apprehension and conviction of the guilty parties, no one stepped forward. There were additional instances of "wanton destruction of property by the strikers."[25]

Although acts of sabotage troubled the public, the G&F firemen found considerable support. In a classic statement of what labor scholars call the "Gutman thesis," namely the conclusion reached by historian Herbert Gutman that residents of smaller communities usually backed strikers against their employers, an online editor opined: "The situation has reached rather a serious stage and while the public regrets that the present state of affairs exists, and is anxious for a speedy settlement, it heartily endorses the firemen's stand and wishes for them in the end—victory."[26]

When in mid-October a settlement at last occurred, neither labor nor management could claim a decisive victory. Wages were only slightly adjusted upwards and the G&F had suffered property destruction and loss of traffic revenue. Williams told stockholders that "this [strike] proved especially costly, coming as it did at the time when the autumn business was at its height." And the anger continued: "The public does not realize to what extent the railroads have to submit to the dictates of the Brotherhood of Engineers and Firemen. Every man should be paid a reasonable wage, but there is a limit to what a railroad can pay and remain solvent."[27]

Although labor conditions stabilized, the weather did not. The growing season of 1912–1913 remained abnormally wet and "so seriously affected the yield of cotton throughout the Railway's entire territory as to shorten the yield fully 40%." Freight tonnage dropped and the volume of passenger traffic also dipped. But toward the latter part of 1913 rainfall lessened and agricultural conditions improved; in fact, 1914 became a good year for the production of cotton and other field crops.[28]

Much less discernable to casual observers, but nevertheless affecting the G&F financially, was the decline in the overall rate of growth in the Wiregrass Region. The boom that had begun at the turn of the twentieth century had largely run its course by the eve of World War I. "Population seems about at a standstill," noted a knowledgeable visitor in his diary for 1913. "Few trees being cut, & no history being made outside of the cities."[29]

Even though operating income rose modestly between 1911 and 1914, by 1913 management realized that financial matters needed to be addressed even more aggressively. No one wanted the G&F to stumble into bankruptcy. The man now at the throttle was R. Lancaster Williams, a younger brother of John Skelton Williams. The senior Williams had not severed his ties with the railroad that he had headed since its inception, but he relinquished the presidency in order to join the Woodrow Wilson administration in Washington, D.C., as a top official in the Department of the Treasury, first as Assistant Secretary and later as Comptroller of the Currency.[30]

A financial strategy for the G&F quickly emerged. On November 29, 1913, Lancaster Williams told the Board of Directors that "having come to the conclusion that it is impossible for the road to continue to carry the burden of interest on it, a plan has been promulgated [by the Executive Committee] for the lifting of this burden of interest for a period of three years." The Board asked holders of the first mortgage five percent bonds to allow conversion of the next three years of interest coupons into five percent notes that would become redeemable in five years. It did not take long before the vast majority of these debt holders agreed; they understood the plight of the railroad.[31]

The plan to keep the G&F out of the hands of court-appointed receivers might have worked had external forces been more favorable. The outbreak of world war in August 1914 badly disrupted money markets and drove down domestic commodity prices, especially for cotton, lumber, and naval stores. Although the G&F labored hard to generate new sources of carload traffic, most notably fruits and vegetables, the railroad remained heavily dependent on the movement of traditional farm and forest products. "The Railway handled during the season of 1914–1915 a total of 115,866 bales of cotton, compared with 93,860 bales during the preceding season, or an increase of 22,006 bales," noted Lancaster Williams in the latter part of 1915. "Unfortunately, however, the producers did not realize as satisfactory prices and this condition affected the Railways's earnings from both local passenger travel and merchandise shipments." The impact of a depressed forest product industry was more severe. "The most important commodities the Railway has handled since its construction are products of the forest; during the [fiscal 1914–1915] year this tonnage, including shipments received from connecting lines, aggregated 114,596 tons, comparing with 189,139 tons the preceding year, indicating a decrease of 74,543 tons, or 39 per cent," explained Williams. "The producers of these commodities also received less favorable prices than under normal conditions, which further reduced earnings in other directions."[32]

In early spring 1915 the G&F succumbed to these largely uncontrollable negative economic forces. The Board of Directors admitted insolvency and sought protection of the court. On March 27 Henry C. Hammond, Judge of Superior Court of Richmond County in Augusta, placed the railroad in bankruptcy effective the following day. On March 29 M. F. Horne, Judge of the Third Judicial Circuit for Madison County, Florida, concurred with Judge Hammond and replicated his actions. As Lancaster Williams told the financial press, "I regret extremely it has finally been necessary for the Georgia and Florida Railway to seek the protection of the court, but under the circumstances there was no other way to bring about a proper adjustment of the situation." He added, "When I was elected president about three years ago I hoped to bring about the development of its business and such a rearrangement of its securities as would be necessary without a receivership." Management willingly consented to the appointment of three receivers.[33]

The G&F was hardly the nation's only failed carrier. The disruptions caused by World War I threw other railroads into bankruptcy. In 1913, 16,286 miles of railroads nationally were operated by receivers or trustees. The following year that mileage increased to 18,608 and then in 1915 spiked upwards to 30,223 miles, climaxing a year later with 37,353 miles. The total of 1916 would not be surpassed until the Great Depression of the early 1930s.[34]

The new receivers were good and logical choices, and they were knowledgeable and friendly toward the property and its investors. Harry R. Warfield, vice-president of the Baltimore Trust Company in Baltimore, was closely tied to the Williamses' financial interests as was W. R. Sullivan, a transportation expert from New York City who worked for the investment banking house of Redmond & Company, and Colonel James M. Wilkinson, the Valdosta railroad promoter, who had been associated with the G&F since its inception. These men performed well together, although in early 1916 Colonel Wilkinson died, prompting the court to name Langbourne M. Williams, a younger member of the Williams family, as his replacement. Another change occurred on April 10, 1918, when Warfield resigned because of other business commitments. In his stead the court named John F. Lewis, president of the Citizens Bank in Valdosta. Finally, in 1921, after John Skelton Williams ended his tenure with the Wilson administration, the three incumbent receivers resigned and Williams became the sole court appointee.[35]

AUGUSTA SOUTHERN RAILROAD

Although in the hands of court-appointed receivers, during the World War I era the G&F made an important, strategic acquisition, namely purchase of the Augusta Southern Railroad from the Southern Railway. The G&F paid about $650,000, a reasonable amount since the Interstate Commerce Commission in 1916 had inventoried the property as having a value of $920,000, based on 1914 prices. Finally the G&F owned its own route into greater Augusta, thus ending the earlier track-lease arrangement beyond Keysville. The G&F acquired more than this strategic line; the company purchased an 88.6-mile property that stretched southwestward from Augusta to the thriving Washington County towns of Sandersville and Tennille and served several long-established intermediate communities, including Gibson, the formerly railroad-starved seat of Glascock County. By the time of the G&F takeover the service territory had become an important cotton-growing region, and later, in the 1920s, the kaolin (white clay) industry started to develop, primarily in Washington County.[36]

Resembling the shortlines that constituted the core G&F, the AS itself possessed a complex corporate past. But unlike those other once independent properties that made up the G&F, the AS began as a narrow-gauge (three-foot) line. Following the Civil War some railroad promoters in Georgia caught the narrow-gauge fever that raged nationwide, believing incorrectly that these slim-width pikes could be built and operated much more economically than could railroads constructed to standard gauge. Although Georgia never became a center for narrow-gauge activities, during the height of the craze, which lasted from the early 1870s to the late 1880s, nearly a dozen of these common carriers appeared. Most of the roads were modest in length, although the Marietta & North Georgia Railroad extended 112 miles between Marietta and Murphy, North Carolina, and the Americus, Preston & Lumpkin Railroad (AP&L) stretched 106 miles between Abbeville and Louvale in the southwestern corner of the state. The Augusta, Gibson & Sandersville Railroad (AG&S), the future AS, proudly claimed to be the third longest of these largely disconnected narrow-gauge operations.[37]

Near the end of the narrow-gauge boom the AG&S project took hold. Spearheaded by two Augusta businessmen, R. M. Mitchell and W. B. Young, the plan was to open an inexpensive line through an area largely underserved by the iron horse. The new road would offer a convenient and economical way to transport cotton, lumber, and other freight and would provide an attractive way for area residents to reach Augusta, an already established railroad hub. Rails would not only link Augusta with Sandersville, but they might reach further to the northeast, most probably to Newberry, South Carolina, about eighty miles from Augusta, and also to the southwest for approximately seventy-five miles to Americus. These promoters also considered a branch that would extend from Mitchell, located nearly midway between Augusta and Sandersville, to White Plains, about thirty miles to the northwest. If completed as discussed, the AG&S would have been one of the largest narrow-gauge operations in the South, with a network approaching 275 miles. Newberry would provide a connection with the well-positioned Columbia & Greenville, an affiliate of the Richmond & Danville Railroad; Americus offered a tie-in with the AP&L, which soon became the standard-gauge Savannah, Americus & Montgomery Railway. Savannah, its operating headquarters, was already a major transportation center.[38]

Construction funding for the AG&S came from traditional sources. Money was raised largely through sale of stock to investors who lived along the core route and from the several counties and communities to be served, and from bonds sold through a New York underwriting house. The timing was not particularly auspicious for railroad building, no matter the gauge. There was the "short [cotton] crop of 1883, the yet more disastrous season of 1884 and the general financial depression" that a Wall Street panic triggered in 1884. Nevertheless, the AG&S took shape, a badge of pride for its promoters. "Your railroad has steadily progressed toward completion," noted President Mitchell at the board of directors meeting held in February 1885. "Work on the road has never ceased for a single day since the first spade of earth was thrown [April 25, 1884]." And he continued, "The entire line, 78 miles long, has been surveyed, located . . ., deeds of right of way secured except at a few points from terminus to terminus, and valuable terminal facilities obtained." By early 1885 laborers with their plows and scrapers pulled by teams of horses and mules had shaped more than fifty miles of roadbed. More grading and track work followed. Then on December 10, 1885, the road opened for revenue service between Augusta (and a connection with the three-mile standard-gauge Augusta & Summerville Railroad, a terminal switching road) and Gibson, fifty-one miles. It would not be until November 28, 1886, however, that the spindly rails at last snaked their way to Sandersville. The building process included a large number of wooden trestles, including 2,658 feet of timber spans over the Ogeechee River. As of February 1, 1887, the company indicated that it had spent $568,337.67, including $464,348.83 on "Road and Equipment."[39]

Typical of narrow-gauge roads, the AG&S was inexpensively built and poorly engineered. Its steel rails, resembling those laid by street railways, weighed only thirty pounds to the yard rather than the fifty-six-pound or heavier rails used by standard-gauge steam railroads. Until the mid-1890s the company's four small locomotives burned wood, a cheap and plentiful fuel source. "Locomotive fuel consisted of lightwood knots, which was found to be not only economical as fuel, but it did away with the necessity of a second class [or segregated Jim Crow] coach," wrote veteran employee G. P. Turner tongue-in-cheek, "as after five miles all the passengers were of the same color."[40]

The AG&S failed to create an "air-line" between its two terminals. Instead, the company operated a highly circuitous route. "This little road I believe was the crookedest in the United States, certainly of any of which I have knowledge," reminisced Turner. "This condition was attributable to the fact that in order to get subscription to stock, it had to agree to run through the plantation of practically every farmer adjacent to its right-of-way." Part of its excessive length between Augusta and Sandersville also involved the desire to keep grading costs to a minimum.[41]

The joy of completing a relatively long albeit inexpensive narrow-gauge project did not guarantee the financial future of the AG&S. Money problems mounted, which prompted President Mitchell in September 1889 to tell associates that immediate prospects looked bleak. "In June 1888 it was evident as almost universally with all Southern roads that the Company could not pay its [bond] coupons maturing July 1st from the earnings on operating expenses for the past six months of 1888." A juggling of finances merely postponed disaster. In 1891 the railroad defaulted on interest payments on its first mortgage bonds, prompting a receivership that began on January 1, 1892.[42]

Court protection led to a reorganization. On May 1, 1893, a new corporation, the Augusta Southern Railroad, made its debut. The timing was bad, for a few days later a crisis hit Wall Street, which according to James U. Jackson, company president, "caused the greatest monetary panic this country had ever known." The negative effects persisted, not fully lifting for another five years. Although the debt was restructured, the property was "in rather a dilapidated condition" and it faced difficulty in meeting its monthly payroll. Still, the railroad continued to operate and a few betterments took place, mostly strengthening the weakest wooden bridges, replacing rotted ties, and installing some heavier fifty-six-pound rail. The new leadership, though, believed that two improvements would significantly enhance the property, namely, purchasing the 3.5-mile Sandersville & Tennille Railroad (S&T) and widening the gauge to standard width.[43]

In early 1894 the AS took control of the S&T. Organized on June 23, 1876, this five-foot-gauge property, subsequently regauged as with nearly all wide-gauge Southern roads to 4 feet 8 1/2 inches, had opened on October 1, 1876, southward from Sandersville to Tennille, a station on the Central Railroad and Banking Company of Georgia (CofG). For all practical purposes, this little line was an appendage of the CofG, although it was locally owned and managed. Subsequently the S&T connected with the Wrightsville & Tennille Railroad, a sixteen-mile shortline that in 1884 had begun service between its namesake communities and later, under CofG control, expanded to become a 104-mile road that linked Tennille with Hawkinsville and Dublin with Eastman. To make the S&T compatible with the gauge of the AS, management spent $6,000 to install a third rail, a common approach to gauge differentials.[44]

But realizing that narrow gauge was an impediment to operations and earnings, AS management ordered that the entire line be standardized. On September 30, 1895, this task was completed, made possible through the sale of $280,000 of five percent "Standard Gauge Issue" bonds. This was a wise expenditure. Not only did interchange of rolling stock now become practical, but overall operating costs dropped noticeably. "An engine of standard gauge delivers to us 20 loaded cars [and] it takes three of our [narrow-gauge] cars to receive the load of one standard gauge [car] and thus for this train 60 of our cars are required," noted President Jackson by way of example. "Our Engines will haul but 6 loaded cars, and therefore ten trips have to be made to deliver this freight. This means the fuel, the wages of engineer, fireman and a train crew ten times to do the work that could be done by one crew, and the transfer has to be made to our cars." No one questioned or criticized Jackson's assessment.[45]

Although the S&T became integrated into the AS, it came at a price. The CofG did not take kindly to the takeover, considering the S&T to be a friendly feeder. Residents of Sandersville also wondered about being wholly dependent on the financially shaky Augusta road. And, too, they wished to "remove the menace of monopoly and restore the advantages of competition." In September 1893 this sentiment prompted the chartering of the four-mile Sandersville Railroad, backed by the CofG, that soon became an operating reality. On August 16, 1894, the first train steamed over the shortline. "Mr. [H. M.] Comer, the Receiver of the Central, has done everything in his power to injure your property and prejudice the people of Sandersville against it," related President Jackson to fellow directors in May 1894. "Aided by him they are building a line to parallel us between Sandersville & Tennille." However, a later proposal to construct an electric trolley between Sandersville and Tennille came to naught.[46]

Soon worry about the CofG and S&T became moot. On March 1, 1897, the South Carolina & Georgia Railroad (SC&G), a 244-mile carrier whose main line stretched between Charleston, South Carolina, and Augusta on the historic trackage of the South Carolina Canal & Rail Road Company, leased the AS "in perpetuity." About two years later the SC&G joined the burgeoning Southern Railway that sought to strengthen its presence in the Palmetto state and to gain access to the flourishing Charleston seaport. Yet, the AS did not long remain a part of the SC&G. On April 1, 1901, the SR bought the SC&G outright and annulled the lease of the AS. The SR preferred stock control of the AS, acquiring at a dirt-cheap price 2,960 shares of the 3,500 outstanding shares of preferred and 2,952 shares of the 3,500 shares of common. The SR operated the property as a subsidiary and feeder.[47]

Under its own management the AS struggled to serve the needs of shippers and travelers. Profits were rare, and scant funds were available for improvements. During the ten-year period beginning in 1905, the company generated a small, positive balance in only four years. At times the tight financial situation allowed for a few troublesome grades to be reduced, a limited number of modern locomotive and rolling stock to be acquired, and some heavier rail to be installed. Of significance, the AS in 1909 was able to eliminate a bad reverse curve at Milepost 23 near Hephzibah, and to purchase two all-purpose Ten-Wheelers (4-6-0) from the Baldwin Locomotive Works in Philadelphia.[48]

The AS was seemingly a welcomed part of the communities that it served. While patrons may have fussed about service and equipment, they understood the nature of this shortline, even though it had become affiliated with the giant SR. "We are bound by ties of steel to Augusta, Gibson, Sandersville, Tennille and all intermediate points," commented a resident of Hephzibah in 1909, "while our 'Big Road's' [SR] connections cover practically the larger part of North America." This same individual so admired the local express agent in Hephzibah that he penned a poem to honor his dedication, concluding:

> The days may come and the days may go,
> But in summer's heat and in winter's snow,
> Unless there's a wreck on the curving rails,
> The "Package" business never fails.[49]

Although far from being a stellar property, the AS proved attractive to the G&F. It provided convenient entry into Augusta, via the tiny Augusta & Summersville Railroad, for all trains and to the Augusta Union Station Company (AUS) for passenger, mail, and express operations. Since August 1, 1903, the AS had been party to a lease agreement with AUS, a company formed April 17, 1901, shortly before the opening of this facility. When representatives of the G&F in 1909 asked the AS for a trackage-rights agreement between Keysville and Augusta, management happily considered the proposal. Indeed, one director, who remained independent of the SR, formally recommended "the sale of the Augusta Southern property to the Georgia & Florida, or any other Company, upon such terms as would be fair." Although his suggestion failed, the lease won unanimous approval.[50]

The AS-G&F accord lacked any unusual features. Specifically, the G&F received these privileges:

> The joint use with the Augusta Southern of this Company's main and side tracks and certain other property from point of connection at Keysville, Georgia, to Augusta, the business of the Florida Company [G&F] thereover to be confined to through traffic only, that is to say, traffic from points on, or reached via, the Florida Company's lines south of but not including Keysville proper to points beyond and to the city of Augusta, and traffic from Augusta and points north, east and west thereof, moving through Augusta, and destined to points south of Keysville, but not including Keysville proper, on or reached via the Florida Company's lines.[51]

There were, of course, rental considerations. Based on the value of the Augusta-Keysville line, the G&F paid an annual fee of $7,048.60 and accepted the caveat that "the rental was to be increased from time to time in the event of certain improvements being made to the properties in joint use, etc." Both companies agreed that after five years either party could abrogate the agreement by giving a six-month notice. If the G&F should fail to meet any of the agreements, "the Augusta Southern would have a right to declare the contract forfeited."[52]

The lease worked out satisfactorily. Since the AS did not operate many trains, only two daily-except-Sunday mixed runs and a movement each way on Sunday, the addition of G&F traffic apparently did not cause undue congestion or repeated delays. The only negative result involved increased wear on the light, mostly fifty-six-pound rails, prompting a long discussion of acquiring seventy- or seventy-five-pound steel for use between Keysville and Augusta. And this occurred by 1912, permitting the G&F to use its heaviest freight locomotives to and from Augusta and to increase tonnage on these trains.[53]

When the G&F officially took possession of the AS on October 31, 1919, however, the property continued to possess considerable limitations. The former narrow-gauge line lacked good engineering, consisting of numerous curves and grades, forcing the G&F to cope with these legacies between Keysville, Sandersville, and Tennille until 1934 when that section was abandoned, and over the remaining portion until the SR assumed control in 1963. For years the AS had tonnage restrictions. On the eve of World War I, the company issued this warning: "Limit of load allowed to pass over this line in excess of marked capacity [of freight equipment], 10 per cent."[54]

Still, the G&F made the correct choice with the AS acquisition. With this property under its wing, the company no longer needed to worry about access to Augusta, the most important city on the system. Having the Keysville to Augusta segment meant that constructing connecting trackage between Keysville or St. Clair (the latter an extensively discussed proposal) and Augusta became unnecessary, avoiding what would have been a more expensive proposition. Moreover, the railroad could serve customers along the formerly leased mileage and could control train operations. And, of course, the G&F could now make some much-needed improvements, including strengthening of the track structure. The company also took ownership of an assortment of rolling stock, including six coal-burning locomotives, eleven flatcars, nine work cars, and seven pieces of passenger equipment, some of which would remain on the roster for years.[55]

WORLD WAR I AND THE CRISIS OF 1919–1920

During the presidential campaign of 1916, Woodrow Wilson promised that if he won reelection he would keep the nation out of the world war. But on April 6, 1917, because of the fear of an Allied defeat, the recently reelected chief executive sent a war message to Congress. Although considerable political dissent erupted, lawmakers approved a declaration of war against the Central Powers of Austria-Hungary, Germany, and Turkey, and the nation mobilized "to make the world safe for democracy." For the railroad industry this meant an enormous increase in freight business. Unfortunately, though, shippers needed to bill this traffic mostly to Atlantic and Gulf ports, resulting in a badly snarled transportation network. Even though industry representatives attempted to rectify the logistical woes, the situation grew more desperate in the territory east of Chicago and St. Louis and north of the Ohio and Potomac rivers. The chaos was exacerbated by long-standing rivalries between major roads and escalating costs, especially for wages, and by the failure to win meaningful rate increases from the Interstate Commerce Commission (ICC). Finally, the Wilson administration and Congress opted for "federalization," and on December 28, 1917, nearly all Class 1 railroads, large and strategic electric interurbans, and certain steamship lines came under the control of the hastily organized United States Railroad Administration (USRA). A few months later lawmakers passed the Railroad Control Act that officially promised railroad owners that their financial position would be protected and that following the "emergency" their properties would be returned "in substantially as good repair" as at the time of seizure.[56]

Federalization by the Wilson administration encountered widespread public support. The Madison, Florida, newspaper, for one, commented: "the taking over by the government of the railroads of the country will do away with competitive freight hauling, as existed with the private lines, and that will do something towards relieving the freight congestion." This publication further noted that "it will also obviate the danger of strikes, and that is important any time and doubly so now." Indeed, the USRA functioned reasonably well in some cases, contributing heavily to the war effort by making the flow of goods more efficient and satisfying the demands for higher pay by the railroad brotherhoods.[57]

Initially the G&F was one of the railroads *not* placed under USRA control, even though some smaller carriers encountered immediate federalization. USRA personnel concluded that the company did not offer strategic trackage for the national rail grid. G&F management probably accepted this decision willingly, perhaps worrying that federal operations might become permanent. Yet for a small Class 1 road the company had unusual clout in the highest circles of government. John Skelton Williams, then serving as Comptroller of the Currency, enjoyed excellent ties to top-ranking Wilson administration officials, and his fast friend, William Gibbs McAdoo, was not only President Wilson's son-in-law but also served as director general of the USRA.[58]

The reality of the USRA soon caused the G&F to wish for inclusion, however. Most of all, the railroad felt the financial sting of traffic diversions.

Interchange or "bridge" shipments largely went over the rails of competitors, usually the ACL, SAL, and SR, as the USRA sought to save car, ton, and train miles by sending freight over the fastest and shortest routes. "During the war there was diverted from [G&F] lines the stable business which it had spent ten years building up and which had finally put it on the basis of earnings of $100,000 a year over its operating costs," noted E. C. Laird, editor of the Atlanta-based *Railroad Herald*. Before the eventual takeover by the USRA in the summer of 1918, G&F General Manager D. F. Kirkland told shippers that "the Government having seen fit not to control this line, [the G&F] is now dependent upon the public for sufficient business to continue operation." Added Kirkland, "the officials of the road have been advised by representatives of the government that the independent lines should continue the solicitation of business and routing in their favor [that] should be respected by the shippers and the government controlled railways. Your help is needed and we sincerely hope that you will give it." Ultimately, however, the G&F entered the USRA fold, likely due to Williams's insistence. On November 1, 1918, the company officially became federalized, only eleven days before the signing of the armistice in France. The USRA remained in control until March 1, 1920, when federalization ended.[59]

Joining the USRA did not mean a brighter day for the G&F. In fact, 1919 and 1920 became two of the most difficult years in the company's history. Pressed by several creditors "for a settlement of accounts," bankruptcy judge Henry Hammond, who continued to have power over the railroad, decided in December 1919 that the road should be sold at public auction on the first Tuesday in February 1920. Three possible scenarios would then unfold: sale of the G&F as a complete unit, sale in sections to buyers who wanted to operate portions of the line, or sale of most or nearly all of the road for scrap.[60]

Alarm bells sounded in the Wiregrass Region. News of the possible dismemberment or junking of the G&F immediately caused concern among residents throughout the length and breadth of the road. "To let this railroad be torn up without doing anything to help it, could be hardly short of criminal," became the commonly expressed sentiment. "If the Madison-Valdosta end of the road is to be continued by the purchasers then there is nothing for us to be worried over as yet," observed the Madison editor, "but accounts that we have read of the condition of the railway and its business lead us to believe that if any of the road is to be scrapped, the Madison-Valdosta end, unless something is done, will be the most likely to be scrapped." Continued this writer, "Such a result would be of untold injury to our town, damaging to Valdosta and almost annihilating to Pinetta, and something should be done NOW to protect our interests in the matter." In a similar vein the Swainsboro newspaper believed that "The scrapping of this road would mean utter financial ruin to hundreds of people in this section of country, and you can not afford to let it be done!"[61]

No one denied that some railroads, including the G&F, were vulnerable to dismantling. Nationally, the 337-mile Colorado Midland Railway, in part a victim of USRA traffic policies, shut down in 1918, and three years later most of the trackage fell to the wrecker's torch. Then in 1923, the 255-mile Chicago, Peoria & St. Louis Railway ceased operations, retiring much of its line and selling off several viable portions.[62]

In the Southeast, most significantly for the G&F, parts of the fabric of shortline railroads had begun to unravel. Immediately after World War I several carriers in north Florida and south Georgia were scrapped. The *Wiregrass Farmer,* published in Ashburn, Georgia, believed that G&F patrons had reason to worry. "From present indications and more especially that the roads in a position to become purchasers, after they get back into the hands of their original owners, will have enough trouble on their hands without buying any more, the logical result is the road will follow the course of the Georgia Coast & Piedmont road, that a few weeks ago was sold for junk."[63]

There was more than scary commentary as efforts to save the G&F unfolded. Soon the Augusta Chamber of Commerce and the Augusta Cotton Exchange spearheaded the "Save the G. & F. Railway" campaign. In mid-January 1920 members traveled over much of the property to discuss strategies to keep the railroad operating as a single entity. "Meet the Augusta people when they arrive here," commented the Swainsboro editor, "and see if some understanding can be reached by which this road can be saved to the country through it traverses." When the special stopped, a public gathering followed. In Nashville every business house and office closed, allowing a large crowd to attend a two-hour Saturday morning meeting. The public heard two related messages: protest any dismemberment by writing public officials, including regulatory authorities, and subscribe to $750,000 of receivers' certificates, allowing the road to appease creditors until better times permitted a workable reorganization.[64]

The grass-roots campaign kept the G&F intact. Not only did bondholders subscribe to $200,000 of receivers' certificates, but online communities made substantial contributions. Augusta businessmen invested $300,000 and Douglas interests committed $40,000. In some of the smallest places served by the railroad, including Gough and Pinetta, public-spirited citizens took thousands of dollars of these promissory notes. With money available to satisfy creditor demands, Judge Hammond called off the scheduled sale. "Now that business men along the line and the bondholders have pulled the G. & F. Ry. across the danger line," observed an encouraged editor, "we hope the road will do its very best, stopping up all leaks, and give us good service and make some money too." Management breathed a sign of relief and publicly thanked communities. "The Receivers and Officials of the Georgia & Florida Ry. take this opportunity of expressing their sincere appreciation and thanks to the business men for their valuable aid in financing the recent issue of Receivers' certificates and for the patronage they have given us in the past."[65]

Although escaping financial disaster, the G&F continued to encounter money problems. Operating expenses had increased markedly due to rising material costs, higher wages for labor, meager regulatory rate increases, and disrupted patterns of freight traffic. The stinging postwar recession of 1920–1921 caused further distress.[66]

In the latter part of 1920 another struggle occurred. The receivers applied to the ICC for a loan of nearly $2 million that the Transportation Act of 1920 (Esch-Cummins Act) could provide. When a formal response failed to be forthcoming, the railroad instigated a letter-writing campaign to politicians, regulators, and other potentially influential people to show that "the G. & F. Ry. is an essential and a necessity" and that funding was needed only because of "the present temporary depression."[67]

Eventually the lobbying campaign worked. In late March 1921 the ICC endorsed a government-backed loan for $1.6 million. Specifically, the G&F won permission to issue receivers' certificates that unfortunately carried a hefty interest rate of eight percent. Still, this financial shot in the arm enabled the G&F to retire some of its floating debt and to provide working capital for much-needed betterments. The latter ranged from repairing rolling stock to painting the depot in Swainsboro.[68]

Although still bankrupt and feeling the effects of a sluggish economy, the 405-mile G&F appeared to have become a more stable property. Revenues grew from $1,389,678 in 1921 to $1,780,889 in 1924. This was an increase of approximately ten percent annually, or about double the average rate of growth for American railroads. Even prior to the encouraging revenue reports, the *Augusta Chronicle* told readers on December 6, 1922, that "the great showing made by the G. & F. financially during the past sixteen months under John Skelton Williams is one of the remarkable achievements in modern railroad operation." Crowed the newspaper: "To change an operating deficit of nearly $1,000,000 for the eight months prior to July 1, 1921, into a net operating revenue of $250,00 for the sixteen months since July 1, 1921, is indeed a noteworthy achievement." The performance was both satisfying and hopeful, with the ratio of operating expenses to operating revenues plunging from 149.5 percent for calendar year 1920 to 77.8 percent for the twelve months that ended April 30, 1923.[69]

Not only did the G&F benefit from an improving economy, but also the company avoided the long and bitter shopmen's strike that crippled many Class 1 carriers during the summer and fall of 1922. In Augusta, for example, nearly 1,000 shopmen on the Charleston & Western Carolina (ACL), Georgia, and Southern railroads walked out. For several months these men remained on strike, ultimately losing their wage demands and suffering dismissal or loss of seniority. The explanation for the more harmonious labor relations that the G&F enjoyed was succinctly stated by General Manager Kirkland: "the G. & F. shopmen are not affected by the wagecut." Company employees and those of many small carriers were not covered under the national shopmen's agreements.[70]

A few months earlier the G&F management also quelled a potentially disruptive dispute with its trainmen. The road had ordered a wage reduction of ten percent from the prewar scale then in effect. In the case of the highest paid brakeman, the daily rate would drop from $1.65 to $1.49. Predictably, workers responded by authorizing a strike. But a last minute conference led to an "amicable settlement"; union representatives convinced John Skelton Williams, the newly appointed sole receiver, that "these men had never received advances given employees on other [Class 1] roads [during World War I] and that the latest wage reduction placed their wages to the point where it was impossible for them to live." Williams once again held the carrier together in the face of a real crisis.[71]

HAPPIER DAYS

Although it would be an exaggeration to suggest that the G&F had become a happy, thriving railroad, the growing prosperity of the 1920s meant regular jobs for office, shop, train, and track workers and black ink in the ledger-books. The freight and even the passenger business generally improved, and no one suggested that the G&F might become a corporate casualty as had the smaller and neighboring Georgia Coast & Piedmont; Hawkinsville & Florida Southern and the Valdosta, Moultrie & Western railroads.[72]

By the early 1920s the public sensed a "new" G&F, even though the railroad remained under the control of a judge and receiver. The reason for this feeling was generated not so much because of the more frequent and longer freights that rumbled over the main line and the sight presented by various betterments, as by the appearance of a bona fide name-train, the *Bon-Air Special,* that offered much improved service between Augusta and Valdosta. Indeed, this would be the *belle epoque* of passenger operations on the G&F.

One area where the G&F needed to improve markedly was with passenger operations. During the era of the world war, the company pressed state regulators to reduce service and mostly succeeded. For main line patrons "double-daily" runs had become only fond memories, and the traveling public resented this retrenchment. "The service given the people by the Georgia & Florida Railroad is just about equal to no service at all, so far as passenger accommodations go," wrote a disgusted W. E. Boatright, editor of the *Swainsboro Forest-Blade.* "Only one train each way [on the main line] is operated daily, that makes a pretense of carrying passengers, and this can not be termed a passenger train, for it is very often the case that it is loaded down with freight, has to do switching along the line while the passengers patiently—or impatiently—wait while this work is being done." Boatright was particularly annoyed that "to go to Augusta from Swainsboro and attend to any business at all, one has to be away from home two days, when as a matter of fact it should not take but one day."[73]

Throughout its corporate existence, the G&F hustled for business. In the early 1920s a photographer captured four employees in the Traffic Department in the spartan general office building located in downtown Augusta. (Robert H. Hanson Coll.)

Boatright's criticisms were reprinted and widely discussed. A writer for the *Augusta Chronicle,* for one, was sympathetic, knowing that local businesses needed patronage from residents of "G&F towns." Yet this commentator admitted that the G&F "is hampered and embarrassed these days," although holding out hope that better service would be forthcoming. "It is believed that [the G&F] will be found lending a willing and eager ear to every suggestion which will work to the convenience and comfort of its patrons."[74]

The *Chronicle* assessment proved largely correct. Yet service would not be improved on every piece of G&F trackage. Management rightly realized that it would be foolish to restore or upgrade passenger trains on the several branch lines. This local traffic was being lost to the growing number of automobiles and an amazingly large number of recently launched "jitney" and bus companies. These private and commercial vehicles traveled over an ever-improving network of public roads. In fact, following the war several counties served by the G&F passed bond issues for road improvements and agitation grew for more all-weather arteries. The wiser course of action for the railroad involved focusing on upgrading travel opportunities for residents of the major communities along the core route.[75]

The first response to solving the passenger "problem" on the main line was simple and inexpensive. In the spring of 1920 the company decided not to handle freight cars on Nos. 4 and 5, the principal passenger trains between Augusta and Valdosta. (By this time the Valdosta-Madison line had only a mixed train that offered daily service between Madison, Valdosta, and Vidalia, but by March 1922 operated only between Madison and Valdosta.) Train speeds could be increased and the advertised times more likely met. As for the latter, in late 1924 the company boasted that "for the past six months 98 per cent of our passenger trains have been on time." The consist adjustment, of course, met with resounding applause.[76]

But a larger ovation came with introduction of the *Bon-Air Special*. The name for the G&F's first true "varnish" was an appropriate choice. Bon Air held meaning for those familiar with Augusta, which by the late nineteenth century had become a popular winter haven for well-to-do northerners. The city had a fashionable "Bon Air" residential section and claimed the popular, large, first-class Bon Air Hotel.[77]

The decision to operate a name train came not from a desire to promote or recognize Augusta. Rather, G&F management saw the opportunity to tap two potential markets: patrons who lived in the larger communities south of Augusta, and those residents of Augusta and the north who sought a pleasant, convenient way to travel to and from increasingly popular Florida destinations for business or pleasure. Although the company might have worked out a joint arrangement with the SAL to move the *Bon-Air Special* through the interchange at Madison to Jacksonville—"Florida's Gateway City"—the Georgia Southern & Florida Railway (GS&F), the SR affiliate, provided a more attractive and faster connecting link between Valdosta and Jacksonville. While not openly admitted, management likely saw the *Bon-Air Special* as having a marquee value. Surely the hope, even expectation, was that if satisfied passengers had freight to ship, they would route "via G&F."[78]

On Sunday, December 17, 1922, service began with extensive publicity: "The Quick New Route to Jacksonville and all Florida Points Through the Heart of South Georgia. DEPENDABLE AND COMFORTABLE SERVICE." This advertising copy continued: "You have the opportunity to visit Jacksonville and other Florida points and return to Augusta with only one day away from home or business. Direct connections at Jacksonville with Seaboard Air Line, Atlantic Coast Line, and Florida East Coast trains for all south, east and west coast Florida points." The first train, officially No 9, with its Pullman sleepers (the two G&F sleeping cars acquired in 1911 were not used), steamed out of Augusta Union Station at 7:45 p.m. and arrived in Valdosta at 3:40 a.m., after having made stops in Midville, Swainsboro, Wesley, Vidalia, Hazlehurst, Douglas, and Willacoochee. Then traveling over GS&F rails, No. 9 arrived in Jacksonville Union Station at 8:00 a.m. The companion train, No. 10, departed Jacksonville at 9:05 p.m., reaching Valdosta at 1:00 a.m., and entered the Augusta terminal at 8:50 a.m. Admittedly, this schedule meant that most online patrons would need to board during the night, including the wee hours of the morning.[79]

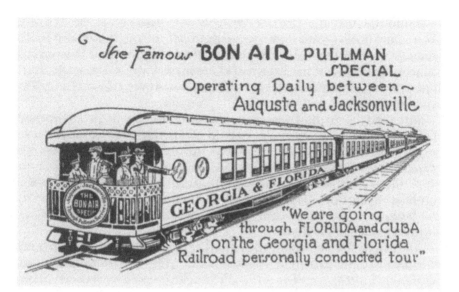

The Famous **BON AIR** PULLMAN
SPECIAL
Operating Daily between~
Augusta and Jacksonville

GEORGIA & FLORIDA

"We are going
through FLORIDA and CUBA
on the Georgia and Florida
Railroad personally conducted tour"

During the 1920s the G&F eagerly promoted the *Bon-Air Pullman Special* between Augusta and Jacksonville, Florida. This train, which operated on an overnight schedule, was the company's only name-train. Management hoped that the *Bon-Air Special* would have marquee value, prompting satisfied customers to request a G&F routing for their freight shipments. (Author's Coll.)

While the G&F ballyhooed the *Bon-Air Special* as a luxury name-train, the new service was a pale imitation of the best varnish operated by the major Class 1 roads of the region. Nos. 9 and 10 were not particularly fast, traveling the 223 miles between Augusta and Valdosta at an average speed of only twenty-eight miles an hour. Although this night train provided comfortable Pullman Company sleeping accommodations, it operated without a dining car. The railroad urged passengers to eat before boarding, and for good reason.[80]

The public liked what the G&F had done. The previously critical Swainsboro editor believed that "the Georgia & Florida Railway deserves all the patronage of the people along its line." As he explained, "It deserves this patronage for the reason that it is giving the best service possible, as good a service as any people could ask for. Two trains each way everyday, scheduled as they are on this road, is all that could be asked or expected." What really pleased this journalist was that "we have over this road an inlet into Augusta, giving us an opportunity to spend the entire day transacting our business, returning the same day, without losing sleep. Then we have a through train to Jacksonville, quick service without the inconvenience of changing."[81]

During the 1920s the G&F was not alone with passenger-service upgrades. Even some smaller roads in the region opted for enhanced amenities. In the summer of 1923 the ACL in conjunction with the Columbia, Newberry & Laurens Railroad and the Laurens & Carolina Railway, for example, introduced through Pullman-buffet parlor car service between the South Carolina cities of Charleston and Greenville.[82]

Although the ridership figures are unknown, the *Bon-Air Special* operated daily throughout the remainder of the 1920s, largely aided by such factors as its dependability, sensible scheduling for through riders, and the mid-decade Florida land boom. The G&F passenger department used Nos. 9 and 10 for heavily advertised special events, usually held in Augusta. After all, a breakfast time arrival allowed patrons to spend much of the day in the city for business or pleasure even though they might climb into their Pullman berths at midnight or later![83]

The *Bon-Air Special* became the train that the G&F utilized in a successful "Personally Conducted Tour" to the "Land of Flowers," Florida and Cuba. Beginning in 1924, J. E. Kenworthy, the railroad's aggressive general passenger agent who worked closely with the Augusta Business Woman's Club, fashioned a twelve-day visit to various locations in Florida, including Key West, Miami, and St. Augustine, and Havana and Mantanzas in Cuba. Several hundred people participated in this semiannual event that the company called "A Vacation without Care or Worry with a Congenial Party." The response was highly positive. "It was my first trip on a 'Personally Conducted Tour,'" wrote Katherine Reid of Decatur, Georgia, to Kenworthy, "and, I must confess, I had my doubts as to the pleasant features of such method of travel; now, that I have been so happily introduced to it, I shall, doubtless, be seizing the first opportunity to use it again."[84]

During the 1920s the G&F made an additional improvement to main-line passenger service. At the end of 1924 a Pullman parlor car was added to daytime trains Nos. 4 and 5. The public seemed appreciative. "The G. & F. Ry. is steadily making improvements in their passenger service, and it is only a question of a short time when they will be giving people along their line of road every convenience of travel that the Trunk lines give to their patrons," observed an online newspaper.[85]

As with the G&F throughout its history, a steady variety of "specials" operated over the road. The company either dispatched an extra train or added coaches to scheduled movements. Baseball games, circuses, fraternal gatherings, motion pictures, and picnics were the most popular events. Ominously in the 1920s, there was a different kind of outing designed for members of the rapidly growing Ku Klux Klan. In October 1923 the Douglas Klan chartered a special train that carried about 100 members and their families to a Klan initiation in Valdosta. "The local lodge marched from their meeting place to the train, all masked, and made quite an impression on the onlookers," and "hot refreshments was [sic] served on [the] special train from Douglas." Ironically, the odds were good that an African-American "fireboy" (fireman) labored in the locomotive cab of this special.[86]

STATESBORO NORTHERN RAILWAY

The 1920s would also be a time of significant expansion for the G&F. Until the company built between Augusta and Greenwood, South Carolina, toward the end of the decade, control of what officially became the Statesboro Northern Railway (SN) in 1924 captured local attention. However, before the G&F leased this thirty-nine-mile line between Stevens Crossing (near Midville) and Statesboro, speculation appeared that the G&F would open a six-mile appendage from Ellenton, located about midway on the Sparks to Moultrie branch, southward to Berlin. Construction costs would be modest, and the G&F could exploit portions of the roadbed used by the recently abandoned Valdosta, Moultrie & Western Railway. Although there may have been the attraction of the promise by local boosters of 1,000 cars of watermelons annually, nothing happened, likely because trucks could transport the crop to Ellenton, Moultrie, or Sparks. Still, an area newspaper remarked that "the people [in Berlin] claim they never knew how valuable a railroad was until the V. M. & W. was dismantled."[87]

As with earlier components of the G&F, the SN possessed a complex past. It, too, was part of the explosion in railroad trackage that made the Wiregrass Region so popular with promoters during the early years of the twentieth century. Resembling some of these small properties, the road offered attractive features.

Just as John Skelton Williams emerged as the driving force behind the G&F, George M. Brinson, "the greatest railroad genius in Georgia," shaped the future SN. Instead of being an investment banker, Brinson was a rags-to-riches businessman who progressed from being "a country store keeper to turpentine operator to sawmill man" and then headed the Brinson Manufacturing Company. "This firm owns a $100,000 creosoteing plant at Springfield [Georgia] for creosoteing ties, bridge timbers, etc.," reported Harvey Fisk & Sons, a Wall Street investment house, in 1908. But Brinson did more than develop a commercial connection between his wood-treating facility and railroad customers; he became a railroad builder and owner himself.[88]

While hardly a "railroad genius," Brinson developed a small, viable property. Initially construction involved trackage between Springfield and Savannah, a distance of twenty-four miles. Chartered in 1906, this company, immodestly named the Brinson Railway, steadily expanded after opening its first segment in 1907. Two years later Brinson acquired a forty-mile, privately held logging company, the Savannah Valley Railroad, that linked Egypt in northwest Effingham County with Millhaven in northern Screven County. Although Brinson tore up a portion of this road, construction in the Newington area made for an "airline" route that contained only a single, short one-percent grade between Millhaven and Savannah. By the summer of 1911 Brinson trains began serving Waynesboro, seat of Burke County and a few miles northwest of Millhaven. Then in spring 1913 rails met the G&F at St. Clair, twelve miles northwest of Waynesboro, and on April 15, the two railroads established an interchange connection. Yet Brinson had his eyes on Athens and maybe Atlanta. He soon severed ties with his namesake railroad when in the summer of 1913 a dispute with investor James Imbrie, partner in the New York banking house of William Morris Imbrie & Company, prompted Brinson to sell his holdings for approximately $350,000. The new administration renamed the company the Savannah & Northwestern Railway, and subsequently the property became the Savannah & Atlanta Railway (S&A). In 1916 the S&A completed a link between the G&F at St. Clair and the Georgia Railroad at Camak, making for a 147-mile route that was better positioned and hence potentially more profitable.[89]

With important railroad experience and money in hand George Brinson took charge of another carrier, the Midland Railway of Georgia (MR), that incorporated officially on May 17, 1915. This railroad was successor to a distressed shortline, the Savannah, Augusta & Northern Railway (SA&N), that operated between Stevens Crossing and Statesboro (see Chapter 2). The G&F may have been behind this scheme, using the friendly Brinson as a stalking horse. Whatever the relationship, if any, Brinson pushed the MR southeastward, reaching Saxonia in 1917 and Savannah the following year. Reports circulated that he contemplated extending the MR northwestward to Milledgeville and later perhaps to Athens or Atlanta.[90]

Unlike the Brinson Railway, the eighty-eight-mile MR quickly hemorrhaged red ink. Brinson did what he could to save what residents incorrectly called the "Brinson Railroad," including the introduction of overnight package-car service between Savannah and Swainsboro via the G&F, but the postwar recession threw the company into bankruptcy and then liquidation. Early in 1924 trackage south of Statesboro was scrapped. The more viable section northwest of Statesboro, however, entered the G&F fold soon thereafter, initially through a five-year lease that called for an annual payment of $7,500, and later by purchase. On March 24, 1924, the first G&F train rolled over the former MR and the company announced "the schedule provides for two mixed trains daily, and as the demand grows, other trains will be added."[91]

Acquiring the SN was not a foolish decision as the railroad was in reasonably good shape and generated a respectable volume of car loadings. "The roadbed and rails are represented to be in excellent condition," noted an ICC examiner, although admitting that many crossties needed to be replaced. Statesboro, itself, with a population of nearly 4,000, was an important agricultural center in addition to being seat of Bulloch County and home to a small teachers college. There were freight prospects, although increased truck traffic was potentially damaging.[92]

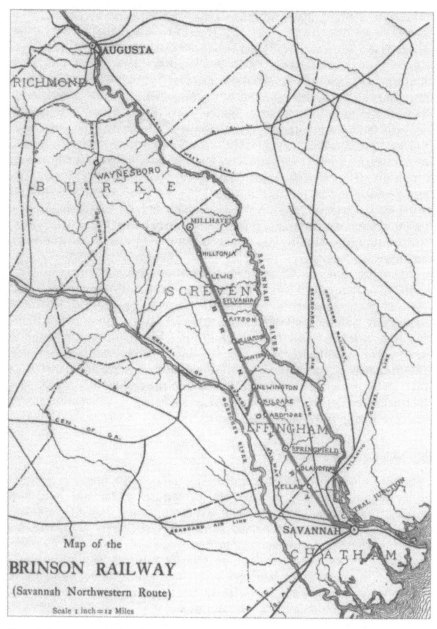

Map of the

BRINSON RAILWAY

(Savannah Northwestern Route)

Scale 1 inch = 12 Miles

One of the numerous shortlines of the early 20th century that had a relationship with the G&F was George Brinson's Brinson Railway, later the Savannah & Northwestern Railway and still later the Savannah & Atlanta Railway. This ca. 1914 map depicts the "air line" qualities of Brinson's most successful railroad venture. (Author's Coll.)

Even though scrappers quickly lifted the former MR rails between Statesboro and Savannah, the G&F remained interested in serving the greater Savannah area. The avenue would not be control of the Savannah & Atlanta, nee Brinson Railway, or re-railing the MR, but rather use of another shortline, the Savannah & Statesboro Railway (S&S). This little pike dated from the mid-1890s with opening of the thirteen-mile Cuyler & Woodburn Railroad that linked the sawmill villages of its corporate name. When that company failed during the depression of the 1890s, it found renewed life as the S&S. Shortly after the turn of the century, the S&S served both cities of its moniker, the former made possible by trackage rights over nineteen miles of the SAL. (Only S&S passenger trains reached Savannah; freight was interchanged with the SAL at Cuyler.) In 1911 the S&S leased the SA&N from its owner, W. J. Oliver of Knoxville, Tennessee, although this arrangement lasted for only four years. Throughout much of its existence the S&S maintained a close relationship with the SAL, which guaranteed interest on the shortline's first-mortgage bonds.[93]

About the time the SN evolved, speculation abounded that the G&F would take charge of the S&S. Although the status quo continued, in May 1931, a new day dawned for the S&S. By this time the road had fallen into receivership and the bankruptcy court named Hugh W. Purvis, who also led the G&F, as receiver for the S&S. Now the G&F could operate trains to Savannah in conjunction with the S&S and supervise the S&S terminals. Unfortunately, as the depression intensified the property deteriorated, forcing a petition for abandonment. Almost immediately the ICC agreed, and the road ended service in February 1933. The dream of having direct entry into Savannah for the G&F faded forever.[94]

BEFORE GREENWOOD

In the years prior to the economic travails of the 1930s, the G&F appeared to be gaining strength. In 1927 its bankruptcy ended and long-term prospects looked encouraging. Much satisfaction came from the railroad's hard work at diversifying Wiregrass agriculture (see Chapter 5) that already yielded promising dividends. Furthermore, the general "Coolidge Prosperity" of the mid-1920s, it was widely believed, would continue, including the remarkable land boom in Florida and the lucrative traffic transporting automobiles to Georgia and Florida destinations. Gross earnings for November 1925, which amounted to more than $200,000, were the highest in company history, and cause for genuine optimism. Management, in fact, decided to share the new-found wealth. In December 1925 all G&F employees received a bonus of five percent of their monthly earnings, with a maximum allowance of ten dollars. Collectively this generosity meant expenditures of several thousand dollars. Somewhat earlier the company raised the wages of most personnel, particularly those men in train service. Workers likely felt better about the G&F and there was even more excitement in the air as the widely discussed extension to Greenwood, South Carolina, seemed to offer lucrative new traffic routes and lasting economic health.[95]

Unfortunately, even as hope for a bright future for the G&F rose, fate intervened with suddenness. On the morning of November 4, 1926, John Skelton Williams, only sixty-one years old, died from a massive heart attack at his Virginia estate, "Paxton." An elaborate funeral followed in the historic St. Paul's Episcopal Church in Richmond with interment in stately Hollywood Cemetery.[96]

The flood of eulogies was heartfelt. "The death of Mr. Williams comes with peculiar pathos at the present time, being coincident with the culmination of the plans for the reorganization of the Georgia and Florida Railway, for the success of which he worked with such great ability and zeal," wrote James M. Hull, Jr, the general counsel for the G&F. "Ever since his appointment as sole receiver in July, 1921, he has devoted his unusual talents with untiring energy and conspicuous success to the task of improving the Georgia and Florida Railway, assisting in the development of the territory which it traverses, and planning for its extension to Greenwood, S.C., where connections could be effected which are confidently expected to insure future growth and progress of the road."[97]

Residents of the Wiregrass Region hoped that the death of the founder and leader of the G&F would not have dire consequences, but many feared for the future of the railroad. The immediate and most daunting challenge was now to "expand or die." Perhaps the anticipated Greenwood extension, the best current hope for financial success, would become the most fitting memorial to John Skelton Williams.

CHAPTER FOUR

"Expand or Die," 1926–1930

THE PLAN

By World War I the main stem of the Georgia & Florida (G&F) had jelled between Augusta, Georgia, and Madison, Florida. Nevertheless, John Skelton Williams, company officials, bankers, and advisors rightly sensed that the railroad needed to review its mileage and overall service territory. The receivership, which had begun on March 27, 1915, meant that the railroad had to consider carefully its future, and the financial crisis of 1919–1920, which easily could have led to dismemberment or abandonment, reinforced this thinking.

The most obvious weakness that the G&F faced involved the Augusta Gateway. Even though the Richmond County seat had become a teeming city of more than 50,000 and a good source of car loadings, ranging from lumber and millwork to brick and hollow tile, the G&F struggled with the lack of "friendly" connections, especially for traffic destined to and from northern points. Indeed, the Charleston & Western Carolina (C&WC), an affiliate of the Atlantic Coast Line (ACL), repeatedly proved to be uncooperative, delaying interchange movements and blatantly telling shippers not to route "via G&F." Moreover, the C&WC seemed oblivious to persistent pleas for unrouted freight. In 1926, for example, R. C. Hicks, G&F traffic manager, asked the general freight agent of the C&WC, "Can't you route more traffic via our line so as to even up this interchange?" The answer was no. The Southern Railway (SR), the other principal interchange partner, never seemed thrilled about the presence of the G&F in Augusta either, although it had made available the Augusta Southern Railroad (AS) for better entry into the city. Unfortunately for the G&F, these two large railway systems dominated Augusta.[1]

The belief that Augusta was not an ideal northern terminus was hardly new. Shortly before the world war erupted, discussions occurred among G&F officialdom about building to Columbia, South Carolina. An approximately sixty-mile extension to the South Carolina capital would permit the company to benefit from a longer haul before interchanging with the SR at that point and, most importantly, allow the Seaboard Air Line (SAL) to become the favored connection. The main line of the friendly SAL ran between

Washington, D.C., and Florida through Columbia. In March 1913, R. Lancaster Williams revealed that the G&F's intention was "ultimately extending the line from Augusta to Columbia" and that "plans will soon be underway toward this improvement." The specifics were not clear, although the G&F appeared to be interested in working closely with James U. Jackson, vice president of the Augusta-Aiken Railway & Electric Company and former president of the AS, whose twenty-six-mile interurban between Augusta and Aiken might be used for part of the distance. Some leading investors in the G&F also held major financial positions in the traction road.[2]

Also prior to the war (and for more than a decade to come) rumors flew that the G&F would extend southward. It was widely expected that the railroad would push from Madison to Tampa, Florida, or some other location along the gulf coast. Although the G&F was experiencing traffic growth, negative economic forces, including critical problems in the financial world, threw the company into receivership, stymieing any efforts either to break out of the Augusta Gateway or to reach deep water.[3]

With the end of the war and the "roarin' twenties" at hand, the possibility increased for *some* line expansion. By the early 1920s even "outsiders" believed that the 444-mile G&F would likely build northward, not to Columbia but rather to Greenwood, South Carolina. Presence in this thriving trade and manufacturing center of about 12,500 residents would enable the company to benefit from a connection with the well-positioned and well-managed Piedmont & Northern Railway (P&N), "The Great Electric System of the South." This profitable interurban rightly claimed "A Mill to the Mile" along its 104-mile Southern Division that linked the South Carolina cities of Greenwood, Anderson, Greenville, and Spartanburg, the heart of the Upstate's thriving cotton-textile manufacturing district. By the 1920s the P&N bragged that its electric-powered freight trains served 133 cotton mills that collectively operated nearly 3 million spindles. Together these plants consumed about 500,000 bales of cotton annually, of which about 50,000 bales moved northward from Augusta. Significantly, the P&N possessed a favorable interchange partner, connecting at Spartanburg with the Carolina, Clinchfield & Ohio Railroad (Clinchfield). This 300-mile heavy-duty bridge and coal road offered a direct route via an interchange at Elkhorn City, Kentucky, with the Chesapeake & Ohio Railway that led directly to various destinations in the Midwest, including Chicago, Cincinnati, and Toledo. Access could also be conveniently gained through Pittsburgh to eastern and northeastern points.[4]

The P&N potentially possessed even more attractive features. There existed the possibility that this impressively built interurban would unite its Southern Division at Spartanburg with its smaller Northern Division at Gastonia, fifty-one miles away. Not only did the P&N serve this thriving Tarheel state mill town but along its twenty-four-mile line to Charlotte, a strategic railroad hub of the Southeast, it tapped a variety of businesses,

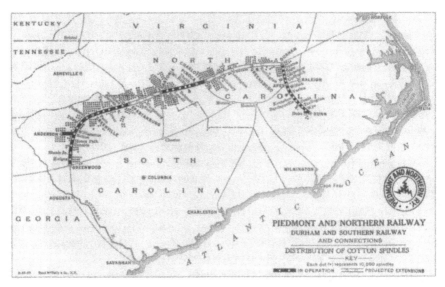

Fortunately the G&F became involved with one of America's greatest electric interurbans, the Piedmont & Northern Railway (P&N). With entry to the Greenwood gateway in 1929, the G&F established a through connection for carload freight to various northern destinations via the P&N at Spartanburg, South Carolina. However, if the P&N had been able to unite its North Carolina and South Carolina segments as planned, the interurban would have offered the G&F additional interchange options. (Author's Coll.)

mostly textile-based. It appeared likely that the P&N would build more trackage; reports spread that the road would link Charlotte with Durham, making for a 320-mile system. Indeed, company maps of the period included these two projections. Rumors also flew that the P&N would build the eighty miles between Charlotte and Winston-Salem, North Carolina, providing service to a city of economic importance and additional steam-road connections. Another possibility, but not shown in published maps, involved the P&N taking over the 949-mile Norfolk Southern Railroad, which operated adjoining electric and steam divisions, and whose 400-mile main line (steam) connected with the P&N at Charlotte and extended northeastward to Norfolk, Virginia, a major east coast port. No one would deny that the economically and politically powerful Duke tobacco interests, which owned the P&N along with the fifty-seven-mile steam-powered Durham & Southern Railway, had the wherewithal to make these projects happen.[5]

Largely coinciding with talk of the Greenwood extension came press reports that a southern extension was hardly dead. In August 1923 the *Florida Times-Union* in Jacksonville believed that it had compelling evidence that the G&F would build to the Gulf of Mexico. The Madison line would be lengthened to "either . . . the mouth of the Suwanee river or to Dead Man's bay." Noted the newspaper, "Arrangements have been made for a boat line from this port to St. Petersburg and Tampa, also a boat line into Cuba and South American ports." And the story suggested that "the extension of the road to the gulf will open up a new section and develop a large region." As it happened, it would be Greenwood, not the Gulf. Yet contemporary sources anticipated that the G&F would prioritize its construction, moving first to the north and then possibly building about 200 miles to the south. "The extension from Madison, Florida, to Tampa," editorialized the Greenwood *Index-Journal* in spring 1925, "is understood generally to be . . . a part of the plans for future enlargement and development." The editor of a Douglas, Georgia, newspaper envisioned that if these extension plans succeeded, they "will place the Georgia and Florida in a class with the big railroads, and give connections with lines that will mean much to the road."[6]

Although the exact date that Williams and his associates finally decided to push beyond Augusta is not known, in March 1924 the company released to the press an announcement that "with two million dollars available and three nationally known banking houses ready to lend other financial support, the extension of the Georgia & Florida . . . from Augusta to Greenwood by way of Edgefield is assured." Investment banker Edward Sykes, who represented Charles E. Doyle & Company of New York, a G&F creditor, told the news media that "we have gone over the route and have studied the situation from every angle, and we are assured that the building of a railroad line . . . [will develop] the sections of South Carolina through which the road will pass as well as the Georgia & Florida Railway Company and the city of Augusta." Similarly, newspapers along the G&F and the proposed extension were abuzz with positive commentary, believing that the railroad would surely prosper with construction in the Palmetto state.[7]

When Sykes indicated that the G&F had "studied the situation from every angle," he was somewhat premature. Officials thought it wise to engage a prominent firm of consulting engineers, Coverdale & Colpitts, headquartered in New York City, to review the property and to assess the economic benefits that might be derived from the Greenwood extension. This company was probably selected because Coverdale & Colpitts partner William H. Coverdale served on the G&F Board of Directors. In mid-February 1925 the process began and in late May directors received copies of a 111-page report along with a set of statistical appendices.[8]

Coverdale & Colpitts told the G&F that entrance to the Greenwood Gateway made sense. The major point of the study was that if the pending company reorganization were to work out successfully, "we strongly recommend" construction. Specifically, the consultants argued that "the proposed extension will, in our judgment, change the whole character of the Georgia & Florida Railway from a purely local line to a line forming an important link in new through routes between south Georgia and Florida on the south and the Piedmont District and the large commercial and industrial centers on the north." The report offered substantial evidence to support this position. For one thing, it emphasized that the G&F would surely garner considerable interchange traffic, likely thousands of cars annually. "The Greenwood extension of the Georgia & Florida Railway will open a new and direct route to the Piedmont & Northern and Seaboard Air Line railways from Greenwood through the port of Savannah and all of south Georgia and Florida points." Of course, these connecting roads would also benefit. The P&N, for example, had no rate divisions in force with the ACL south from Greenwood, and consequently it was unable to handle freight that it might otherwise control for shipment to interior southern points and coastal ports.[9]

Coverdale & Colpitts recognized the importance of other expansion schemes by smaller Class 1 roads. The report suggested that history might happily be repeated based on the case of the New Orleans, Mobile & Chicago Railroad (NOM&C). This 402-mile carrier, the self-proclaimed "Panama Route" headquartered in Mobile, Alabama, strongly resembled the G&F, being made up of an assortment of smaller, former lumber-carrying roads. Like the G&F the NOM&C depended heavily on locally generated traffic and served only one large community. The 369-mile NOM&C main line, which extended from Mobile though the piney woods of east Mississippi to Middleton, Tennessee, where it connected with the SR, failed to generate an adequate business. After a troubled financial existence, which dated back to the 1870s, the company went through a reorganization in 1909. Then four years later, the carrier found itself in receivership. In 1913 the road's bondholders committee hired Coverdale & Colpitts to review the property and make suggestions for improvements. What consultants found was that Mobile, especially its port traffic, offered a bright future for the NOM&C but Middleton was a poor northern terminus since the railroad "had no cooperation from the Southern." Yet there was a practical solution. The report urged the owners to construct a forty-mile extension from Middleton north to Jackson, Tennessee, for better interchange opportunities, namely with the Illinois Central, Mobile & Ohio and Nashville, Chattanooga & St. Louis railroads. Between 1916 and 1918 this trackage was built and the reorganized company, the Gulf, Mobile & Northern Railroad (GM&N), benefited greatly. The consultants crowed that gross revenues per mile for the old NOM&C stood at only $4,400 in 1912 but by 1924 had soared for the GM&N to $13,000 per mile. What seemed so obvious to Coverdale & Colpitts was that the tributary territory of the G&F was far "superior" agriculturally to the NOM&C-GM&N and that in 1925 the gross revenues per mile of the G&F were almost identical to those of the NOM&C thirteen years earlier. G&F personnel must have found the Coverdale & Colpitts document fascinating reading, indeed.[10]

REORGANIZATION

Armed with the findings and suggestions of Coverdale & Colpitts, the G&F, led by Franklin Q. Brown, chair of the railroad's bondholders' committee, moved ahead with plans for both its corporate reorganization and the

Greenwood extension. The process involved winning approval from the Interstate Commerce Commission (ICC) for each part. Therefore on December 3, 1926, the company filed the appropriate papers that sought "authority for the issuance of securities and the assumption of obligations incident to the reorganization of the Georgia & Florida Railway, which has long been under receivership, and for the extension of its line with a view to such increase of earnings as will render its operations profitable." It did not take long for the ICC to decide favorably on G&F's requests; a few weeks later the body approved conditionally creation of a new company, the Georgia & Florida *Railroad,* to acquire the assets of the Georgia & Florida *Railway* and endorsed the plan "to construct and operate" the Greenwood extension. The consultants' findings had impressed the ICC; the body recognized the importance of strengthening the G&F.[11]

The swift response by the ICC pleased G&F officialdom. R. Lancaster Williams, who had taken over the throttle after his older brother's sudden death in November 1926, saw the Commission endorse what reorganization representatives had sought and the federal bankruptcy court had approved. As with all railroad restructurings the final plan contained the usual complexities. In this case holders of the Railway's $1,000 first-mortgage bonds were required to pay the Railroad (new company) $250 in cash and in return they received $250 of income non-mortgage six percent debentures, $1,400 preferred stock, and twelve shares of common stock. All owners of preferred stock would be entitled to dividends, when declared, at the rate of six percent per annum. Those parties who held the Railway's (old company) general mortgage bonds acquired securities on the following basis: for each $1,000 of their general mortgage notes a cash payment of $25 gave them scrip for one-quarter of a share of preferred Railroad stock and five shares of common stock. As commonly occurred with railroad bankruptcies, holders of common shares in the former Railway saw their investments vanish. Significantly, bankers and managers believed that the financial structure of the reorganized company was realistic; final capitalization would be nearly $4 million less than it was for the old corporation and fixed interest charges would drop from $621,020 to $427,020 annually. The Greenwood extension, however, would increase the interest level; the new strategy would be to sell first mortgage bonds to cover construction costs. Still, the ICC concluded that the reorganized G&F "should be able to meet its fixed interest charges."[12]

The ICC expressed some concern, though, about the financial details of the reorganization. An independent and often iconoclastic commissioner, Joseph B. Eastman, thought that the reorganized company bore too much of the burden of restructuring expenses, complaining that the law firm of McAdoo, Neblett & O'Conner, which provided legal counsel, charged excessive legal fees. But G&F interests responded by making some reductions in overall expenses. In the final ICC report, dated February 12, 1927, Commissioner Eastman opined that "so far as the merits of the items of expense now before us are concerned, some of them impress me as being unduly large, taking all things into consideration." But this would not be a roadblock in creating the *Railroad*. "However, we [ICC] ought not to inter- fere in such matters unless the facts clearly justify interference, and it can not be said that this is the situation here."[13]

The ICC lauded the Greenwood extension. The arguments largely echoed those of the Coverdale & Colpitts report, although the regulatory body, always sensitive to protecting the public interest, rightly observed that "abandonment of this railroad would be a calamity to thousands of individ- uals and many communities." Building into South Carolina would surely enhance the G&F's earning power, making the railroad capable of serving the transportation needs of its expanded service territory.[14]

The Greenwood extension also won enthusiastic approval from South Carolina politicos. In documents submitted to the Secretary of State for a charter, lawmakers from Aiken, Edgefield, Greenwood, and Saluda counties saw the project as being "very desirous." And they expected the new line to "bring about $2,000,000.00 taxable property into the State," generating income that the chronically strapped South Carolina economy badly needed. The chapter application, then, brought only kudos.[15]

CONSTRUCTION NORTHWARD

Even before the Coverdale & Colpitts report and the G&F's exit from receivership, representatives of the G&F carefully reconnoitered the territory between Augusta and Greenwood. In early January 1925, Hugh W. Purvis, gen- eral manager and after 1926 president, informed J. H. Cantelou, an attorney in Edgefield, a county seat of approximately 3,000 residents located nearly mid- way along the proposed extension, that detailed survey work would begin by March, concluding that "I certainly hope nothing will arise to prevent this being done." By spring rumors spread along the projected route that construc- tion would start shortly. The *Index-Journal,* which billed itself the "Leading Newspaper of Western South Carolina," was more restrained (and accurate), reporting in March that the G&F was focusing on preliminary work and indi- cating that "two or three new surveys have been ordered and these are now being made" and "work has not yet been ordered." Shortly, though, surveyors completed their tasks. Part of the route they selected largely followed a survey made in 1913 by the ill-fated Augusta & Edgefield Railway between Edgefield, Pleasant Lane, Kirksey, and Greenwood. This "paper" road sought to serve these communities and to take advantage of a connection with the P&N, which had arrived the previous year in Greenwood.[16]

Even though the G&F anticipated that the Greenwood extension would cost about $2.2 million (later revised downward to $2.1 million) and made plans for these expenditures in its reorganization plans, financial matters still required close attention. In May Purvis again wrote to Cantelou, indicating that "this work is going to cost us more than we originally figured on." And he asked the Edgefield attorney "if there is any probability of our being able to get some concessions from the landowners in the way of crossties and other timbers."[17]

Yet the major roadblock that the G&F faced involved crossing the Savannah River at Augusta. Throughout much of 1925 and 1926 Purvis had ongoing discussions with the SR about use of that road's bridge. The SR moved slowly and Purvis repeatedly pleaded with F. S. Wynn, a company vice president in Washington, D.C., about resolving this matter. Early on in the negotiations Purvis wanted the SR to consider a trackage rights agreement between Augusta and Edgefield, using the SR's Augusta to Columbia line between Augusta (and the Savannah River bridge) to Trenton, South Carolina, a distance of twenty-six miles, and the six-mile branch that extended from Trenton to Edgefield. In time, however, Purvis dropped the request for trackage rights over what railroaders called the "CC&A line" (the former Charlotte, Columbia & Augusta Railroad) between Augusta and Edgefield, and focused on the bridge. A stumbling block involved anticipated interference of G&F trains with SR freight and passenger movements. But Purvis personally observed travel over the bridge and in November 1926 told Wynn that "I do not see how the amount of traffic that we will have over this bridge can in any way interfere with your operations." Then in December an agreement was struck between the companies and involved the G&F paying the SR an annual rental of $20,000 for use of its tracks and bridge "from a point from the center of Reynolds Street in the City of Augusta to a point 287 feet north of the bridge, including 3,243 feet of Southern Railway's industrial tracks leading from their Hamburg yard to North Augusta industrial territory, but not including tracks serving industries." The fee was not insignificant; moreover, the G&F agreed to treat the SR as a preferred connection on unrouted freight traffic. Still, at the time, this arrangement for the G&F was more attractive than building its own bridge over this navigable stream that would necessitate installation of a lift span and require a bridge tender. If the SR had not agreed to a lease, the G&F would have found the extension much more costly. Whether it was true or not, Purvis told Wynn shortly before the agreement was finalized that "the good citizens of Augusta have very kindly agreed to help us find a way out if for any reason we cannot make arrangements for the use of your bridge." Perhaps this veiled threat worked on Wynn and the SR.[18]

The slowness of construction troubled some observers, including several online editors. Throughout 1925 this was a frequently expressed concern. Yet the feeling persisted that work would eventually begin on "the most talked of railroad proposition in the South Atlantic today." After all, "[The G&F] must expand or it will be dried up," concluded the *Index-Journal,* echoing the conclusion reached by Coverdale & Colpitts and other commentators that the railroad's survival depended upon becoming less a localized property.[19]

To the G&F 1926 seemed to augur well for building to Greenwood. There were the negotiations between Purvis and Wynn that ultimately succeeded, and the survey work between the bridge area near Augusta and Greenwood had largely been completed. Also, most land for the right-of-way had been acquired. This prompted Purvis to take to the road on office car No. 100 and remind everyone that construction was imminent. On a Sunday in March he addressed about seventy-five employees at a gathering in the Masonic Hall at Douglas, telling them that "actual work on this extension would begin during the early summer." But that declaration proved to be too optimistic. It would not be until February 1927, nearly a year later, that the railroad opened bids submitted by about thirty parties. The winners were Winston & Company, based in New York City and Richmond, Virginia, for general construction and the Virginia Bridge & Iron Company, also of Richmond, for the major steel bridges. Both of these experienced firms seemed to be good choices. As with most railroad building projects of the era, the two principals, particularly Winston & Company, would hire various subcontractors.[20]

With all the excitement for what proved to be the last important new railroad construction project in South Carolina, the G&F decided not to conduct any first-shovel-of-dirt-turned ceremony; the hoopla would come later. Even though contracts had been let, it would be several months before actual building began; in fact, work did not officially commence until July 1927. Surprisingly, the G&F still was not absolutely certain about the exact location of the southern portion. As late as March 25, 1927, Purvis informed SR's Wynn that he personally remained interested in using the SR trackage beyond the immediate Savannah River bridge area. "Our people have all along felt that it would be to our advantage to build the line we have arranged to build but I have felt that we might utilize the Southern Railway's C.C.& A. line and in the long run be as well off as we would be by building our own line." What Purvis was thinking involved using SR rails to a junction ten miles from Hamburg called Warrenville, where the SR's historic line to Charleston turned eastward from the route to Columbia and Charlotte. At that point the Greenwood extension would begin. But the SR was not interested, largely because of growing freight traffic, and Purvis ended the conversations.[21]

By summer 1927 newspapers reported extensively on the construction. Instead of pushing either from the north or the south, work on clearing the right-of-way, shaping grades, and building bridges started at several intermediate points. Most equipment and supplies, including steam shovels, scrappers, and narrow-gauge "dinky" steam locomotives and cars, arrived by rail at Edgefield, Greenwood, and North Augusta, although contractors also used commercial trucks that traveled over the mostly primitive public roads to transport materials. And several Fordson gasoline tractors chugged to the work sites. At times heavy rains hindered building efforts as did severe cold snaps during the winter of 1927–1928, yet workers pressed on as best they could. In February 1928 the *Augusta Chronicle* happily noted that there were "23 gangs at work, with 18 steam shovels and 900 men employed in the work" and that "J. O. Winston, head of the organization, has leased a winter home in Augusta and is on the ground looking after the situation almost daily."[22]

Although large parts of South Carolina are relatively flat, the Greenwood extension traversed some rugged topography. "The country is very hilly," noted an industry trade writer, "and might be referred to as undulating." The more challenging portions were the twenty-five miles between North Augusta and Edgefield. This section necessitated excavating about 80,000 cubic yards to the mile. The most difficult work centered on removing approximately 270,000 cubic yards of earth, which consisted of mica, sandstone, and schist, to construct an eighty-foot cut about eighteen miles from North Augusta. Then two miles south of Edgefield laborers needed to cut through a huge granite ledge. "Engineers are of the opinion that it has commercial possibilities," but that estimate offered little consolation to the G&F. Also along this route several major bridges were installed, including a steel viaduct over Chavous Creek, fourteen miles from Augusta, that measured 540 feet in length and stood nearly eighty feet above the stream. Fortunately the thirty-two miles between Edgefield and Greenwood featured far less rugged terrain, being mostly rolling countryside. Yet, the route crossed five waterways that necessitated steel bridges, including another 540-foot span that carried the line over Turkey Creek, and there was also a large earthen fill near Greenwood.[23]

Although the G&F required station facilities along the Greenwood extension, these additions did not involve major expenditures. The company did not plan to expand greatly in Augusta, and it would use the joint station complex of the P&N and SAL in Greenwood. The G&F needed a depot most of all in Edgefield and turned to a Madison, Georgia, builder, Blackburn & Proctor, to erect a 75x25-foot combination freight and passenger structure, which by spring 1929 the firm had completed. This "artistic" wood and stucco building, with its sweeping hip roof, was a carbon copy of a depot Blackburn & Proctor earlier had erected for the G&F at Statesboro on its newly acquired Statesboro Northern property. Somewhat later G&F employees put up modest wooden structures, usually cotton-loading platforms, at the other established stations of Epworth, Kirksey, Pleasant Lane, and Pittsburg. The Edgefield station site also got a similar platform.[24]

The construction process, however, was not continual. Repeated rains either slowed or temporarily stopped work. Then in fall 1928 the G&F and Winston & Company quarreled over several engineering matters and payment schedules. A legal injunction, won by the contractor, halted work, but soon these issues were temporarily resolved and laborers returned to their assignments.[25]

The physical condition of the Greenwood extension is revealed in this 1948 photograph, indicating substantial earthen fills. The head locomotive of this northbound freight is a Schenectady-built former Florida East Coast Railway 4-6-2, No. 504, and the second unit is an ex-Gulf, Mobile & Northern Railroad 4-8-2, No. 601. The G&F assigned its three Richmond-built 4-8-2's to Greenwood runs because they proved too heavy for sections of the main line south of Augusta. (Hugh Comer photograph, Robert H. Hanson Coll.)

With most of the right-of-way shaped and bridges built, in November 1928 track-laying gangs swung into action. As with the grading strategy, installing the eighty-five-pound rail on mostly locally harvested hardwood ties began at three points. By early January more than ten miles of track, about twenty percent of the total, had been laid: eight miles out of Edgefield, leading north and south, one and one-half miles from Greenwood, and a half-mile from Hamburg. Some of the bridge-building had to be coordinated by the contractors with track-laying. The large span over Turkey Creek north of Edgefield, for one, could not be completed until the track was installed. "The heavy bridge steel can not be transported except by trains, trucks being unable to handle them," observed the *Edgefield Advertiser*. By the end of January about one-third of the track had been laid, and area newspapers reported that "Winston & Company completed all of the grading last week and most of their equipment has been assembled at their shops . . . to be thoroughly overhauled before being shipped north to other jobs." But some Winston employees remained. These men worked mostly near Greenwood where about a mile of track became extremely unstable because rains had caused the mica formation to "have no bottom." "Not only do the ties and rails mire down here almost out of sight," observed the Edgefield editor, "but a pedestrian, if he possessed considerable avoirdupois, would soon find himself knee-deep in this mica mud in places." The application of several hundred cars of cinders and granite screenings helped to stabilize the track structure, yet the problem persisted. At last, on May 1, 1929, the Virginia Bridge & Iron Company finished the final bridge.[26]

The completed line was reasonably well-engineered and constructed. The G&F claimed that it was "one of the best new roads that has ever been built in the south." Yet, it was hardly a speedway. A series of grades, mostly modest and not exceeding one percent, would limit train speeds and at times necessitate the double-heading of the company's steam engines. Locomotive engineers would discover that northbound trips would be more difficult than southbound runs. "It was really a hill-and-dale line and considerable power was usually required."[27]

The end finally seemed near. Crews from the Western Union Telegraph Company installed about 2,000 large wooden poles for the telegraph line, and the G&F busily prepared for its first trains. Even though some track and bridge work remained, J. E. Kenworthy, the G&F's general passenger agent, happily notified communities along the road that "on May 15th, we expect to formally open our Augusta-Greenwood Extension," indicating that a highly anticipated gala was close at hand.[28]

THE LINE OPENS

In the tradition of American civic boosterism that knew no geographical bounds, the G&F worked closely with public-spirited representatives from Augusta, Edgefield, and Greenwood to promote the formal opening. It did not take any arm twisting by railroad officials to convince residents of these communities and elsewhere to participate. The only problem involved *when* the celebration would take place. Although May 15, 1929, became the date extensively advertised, the company initially had indicated that the big day would likely be April 1, but quickly opted for April 20. Torrential rains that fell throughout much of February and continued into March, which pounded the territory along the extension, especially Edgefield and Greenwood counties, triggered mud slides and disrupted final track preparations. Still by early spring the railroad, working closely with civic and government groups in the three communities, had formulated tentative plans for the celebration.[29]

Much of the day-to-day planning fell on the shoulders of the railroad's capable and energetic J. E. Kenworthy. This Boston, Massachusetts, native had honed his professional skills while an employee of the SAL in Jacksonville, Florida, before joining the G&F. It was Kenworthy, working closely with Hugh Purvis, who wanted to run several special trains, including one with at least ten Pullman cars, from Madison northward to Augusta, where the first festivities would occur. Well-wishers would then travel over the extension to Greenwood for the grandest of ceremonies. On the return trip trains would stop in Edgefield, allowing that town to welcome guests. The official finale would take place in Augusta. Yet as an Augusta newspaper reported in early March, special committees locally would not be launched until "a definite date is announced."[30]

By early May plans were more firmly in place. The host communities had created their special committees and named members. In Greenwood the degree of preparation was particularly impressive. Committees included Band and Music, Barbecue, Decoration, First Aid, Invitation and Reception, Parade, Police and Traffic, Publicity, Speakers and Program, and Transportation. The Invitation and Reception Committee alone had more than seventy-five participants and included a chairman and vice-chairman; the committee's roster read like a who's who in Greenwood business, professional, and society circles. It would be the several publicity groups that contacted mayors, civic leaders, newspaper editors, and other interested individuals along the G&F, inviting them to organize local delegations. As an additional incentive to attend, the railroad revealed that corporation lawyer, Democratic presidential contender, and G&F associate William Gibbs McAdoo would be the featured speaker, an announcement that pleased many. "Mr. McAdoo is a Southern man, and has kept in close touch with the South, and he will no doubt have an interesting message for those who are fortunate enough to hear him," opined the *Forest-Blade* of Swainsboro. For Greenwood boosters the cry became "Meet Me in Greenwood!"[31]

But there would be no "Meet Me in Greenwood" in May; rather the new date became Wednesday, June 19. During the first week of May G&F personnel concluded that the 15th was impractical. "The time has been extended on account of delay in the work of finishing the roadbed . . . caused by the heavy rains," were the press reports. "We feel satisfied that by June nineteenth everything will be in fine shape for the celebration," announced Kenworthy. "I think . . . that it is better to postpone the celebration rather than go off 'half cocked.'" It was believed that a train of heavy steel Pullman cars would move too slowly over the new track, making it difficult to show off fully the construction triumph and to maintain a reasonable schedule for what was expected to be the "largest celebration that South Carolina has ever known."[32]

In early May the G&F also announced that on June 1 it would dispatch its first northbound revenue freight train. And the railroad kept this promise. At eleven that morning two ten-wheelers pulled twenty-five loaded freight cars out of the Augusta yards bound for Greenwood, arriving in the late afternoon. The *Index-Journal* was so excited that it ran a front-page banner headline in large bold type (**G. & F. Runs**) and commented positively on the event, noting that the train made "good time considering the newness of the track and several stops." Crew members set out cars along the route, including several at Edgefield and Pleasant Lane, and the doubleheaders steamed into Greenwood with thirteen cars, one containing miscellaneous merchandise for local delivery and the dozen others for interchange with the P&N, SAL, and SR. The destinations and cargoes of this initial freight would be largely representative of the traffic mix for years to come: Albany, New York—poles; Anderson, South Carolina—lumber; Gainesville, Georgia—brick; High Point, North Carolina—lumber; Laughlin, Ohio—clay; Lenoir, North Carolina—lumber; Newberry, South Carolina—building materials; Spartanburg, South Carolina—brick; Spray, North Carolina—cotton; Thomasville, North Carolina—lumber; Winston-Salem, North Carolina—cotton and lumber. A few days later this event prompted the *Index-Journal* editor to write: "The Georgia and Florida Railroad has operated its first freight train over the Greenwood-Augusta extension. All this means more business of many kinds for Greenwood. In every way it is a desirable achievement and now that the corner has been turned to this enterprise, it is our privilege to turn to something else for Greenwood's growth and general good."[33]

Not long after freight service began, representatives of the South Carolina Railroad Commission made an inspection trip. State law required such scrutiny. The special two-car train, which carried public officials, including Chairman Sam C. Blease, and G&F personnel, made a thorough examination. In the Commission's report, issued June 14, the conclusion was positive; indeed, the body was "surprised at the excellence of the road."[34]

A sense of wonderful anticipation for the planned events of June 19 soon spread. Newspapers along the G&F and in nearby cities and towns made much of the forthcoming festivities. On June 13, the *Douglas Enterprise* told its readers that "This is going to be a grand occasion, and every person that can do so, should not fail to make the trip." Local residents had a choice of a low round-trip fare of $5.00 for day coach and $9.00 round trip for "first-class" Pullman. "These rates include free barbecue dinner at Greenwood, supper at Edgefield, and delicious refreshments at Augusta," noted the paper. Moreover, the outing would be convenient. "The schedules that have been arranged for this trip will enable anyone to make it, and only be away from home one day."[35]

The opening celebrations turned out to be a series of smashing successes. The attention to detail, both on the part of the railroad and the host communities, helped to create memorable, festive experiences. Travelers from along the line put on their Sunday best and many wore special buttons. The male delegation from Nashville, for example, placed blue ribbons on their coat lapels that bore the words: "Nashville, Ga., Center of the Georgia Tobacco Belt." On board the special trains local groups entertained, including brass and string bands and various musical groups. As the

Forest-Blade later reported: "a number of Swainsboro's best and most noted singers, among them being Bozie Flanders, Arlis Rountree, Alonzo Wood and G. C. Powell, attracted much favorable attention from people both on and off the train." Throughout the observances "the old and the young, white and black, turned out all along the way to wave, sing and yell greetings of welcome."[36]

Organized events began early. Guests on incoming trains were welcomed in Augusta and treated to breakfast at a local hotel. Then during mid-morning the specials departed from Augusta Union Station for Greenwood with the first train arriving exactly at noon in the SAL yards with 610 passengers. As engine No. 405 and a dozen coaches reached Greenwood "an aeroplane of the Charlotte Flying Circus accompanied it overhead and just as the train pulled into the yards dipped low over the great throng of people standing on almost every foot of ground around the Seaboard station." Once the train stopped, the Augusta Police Band struck up a lively rendition of "Hail, Hail, the Gang's All Here." It did not take long before passengers on the following three trains, numbering about 1,200, joined 6,000 or more residents and visitors to enjoy what officially was called "Greenwood-G&F Day." Soon a parade with bands, fire trucks, and nearly 100 decorated automobiles, which transported distinguished visitors, moved slowly through downtown streets to the fairgrounds where well-wishers dined on ample quantities of barbeque "with all the trimmings." They also heard several speeches from area and local politicians and railroad officials, including Hugh Purvis. The G&F president declared that "we could not have accomplished the results without the support of those who have stood so loyally behind us." Perhaps the only disappointment was the absence of featured speaker McAdoo, who the previous day had wired the Speakers and Program Committee that illness forced him to cancel. Later the *Index-Journal* observed that these fairgrounds presentations "were eloquent and some just speeches." Still, the celebration honored the historic opening tradition of long-winded orations.[37]

In a somewhat ironic twist, "Greenwood–G&F Day" also featured dedication of the city's new, albeit small airport. The formal opening of this facility attracted far fewer spectators and lacked the elaborate trappings that made the railroad festivities so memorable. Still, the local editor thought that the latter might be more significant than was commonly believed. "The airport is still an 'infancy' proposition. To many it perhaps seems comparatively unimportant beside the completion of the line of steel to Augusta and southward. But who can tell?" And he added, "Someday, maybe, Greenwood will look back upon this day and wonder that the railroad so greatly overshadowed the airport in the popular estimation of importance as a community asset."[38]

By late afternoon the specials had departed on time from Greenwood for Edgefield and Augusta, bound for the final two celebratory events. These passengers may have been pleasantly surprised at what they encountered in

Edgefield. This community went "all out" to celebrate the coming of the new railroad. The town was gaily decorated with streamers that read: "Welcome" and "The Georgia and Florida: Active; Edgefield: Attractive," and red, white and blue bunting draped the courthouse, Confederate memorial, and most commercial buildings.[39]

The excitement had been building for some time. Earlier several area businesses had taken out advertising space in the *Edgefield Advertiser* to promote the event and to welcome the railroad. The Service Store, a general mercantile company located near the new G&F depot, used particularly enthusiastic copy:

> Toot! Toot! Toot! Toot! Toot! HEAR HER COMING!
> The train that we have been listening for for the last ten years.
> Ding, Dong Ding, Dingling!
> SHE'S HERE!
> WELCOME GEORGIA & FLORIDA
>
> Words cannot express Edgefield's joy over your coming. The town is unbottled at last, after nearly thirty years of bond issue and paper talk that have failed. We take off our hats, you deserve the 'Cake,' and we wish you much success with your new extension.[40]

Proportionally, more citizens of Edgefield became involved in preparations for the celebration than those who had been active in Greenwood. It is easy to understand the enthusiasm. Residents believed strongly that they required another railroad much more so than Greenwood, which was an established rail center. Edgefield had been "bottled up these many years" in a railroad sense, having access to only a stub of the SR with limited freight service and poor passenger options. Although the giant carrier claimed that "The Southern Serves the South," the town did not agree. "[The G&F] means that Edgefield, one of the oldest and most historic towns in the state, will no longer be handicapped by being situated at the terminus of a branch road, but that henceforth the town will have shipping facilities that are afforded by a trunk line or main artery of transportation." Arrival of the G&F was, in the words of the local editor, "a Red Letter day for this town," and everyone agreed.[41]

The celebration went off well. A party of Edgefield representatives met each train and escorted passengers to the public square where they were "served by the ladies." Bands played and a "quartet of colored men" sang at the "help yourself dinner." A few remarks were made, including "hearty greetings" from attorney J. Strom Thurmond, later icon of South Carolina politics, who represented the Edgefield Chamber of Commerce. At the end of the festivities, which had attracted about 3,000 people, Mayor Harold Norris presented President Purvis with a silver pitcher, goblet, and waiter, and then his wife received "a large, beautifully iced cake from the people of Edgefield." About 6 p.m. trains began to leave the Edgefield station, departing at twenty-minute intervals. The post-celebration commentary was especially laudatory. General Passenger Agent Kenworthy told an acquaintance in Edgefield that "I must tell you a little secret. So many people said, 'Well, I enjoyed the Edgefield reception best of all.'"[42]

The final festivities in Augusta were surely anticlimactic. Some of the undoubtedly weary celebrators took advantage of a banquet hosted by the city at the Hotel Richmond, while others left the party. After the dinner the remaining crowd "was entertained in various ways until about midnight" when coach and Pullman passengers left for the awaiting trains that would make their southbound stops throughout the night and the following morning.[43]

In a sense the celebration continued. There would be an opportunity for African Americans to participate separately. Although not excluded from the June activities, the "colored citizens of Greenwood," backed by G&F management, invited fellow black residents from along the G&F to board trains for a gala to be held at the fairgrounds on Monday, July 22. The highlights would include a baseball game and barbecue. In a message to the Edgefield African-American community, the Reverend Mr. F. A. Weaver encouraged attendance. "I have been in Edgefield for sixty years and I want Edgefield to do her best in showing appreciation of the new railroad. So I urge all of the [black] citizens of Edgefield county to go and we will make that a great day in Greenwood." Several thousand blacks from Valdosta to Edgefield rode the G&F to the Emerald City.[44]

THE AFTERMATH

The festivities were reminiscent of a large wedding, and their aftermath resembled the routine of a newly married couple. There was a honeymoon of sorts. Initially the future appeared promising, a feeling believed to be grounded in reality. Even before the start-up of freight service to Greenwood, "The Heart of Western South Carolina," the SAL announced that in anticipation of a brisk interchange business with the G&F it would spend approximately $60,000 to expand its local yards and facilities. Shortly thereafter the SAL doubled its car-storage capacity. For those South Carolinians who had done so much on June 19 to entertain the flock of out-of-town visitors, civic groups in Douglas, Madison, Moultrie, Nashville, Swainsboro, and Vidalia, encouraged by the G&F, soon hosted the "Greenwood-Edgefield Business Men's Friendship Tour," which showcased the agricultural and commercial activities, most of all bright tobacco production and sales, that flourished in the Wiregrass Region. The well-attended and popular August trip helped to bind together the business leaders of the northern and southern sections of the railroad. Other trips followed, including one taken in October to visit the large and modern Swift & Company packing plant at Moultrie.[45]

Optimism sprang, however, from more than the SAL investment and the goodwill tours. The company found the flow of traffic heartening. A year after the formal opening a Greenwood journalist called the freight business over the new line "splendid." To stimulate use of the extension and the "system that has been created," the G&F soon distributed widely "a very attractive map, showing how traffic should be routed from Northern, Eastern or Western points, also points in Virginia and the Carolinas, in order that it may reach their line at Greenwood." But as with so many marriages, a host of trials and tribulations followed. Indeed, no one could have imagined the problems that appeared in a relatively short period.[46]

Heavy rains, which repeatedly had delayed construction work and had severely damaged the main line and branches in Georgia and Florida, now caused even greater havoc along the Greenwood extension and much of the G&F. Beginning on September 26, 1929, biblical-like downpours flooded water courses large and small; the Altamaha River near Hazlehurst, for example, reached record levels. Destruction mounted as bridges, culverts, and track components washed away. Although trains were able to creep across the mighty steel spans over the Altamaha, the SR closed the Savannah River bridge at Augusta. Train service was badly disrupted with the main line broken between Augusta and St. Clair from September 30 to November 6. Still, the G&F maintained operations between Greenwood and Edgefield and rerouted through freight runs to south Georgia and Florida destinations from Augusta via Waynesboro and St. Clair (Torbit), Georgia, over the Central of Georgia and Savannah & Atlanta railroads. With most schedules annulled, passenger trains stayed in their terminals. The financial costs were high, approximately $150,000 for direct flood damages and about $100,000 in losses caused by decreased operating revenues and detour expenses. "No other railroad in the two states suffered anything like the Georgia and Florida, considering its mileage," observed the *Augusta Chronicle*. "No one could foresee it any more than the people of San Francisco could foresee the earthquake, or the people of Galveston, the tidal wave," added this newspaper philosophically. "It was a visitation of Providence which came suddenly, swiftly, and wrought destruction throughout the length and breadth of a wide area."[47]

Although large railroads could absorb $250,000 in losses, G&F officials found the financial burden too great to manage. Moreover, the Greenwood extension had cost in excess of $3 million, about a third more than initially anticipated, already making discretionary funds scarce. Management sought court protection and on October 19, 1929, the company entered receivership. Federal Judge William H. Barrett of the Southern District of Georgia appointed as co-receivers William V. Griffin, a New York City banker "and a splendid gentleman who is deeply interested in the road," and President Purvis. An ancillary brief filed with the Federal District Court for the Western District of South Carolina in Anderson supported the actions of Judge Barrett.[48]

A widely held expectation among G&F personnel, bankers, shippers, community leaders, and other observers that this second receivership would be of short duration proved highly false as the bankruptcy lasted for thirty-four years! There was also the hope that court protection would enable the G&F to become a much improved property, "repairing of damage in such a way that we will have a better roadbed, better trestles and better bridges, which are better able to withstand the attacks of floods." It was not to be.[49]

When it rained, it poured on the G&F, literally and figuratively. The Coverdale & Colpitts report had emphasized the attractive connections that entry into the Greenwood Gateway would provide, but troubles erupted on this front as well. About the time workers were building the Greenwood line, the ICC, in a split decision, turned down the request of the P&N for a "Certificate of Convenience and Necessity" to close the gap between Gastonia and Spartanburg and to build between Charlotte and Winston-Salem. The P&N subsequently claimed that as an electric interurban it was not subject to ICC jurisdiction. The Commission, though, considered it to be an "electrified Class 1 railroad." Later the U.S. Supreme Court sustained the decision of the regulators. Although construction crews actually started to shape a grade near Gastonia and Spartanburg, a federal court injunction, spearhead by the SR that closely paralleled the proposed P&N between Spartanburg, Charlotte, and Winston-Salem, brought work to a halt. The P&N ultimately decided to abandon its multimillion-dollar expansion plans, thus dashing the hopes of the G&F for new P&N connections in Charlotte and Winston-Salem. A potentially profitable north-south route in connection with the Norfolk & Western at Winston-Salem with the P&N never materialized. Persistent rumors that the P&N might buy the G&F and electrify it, perhaps to Augusta or Valdosta or even the 309 miles to Madison, soon vanished.[50]

The failure of the P&N to provide a better interchange connection was not the only disappointment that the G&F encountered after its arrival in Greenwood. A nasty and expensive fight erupted between the G&F and the ACL, parent of the C&WC, and the Louisville & Nashville Railroad (L&N), the latter recently leasing the Clinchfield, over joint through rates via the Greenwood Gateway. Because of the interstate nature of this issue, the ICC entered the fray. In January 1930 an ICC examiner ruled that the G&F must "short haul" itself. The verdict forced the G&F to relinquish or receive cars at Augusta for movement over the C&WC and the Clinchfield (through a short interchange connection with the SR at Spartanburg), thus depriving the G&F of additional haulage fees over its Greenwood line to the P&N. Through rates could only be levied for traffic that originated or was destined to local points on the extension itself. On June 19, 1930, the ICC overturned the preliminary decision, however: "The effect of the decision is that instead of the Greenwood extension being strangled, it will be able to participate in these rates as a regular carrier," noted a Washington, D.C., news dispatch. "The effect will be that business will not stagnate at Augusta, Greenwood and other nearby cities and towns which probably would have been the case had the decision been otherwise." The ICC argued that it had intended for the P&N and Clinchfield routes to be open when it authorized the G&F to build to Greenwood. Regulators also concluded that the joint lease of the Clinchfield by the ACL and L&N had been violated since the document called for an "independent" Clinchfield management. But the ACL was a sore loser. It then appealed to the federal courts for relief, but in early 1931 a three-judge review panel dismissed the objections. Understandably, this rate dispute had been worrisome for the G&F and the P&N, and there was a collective sigh of relief in the executive suites of both roads.[51]

While some lawyers for the G&F became involved with the ACL-L&N case, other attorneys for the railroad dealt with a dispute that proved to be just as costly. Even before the Greenwood extension opened, bickering erupted between the G&F and its principal contractor, Winston & Company. This dispute involved more than harsh words. In the summer of 1929 Winston & Company went to federal court asking for payment of $421,022.50 for costs and interest for nonpayment of construction services. The G&F responded with its own suit against Winston & Company, contending that the firm failed to complete work on time and that $150,000 in damages should be paid. Nearly a year later following extensive hearings, a federal special master ruled that the plaintiff was due approximately $200,000 and disallowed the counterclaim of the defendant. This was hardly good news for the receivers.[52]

Although the public probably cared little about the legal battle between the G&F and Winston & Company, there was concern about passenger operations over the Greenwood extension. It was popularly believed, even in railroad circles, that the extension would have regularly scheduled passenger trains. As early as late September 1929 Purvis told the Edgefield newspaper that "November 1 has been set for the inauguration of passenger service. Later, as soon as conditions warrant, other trains will be put on." But service did not materialize. Some encouraging news followed in mid-November when General Passenger Agent Kenworthy announced that on the morning of December 16th the first passenger train would leave Greenwood. "The train will furnish mail, coach and express service, and will operate in conjunction with the regular trains from the south, known as trains four and five." If that was not enough to please potential patrons, Kenworthy disclosed what some residents had longed for, namely Pullmans operating through Greenwood. "On December 19 a new sleeping car service will be inaugurated between Augusta and New York . . . [to] be known as the Southern States Special." A proud Kenworthy told *Index-Journal* readers that "this new service will enable the traveler to leave Greenwood about midnight and be in New York the next night in time for the shows." Admittedly, these Pullmans would be running mostly over the rails of the SAL and the Pennsylvania Railroad, but Kenworthy's company would be involved and the *Southern States Special* would join the G&F's other name train, the *Bon-Air Special*, between Augusta, Valdosta and Jacksonville via the SR at Valdosta. Who knew the marquee value of these trains? After all, the feeling existed within the railroad industry that shippers commonly routed their traffic over the roads that they traveled.[53]

Just as the opening date for the Greenwood extension was repeatedly rescheduled, the publicized December dates passed without passenger service on either a local or through basis. In a letter, written on December 6, 1929, Kenworthy told newspapers that "we regret very much to advise that it is necessary to postpone passenger service on the new line until probably February 15th." The reason, explained the general passenger agent, involved track conditions. "On account of the roadbed not being properly settled, due to the heavy rains, we do not feel that we would be justified in the inauguration of any passenger service under present conditions, between Augusta and Greenwood."[54]

Regular service did not begin in February 1930 or at any time. Even though track conditions improved markedly, the deepening national depression, the receivership, and better area public roads contributed to the decision by the receivers and by SAL officials not to offer scheduled passenger accommodations of any type between Augusta and Greenwood. The exceptions involved occasional excursion trains that the G&F operated briefly. In 1929 the South Carolina Railroad Commission reported that the company carried 3,666 passengers, mostly for the opening celebrations, but the following year only 678 patrons were handled. As the economy sank, no more excursionists rode the rails. Only train crews, officials aboard the company's office car, and an increasing number of hoboes, "passengers without tickets," traveled over the fifty-seven miles of track.[55]

Construction of the Greenwood extension proved not the panacea for solving the financial problems of the struggling G&F. It did give the company beneficial connections, however, that increased the flow of bridge traffic. The Coverdale & Colpitts engineers were correct in that the G&F had been a local carrier, but with its South Carolina trackage it became part of another steel thoroughfare between the North and South: C&O-Clinchfield-P&N-G&F, a new "alphabet" freight route of sorts. Early reports of traffic for the line suggested that construction had been worthwhile. Tonnage for an abbreviated 1929 stood at 83,380 and jumped to 270,675 for 1930, but then slipped as the economy worsened. Still, tonnage handled in 1931 exceeded 215,000 and actually rose to 235,132 in 1932, likely the result of farmers dumping cotton as commodity prices fell. The South Carolina Railroad Commission was correct when it observed in 1933 that "the prosperity of the railroad industry is so tied in with the prosperity of all other industries that when the one suffers the others must suffer."[56]

The important "what if" question might be asked. *If* the G&F had marched into Greenwood (or Columbia) during those flush years immediately following the Panic of 1907 and before World War I, construction benefits would likely have been significantly greater. The volume of traffic, with increased mileage haulage, might have kept the G&F from slipping into its first receivership. But construction occurred at nearly the end of railroad building in the Southeast, and for most of North America as well. Increased truck traffic badly hurt small Class 1 roads like the G&F, syphoning off considerable local business, especially farm products. Although the Greenwood extension traversed a sparsely populated territory, its appearance failed to precipitate much local growth. *If* the line had opened a decade or two earlier, the railroad might have contributed much more to town building and online businesses, just as it had done at several points along the main stem in Georgia. As late as 1929 a writer for the *Saluda Standard* believed that the new Greenwood County station of Pittsburg, which honored M. T. Pitts, a large landowner, "with no other town in less than 16 miles," was destined to become a thriving community. Unfortunately, the place never became more than a tiny trading center. Similar communities, spawned by new rail lines during the late 1920s on the Great Plains and on the Canadian prairies, often got off to a much better start. Yet during the hard times and extensive and severe drought of the 1930s most of these railroad-spawned towns faltered or failed to meet the expectations of promoters.[57]

Arguably the "expand or die" strategy worked. Even with a crushing national depression, which struck the service territory of the G&F especially hard, there was no further talk of dismemberment or liquidation. By the early 1930s the real hope for a revitalized G&F seemed to be promotion of the Greenwood Gateway ("Gateway to the Piedmont"), abandonment of unprofitable branches, and patience waiting for that inevitable strong uptick in the economy that would produce enough compensatory traffic. Always there was the expectation that the "New South" would be the place of solid population growth, agricultural maturity and industrial expansion. That feeling remained strong; after all, the G&F tapped "one of the richest sections of the South, the heart of wiregrass Georgia, and . . . the country it traverses is just in the infancy of development."[58]

CHAPTER FIVE

Developing the Wiregrass Region

The Georgia & Florida (G&F) joined other railroads that sought to advance their service territory. Since the mid-nineteenth century, carriers throughout much of the United States and Canada had labored at expanding agricultural, commercial, and industrial activities. Almost from the start the G&F revved up its engines for development along its main and branch lines between Augusta, Georgia, and Madison, Florida, and after 1929 the Greenwood extension. The company's most enduring triumphs occurred in south Georgia, heart of the Wiregrass Region, a legacy that remained long after the company became a "fallen flag" road.[1]

Unlike a Chicago, Burlington & Quincy, Illinois Central, or Wabash that might serve exceptionally fertile regions, the country along the G&F track hardly ranked as the nation's finest. Most of the lands were part of the Atlantic Coastal Plain where soils tended to be rather sandy and spotted by occasional outcroppings of clay. "Barren, oppressive, starved" were words antebellum visitors used to describe the countryside. Indeed, generations of Georgians considered much of what became the G&F's heartland to have limited economic value. The great core of the sprawling Atlantic Coastal Plain was commonly known as the "Rolling Wiregrass Country," a huge, egg-shaped expanse of more than 10,000 square miles. It was covered largely with a dense forest that sustained expansive longleaf or southern yellow pines (*Pinus palustris*) and a thriving undergrowth of wiregrass (*Aristida stricta*). This distinctive plant grew under the tall, overhead canopy in dense, spreading tufts and reached heights of from one to three feet. Wiregrass regenerated quickly after multiple fires; in fact, it depended on regular summer burnings to stimulate flowering and seed production. And this native grass appealed to agrarians, for it "resists the cold and furnishes food to cattle, sheep, and hogs."[2]

A mostly gentle climate contributed to this lush growth of trees and grass. The temperature seldom dropped below twenty degrees Fahrenheit or rose above 100 degrees Fahrenheit. Rainfall was usually abundant, averaging more than fifty inches annually. Killing frosts normally did not arrive until early November, with the last frost coming in mid-March, allowing for a growing season of nearly 240 days. "It is a healthy country where you live an out of door life," remarked a zealous writer in the 1920s, "and where you do not have to keep the winter fires burning continually, and where you enjoy the cool summer breezes and sleep with perfect comfort."[3]

The Wiregrass Region remained one of the last "frontiers" in the Southeast as it was sparsely populated until after the Civil War. The local inhabitants, often described as "frontier paupers," were mostly occupied with lumbering and naval-stores production and raising livestock that wandered over the unfenced terrain. Cotton, the stable crop of the South, was usually absent until the late nineteenth century. The region was an economic backwater, with its isolated, small farms, characterized by their mud-daubed log houses, crudely constructed outbuildings, haphazard cattle lots, and small patches of corn. The Wiregrass countryside was hardly a Dixie showplace.[4]

Following the Civil War some sustained development began, spawning modest population growth and town building. The timber and naval stores industries expanded, largely stimulated by the coming of the railroad, and farming of the thousands of acres of cut-over lands increased, aided greatly by using a mixture of manure and imported guano and phosphates. Unquestionably, "Open Sesame" was spoken through the railroad whistle. After 1870 production of Sea Island cotton or "long cotton" gradually became economically important in scattered sections of north Florida and south Georgia. Unlike the short-staple variety, Sea Island cotton was prized in the making of lace, thread, and fine fabrics, and therefore commanded a price that was double, even triple that received for the much more common fiber. At the turn of the twentieth century, Madison, Florida, southern terminus of the G&F, claimed "the largest Sea Island cotton gin in the world," and was undeniably a center for this valuable crop.[5]

Just as predecessor lines of the G&F relied heavily on hauling lumber and forest products, once assembled and consolidated, the company continued to handle substantial car loadings of logs, telephone poles, fence posts, structural timbers, finished boards, and other wood items. Similarly, turpentine and naval stores traffic remained significant. Cotton, too, became more important as farmers planted both the short and long-staple varieties. Fortunately for residents and the G&F, the emerging twentieth century saw stronger prices in these basic commodities. In 1900 the *Moultrie Observer* happily declared that "cotton is up, . . . spirits and rosin are higher than they have been for ten years, lumber is high . . . labor is bringing a good price. . . . God is surely smiling on this country." It appeared that the "Long Depression," which extended from the end of the Civil War until the Spanish-American War, had mercifully lifted. The new century for the Wiregrass Region dawned bright, indeed, just as it did for nearly all of the nation. This optimism, and accompanying boosterism, led communities to advertise their location and natural resources. By 1911 Douglas, seat of Coffee County, declared itself the "Hub of the Wiregrass," and C. O. DuVall, who represented the Chamber of Commerce, urged local businessmen to use this slogan, especially on their commercial stationery. Almost from its corporate inception the G&F contended that it served "The Heart of an Empire."[6]

LUMBER

By the early years of the twentieth century what had evolved as the dominant commodities that moved over the G&F were about to change. Initially timber products became the most discussed. After all, the region supported a vast longleaf pine forest and impressive stands of hardwoods, including cypress, gum, hickory, oak, and sycamore. But this great natural resource was finite, and persistent logging led to countless acres of cut-over lands. "Before long all the large tracts of timber in this county as well as those that reach over into the adjoining counties will be a thing of the past for the stately pines are now being cut, sawed into merchantable materials which are in turn made parts of the buildings of this country, some even going across the waters," opined the *Swainsboro Forest-Blade* in 1915. "With . . . two big mills running full time it will not be long before this section of the state will be minus its large tracts of timber when the turpentine and lumber interests will merge into small concerns . . . and the vast acres that once were so delighting to everybody will be turned into fields of waving grain and fleecy white cotton." Residents assumed that as loggers cleared the forest, farmers would appear; indeed, throughout much of the late nineteenth century and early twentieth century the local notion was that the plow followed the ax.[7]

Yet it was premature to write an obituary for commercial wood production. The work of professional foresters who hailed from the United States Forest Service, state forestry departments, and land-grant colleges demonstrated that timber could become an enduring and important cash crop. Although the G&F was too poor to afford its own company forester, as early as 1929 it gladly dispatched "Forestry Demonstration" trains. The G&F continued the practice of progressive railroads of educating farmers, landowners, and other interested parties about the potential of agricultural change. Since the turn of the twentieth century these trains nationally had become important in "dissolving rural suspicion of scientific agriculture and in awakening the farmer to its possibilities."[8]

The G&F "Tree Train" lacked great complexities. The special usually consisted of a locomotive, baggage car, and office car and operated on highly publicized schedules. On the eve of the Great Depression the onboard exhibits were prepared mostly by the American Forestry Association as part of its Southern Educational Project. The Georgia Forestry Association and the Georgia State College of Agriculture in Athens also participated. These displays were designed to show what was currently being done in the manufacture of wood products and the potentialities for a timber industry based primarily on the fast-growing shortleaf or loblolly pine (*Pinus taeda*). Specifically, these exhibits included paper of various types, rayon made from local trees, and wood-generated chemicals used in the production of deodorants, insecticides, matches, pharmaceuticals, wire insulation, and other consumer and industrial products. At station stops train personnel, which included forestry professionals and G&F representatives, used public places, whether a courthouse, school, or movie theater, to present lectures that complemented the baggage-car displays and to show films that usually emphasized forestry protection. The G&F made it clear to visitors that it did not believe that all land should be utilized for the growing of forests "but does maintain that all land which cannot be used for agriculture should be used for the production of trees."[9]

Although it is difficult to measure precisely the success of these efforts by the G&F to promote commercial forestry activities, press reports were universally positive. When the train visited Nashville in September 1929, Carl Wilson, Unit Director of the American Forestry Association, and W. E. French, G&F General Industrial Agent, performed admirably. "Two experts well matched," observed the *Nashville Herald*. "The interest they manifested begat interest in others and their power of description drew the attention of the people." Apparently their public presentations offered occasional challenges. "Some of the boys were restless at first and rather boisterous and inattentive. However before Messrs. Wilson and French got through talking they were all attention." Added the Nashville newspaper, "There is no telling what the fruitage of the seed sown in their young minds that night will do in developing forestry in Berrien county, where already the farmers are getting well interested protecting the young growing pine trees that in all probability will enhance vastly in ten or fifteen years the agricultural production of the county." The conclusion was straightforward: "This promising industry got a big boost by the visitation of the forestry car." In time loblolly pines became a significant part of the economy of the Wiregrass Region; the G&F benefited greatly by transporting these commercially grown trees, which were used extensively as pulpwood.[10]

Development personnel did not overlook the long-established production of naval stores. By the beginning of the twentieth century this industry was well established in south Georgia and north Florida, where it would remain concentrated. Although generally in a decline after World War I, naval stores contributed to the G&F's bottom line. In 1921 the railroad enthusiastically backed formation of the Gum Turpentine Farmers Cooperative Association, centered in Vidalia, and provided what assistance it could to producers and marketers alike.[11]

COTTON

And then there was cotton. After the turn of the twentieth century plant-ings of this silky fiber in the Wiregrass Region increased steadily, spiking upwards to a high point on the eve of World War I. Bumper crops appeared in 1911 and 1914. Although the outbreak of war in Europe in 1914 soon closed some markets for regional cotton, prices remained strong. In 1916 Georgia's cotton crop was worth three times what it had been valued in 1900, and prices continued to be good until the end of the conflict. Not only was upland short-staple cotton part of the economy along the G&F, but also Sea Island cotton grew in importance in southern sections. Some of Madison County, Florida's, pine-clad slopes and gently rolling lands, for example, proved ideally suited for the crop. Needless to say, the G&F annu-ally handled hundreds of cars of baled cotton, mostly destined for textile mills in the Carolinas, New England, and abroad. Cottonseed, too, moved in significant quantities.[12]

As might be expected, company personnel did what they could to inform the public that cotton fields were part of the G&F landscape. The railroad rightly had its eyes on relocating experienced cotton farmers, most of whom were tenants, who lived on the worn-out Piedmont lands of Georgia and South Carolina. Not long after operations began, the company took space in the main building of Augusta's Georgia-Carolina Fair held annually in November. "The cotton exhibit [of the G&F] is especially interesting, show-ing different varieties of the staple on the stalk and in the lint," reported a visitor. "The Sea Island cotton attracts the most attention from the farmers, especially the price that being double the amount received from upland cot-ton. Some of the Sea Island cotton stalks were 14 feet in height." For those potential cotton growers who missed the Georgia-Carolina Fair, for several years the G&F awarded an annual prize of $100 for the best five acres of upland cotton and $100 for the best five acres of Sea Island cotton. The rules were simple: the producer, who needed to live within six miles of the rail-road, "shall furnish a statement as to the variety of seed planted, when planted, the preparation of the ground, the quantity of fertilizer used and when and how applied, the method of cultivation and kind of implements used. The Contestant shall furnish a sample of not less than ten pounds of Cotton . . . to be examined by the judges selected to make the awards." A faculty member from the Eleventh District Agricultural College (today's South Georgia College) at Douglas supervised the contest.[13]

Just as timber resources were diminishing by the 1910s, a crisis in cotton developed as the Mexican boll weevil nearly dethroned King Cotton. This voracious insect, described as being "only a bit smaller than an ordinary fly," first appeared in Texas in 1894, and began to move eastward, averaging about seventy-five to 100 miles a year. By 1913 the weevil had reached southeast Georgia and a few years later northern Florida. While infestations only diminished yields of the faster growing short-staple cotton, eventually the "winged demon" completely wiped out the slower maturing Sea Island variety. "After the boll weevil came you could still get half a crop with short cotton," remembered a Madison County farmer, "but the growing season was so long for long cotton and it took so long to mature that the boll weevil ate it up and stripped the stalks bare." Initially cotton yields did not drop markedly, and apathy by farmers toward the impending disaster set in. Even though the U.S. Department of Agriculture suggested that an effective weevil control measure (dusting with calcium arsenate) had been developed, many farmers ignored the treatment. Then the damage skyrocketed. In 1919 a sharp downswing began, and between 1921 and 1923 yields in Georgia fell thirty to forty-five percent below normal levels. Similar declines occurred throughout the cotton belt of the Southeast.[14]

The G&F recognized the crisis and responded. The railroad exhorted cotton growers to use calcium arsenate, delivering large quantities of the chemical to online stations and rural "blind sidings." And the company encouraged farmers to pay heed to the advice offered by a recently created network of agricultural extension agents who were knowledgeable about crop diseases. Yet the G&F was also practical. As early as 1917 the company distributed "Antidotes for the Boll Weevil" circulars. "It is not the purpose of this Company to urge our farmers to grow no cotton," argued a G&F publication. "Georgia is a great cotton producing State and will continue to grow a certain amount. It has been demonstrated that cotton can be successfully grown in boll weevil territory, but it is an up-hill job with increased expense and reduced output per acre, and we will have to get away from it as a single cash crop to ever become financially independent." By the early 1920s, however, as conditions for cotton worsened, the road's several industrial and agricultural agents argued more strenuously for the replacement of cotton with alternative hearty and profitable crops, believing that the boll weevil "has made the cotton planter sit up and take notice; he [boll weevil] has been the means of convincing thousands of good people already living in the South, that he can reduce them to poverty unless they change their old cotton planting methods into the diversified farming system, which is today making up the Nation's Garden [the G&F's service territory]."[15]

TOBACCO

In the minds of G&F officials the best remedy for the woes confronting the cotton belt was tobacco, and here the railroad played a pivotal and impressive role in turning thousands of acres from cotton to "bright" or "flue-cured" tobacco production. This type of tobacco had already been raised successfully in the region around the eastern North Carolina-Virginia border. Even though this particular "thirteen-month crop" required much more work than cotton, bright-leaf tobacco became prized by the burgeoning cigarette-making industry as men gave up pipes and began to smoke cigarettes. As such, profit levels were attractive.[16]

By the mid-1920s the G&F enthusiastically spoke of bright-leaf tobacco as the "CHAMPION CROP OF ALL." The railroad immodestly boasted that "THE HISTORICAL RECORDS ON TOBACCO show that the GEORGIA AND FLORIDA RAILWAY was the first railroad to undertake to commercialize Bright Tobacco in the State of Georgia." This statement may well be accurate.[17]

The role played by the G&F clearly reveals a major, early commitment. Even before the era of World War I the south Georgia press regaled readers about the promotional efforts of a tireless Southern Baptist pastor, the Rev. Mr. W. B. Smith, better known as "Preacher Smith." In 1915 the G&F hired Smith as its representative to encourage tobacco planting in the Wiregrass Region, and he turned out to be the right person for this job. A former resident of the Carolina tobacco belt, Smith had moved to the G&F branch-line community of Broxton, Georgia. It would be under Smith's tutelage that the first tobacco was successfully grown as a commercial experiment, involving four farmers on a total of twelve acres in Coffee County. Appropriately, in 1923 Smith officially became the G&F's "Tobacco Agent."[18]

Since these initial tobacco-growing efforts were profitable, expansion spearheaded by the G&F followed. The railroad gave growers free seeds, and in 1917 encouraged creation in Douglas of the Georgia Tobacco Company, a firm that conducted auctions and stored and shipped tobacco. Later that same year a second tobacco facility opened in Douglas, and similar auction-marketing outlets appeared in Adel, Hazlehurst, Madison, Moultrie, Nashville, Valdosta, and Vidalia. Expansion in Coffee County was particularly noteworthy. In a letter to the railroad's assistant traffic manager in 1939, the station agent at Douglas explained that the first warehouse locally "contained about forty five hundred square feet of floor space and that was the only warehouse in this section. We now have six warehouses in Douglas with a combined floor space of approximately four hundred thousand square feet, exclusive of the Douglas Tobacco Company's plant." Quickly these warehouse owners, too, joined the G&F in promoting production, distributing seeds and providing growing and selling advice.[19]

Another way that the G&F fostered bright-leaf tobacco was to operate an excursion train from south Georgia to the tobacco fields and markets in North Carolina. In September 1920, for instance, the railroad, at Preacher Smith's encouragement, urged large landowners to invest nearly $100 for an extended trip to the Tar Heel state. For that price, which represented the actual cost to the company, individuals received rail fare, sleeping car, and hotel accommodations. Reports indicate that this was a popular venture and again attested to the railroad's "doing everything in its power to encourage tobacco growing. [The company] never misses an opportunity to help the farmer."[20]

The G&F was not alone in promoting a promising replacement cash crop for short and long-stem cotton in south Georgia and north Florida. Agricultural agents who worked for other railroads, most notably the

Atlanta, Birmingham & Atlantic, Central of Georgia, and Seaboard Air Line (SAL), also trumpeted the bright tobacco culture. Individuals associated with the area's land-grant colleges likewise assisted, and community booster groups did what they could. In 1924 the Madison County Chamber of Commerce, for one, took out eye-catching advertisements in the local newspaper that proclaimed "Bright Tobacco is Our Salvation" and explained why farmers should turn away from cotton. These advocates, however, ignored the negative impact that tobacco had on soil fertility; the crop's susceptibility to disease, including black shank, blackroot rot, bluemold, Granville wilt, and nematodes; and how landowners could manipulate tenant producers.[21]

Still, hundreds of farmers took the advice of tobacco enthusiasts. There is little evidence to support the viewpoint that area farmers suffered acutely from deep-seated traditions that made change difficult. Even though the vast majority lacked much formal education and understanding of modern science, the most isolated agrarian seemingly sensed the value of growing tobacco. This cash crop proved to be ideally suited for the small family agricultural unit, which often totaled only forty or fifty acres and was so common throughout the Wiregrass Region. Residents widely recognized the need for finding a way to sustain rural life.[22]

Tobacco production burgeoned. Most of all, statistical data for Georgia agriculture vividly reveal the expansion of the bright-leaf tobacco crop. In 1917 only 440 acres were cultivated, but two years later acreage soared to 25,300. Only a decade later, 115,000 acres were committed to tobacco, which, until 1939, was the peak. As with all agricultural commodities, prices varied wildly. In 1918 the average price per pound stood at 34.5 cents, but plummeted to 6.41 cents in 1931, although New Deal–era price supports pushed the average back to the twenty-cent-per-pound range. By 1930 tobacco-leaf tonnage, while less than that of lumber products, cotton bales, and cottonseed meal and cake, represented a substantial portion of the G&F's freight business. In that year tobacco leaf exceeded 1,600 carloads, producing revenues of nearly $150,000. Although volume fluctuated, especially during the Great Depression, the figures from Georgia (as reported to the Georgia Public Service Commission) for 1944 revealed 22,318 tons, producing $144,272 in revenues, outstripping cotton, the second largest field-grown commodity, in both weight and value. As to the percentage of the total Georgia-Florida tobacco crop handled, the G&F in 1939 claimed approximately forty percent, a figure that remained roughly steady for years. No one denied that tobacco turned out to be enormously beneficial for the company.[23]

Moreover, the G&F seemed highly adept at moving tobacco. In August 1930 Joseph Lawrence, editor of the *Nashville Herald,* praised the railroad for handling the tobacco rush in a "smooth and easy manner." Of course, this was a lucrative business with much of the tobacco traffic traveling nearly the length of the main line via the Greenwood Gateway. In 1938, for example,

55.2 percent of carloads moved through Greenwood, 26.3 percent through Augusta, and the remaining shipments through other junctions, mainly Midville and St. Clair, Georgia. These car loadings came both from online communities and from scattered offline locations, including Live Oak, Florida, and Quitman, Georgia.[24]

The Nashville newspaper went to great lengths to describe the excellence of service in this editorial:

> Ample empty cars were on hand at all times, ready to be placed wherever wanted by the shippers on a few moments notice. The switch engine manned by Mr. W. M. Griffin, conductor, Mr. M. Drew, engineer, has put in full time not alone switching here and at Adel, but acting as a special tobacco train, bringing in here a load of tobacco every morning at 6 a.m. in time to send it on the through early morning train to Greenwood, thus getting it fifteen hours ahead if it had to wait for No. 26 from Moultrie. . . . It became necessary on Thursday the 7th [August] to run a special train from Moultrie with 16 cars of tobacco and another on Saturday the 9th, pulling 26 cars.
>
> Up to Tuesday night there were 159 cars shipped from Nashville that weighted 4,555,902 pounds of tobacco.
>
> The management of the G. & F. are being congratulated on this well planned and executed program, not alone at Nashville, but also all along their lines in the Georgia tobacco belt.[25]

Even though by the 1930s trucks carried more tobacco as public roads steadily improved, the G&F retained much of this business relatively well. The fine quality of service pleased tobacco warehousemen, whose loading facilities were frequently on the railroad's sidings, and these shippers stayed with the railroad until the end. It was hardly a news flash when the Nashville editor reported five years after his initial commentary that "at Nashville they [G&F] will have a switch engine day and night, telegraph operators and every other necessary facility for the annual tobacco rush." Indeed, tobacco needed to be moved rapidly because market prices could change quickly.[26]

The G&F remained ever-mindful of the needs of tobacco growers. In the late 1930s a troubling outbreak of bluemold disease threatened to reduce crop yields. Fortunately, treatment for bluemold was more effective and less bothersome than chemical responses to control the boll weevil infestations. An inexpensive spray consisting of red copper oxide, cottonseed oil, and water, developed in part by a tobacco-disease specialist at the agricultural experiment station in Tifton, Georgia, worked effectively. With this tool at hand, the G&F, cooperating with agricultural extension agents and others, in January 1938 dispatched its "Blue Mold Control" train to inform tobacco raisers of this mold-fighting method. "This special is being operated," according to W. E. Aycock, G&F agricultural and industrial agent, "for the purpose of bringing this valuable information to the tobacco farmers of the Georgia-Florida bright leaf belt and we have arranged the schedule of stops for convenience of the farmers all of whom are invited to the nearest demonstration point, where experts will answer any and all questions to growing tobacco from the seed bed to curing barn and especially controlling Blue Mold." Between January 17 and January 21 the three-car special, which resembled the "Tree Train," paid calls at Adel, Douglas, Hazlehurst, Moultrie, Nashville, Statesboro, Valdosta, and Vidalia. A year later the train operated on a similar schedule.[27]

When the Blue Mold Special arrived in Nashville on January 20, 1938, a large crowd, estimated at approximately 700, met the train when it steamed into the station at 9:30 a.m. The program began with comments made by Dr. J. V. Talley, mayor of Nashville, who deplored the damage done to the tobacco crop of 1937 from bluemold and resulting losses sustained by growers and merchants alike. "We are here today to study the new method to use in combating blue mold, the plant disease that created the loss of thousands and thousands of dollars to tobacco growers of Berrien county last year." Added the mayor, "With this spray, so I am informed, growers may be able to grow healthy, thrifty plants so necessary in producing quality tobacco. Our community appreciates the opportunity presented by the Georgia & Florida Railroad cooperating with the Extension Service and the Experiment Station at Tifton to learn how to mix this new spray." Then it was W. E. Aycock's opportunity to welcome farmers. Next Aycock turned over the program to Homer Durden, an agricultural specialist from the U. S. Agricultural Adjustment Administration, who conducted "a most interesting discussion in regards to tobacco culture." Durden was followed by S. B. Fenne, plant pathologist for the Georgia Extension Service, who explained various types of sprays and how they might best be used. Before the train left town at 11:30 a.m. for Douglas, farmers had an opportunity to ask questions "which were promptly and plainly answered by Mr. Fenne."[28]

WATERMELONS

As tobacco production rose and the accompanying rail traffic increased, yielding vital and substantial revenues, the G&F did not ignore other possibilities for agricultural diversification. The most significant new crop after tobacco that the railroad promoted was watermelons. Like tobacco, watermelons were superbly suited for the modest farming operations that dominated Wiregrass agriculture, and they enjoyed expanding and profitable markets. As the twentieth century progressed, this "most juicy of all herbal fruits" emerged as an important cash crop in south Georgia and north Florida, occupying in fact the lion's share of truck-farming acres in the Peach state. Since the 1880s northern, urban consumption of fruits and vegetables, including watermelons, had been accelerating.[29]

About the time Preacher Smith launched his successful efforts to stimulate bright-leaf tobacco, R. L. Armacost, G&F's assistant industrial agent, began to urge online farmers to grow these profitable melons. It was Armacost who encouraged the planting of at least ten acres on each farm, and during the formative years of production aggressively sought publicity by awarding cash prices for the biggest melons. Likely the best cotton contests inspired this ploy. In 1916, for example, the company paid $25.00 for the largest melon, $15.00 for the second largest, and $10.00 for the next in size. The only rules were that "contestants must have ten or more acres tributary to the Georgia & Florida Railway" and that "not more than one prize will be allotted any individual." Area newspapers offered coverage of the contest, with stories appearing on the front pages of small-town weeklies. This was hardly a novel idea; for some time railroads throughout the country had such contests for livestock and crops. Nevertheless, the cash contest drew welcomed attention to watermelon culture.[30]

But Armacost and other G&F personnel did much more. Farmers appreciated the railroad's efforts to find attractive markets for their watermelons. Armacost worked hard to market the crop through a large fruit and vegetable broker in Cincinnati, Ohio, Leonard, Crossett & Riley Company, being "recognized by melon growers . . . as the best in the business." Similarly, the railroad backed producer efforts to organize and promote marketing associations. The most successful group, headquartered in Adel, was the Southwest Georgia Watermelon Growers Association (SOWEGA), organized in November 1920. As with other agricultural products, the G&F distributed a variety of "circulars" that told producers about the planting, cultivation and marketing of this crop. Special attention was paid to plant diseases, mostly stem-end rot.[31]

In "Timely Talk No. 66," "Eat a Slice of Melon a Day!", one of a series of public-service sheets the G&F issued during the 1920s, President Hugh Purvis urged higher consumer consumption of watermelons. "We do not believe that the public generally knows the nutritive value of the watermelon, because if it did, the consumption would increase many times." And he added, "Every member of the human family should eat WATERMELONS at least once daily during the watermelon season."[32]

The promotional efforts paid off handsomely. As early as 1915 hundreds of cars of freshly harvested melons moved over G&F rails through the Augusta Gateway to northern destinations, including points in Atlantic Canada. As production increased, especially to the south and west of Douglas, car loadings burgeoned. The major center for shipments was Pinetta, Florida, a village located between Valdosta and Madison. By the late 1920s the railroad billed more watermelons from this station than from any other. In 1929, for example, 115 cars left Pinetta, although several nearby locations also did a brisk business: eighty-three cars from Clyattville, Georgia, seventy-nine cars from Madison, and forty cars from Hanson,

Florida. Watermelon raisers discovered that prices were good, especially since growing conditions allowed them to ship their twenty-five- to thirty-pound watermelons to urban markets ahead of crops grown further north. At this time a carload usually gave growers from $200.00 to $350.00 and occasionally reached nearly $500.00.[33]

The G&F did all that it could to expedite the watermelon crop, dispatching during the harvesting season frequent "Watermelon Specials." At times doubled-headed locomotives pulled long strings of boxcars loaded floor-to-ceiling with melons that shippers packed with hay straw to avoid damage in transit. In June 1921 the *Sparks Eagle* noted that "these trains are operated each year during watermelon season and haul melons from this section to Augusta."[34]

When the watermelon rush was in full swing, the G&F expedited these perishable cargoes as best it could. Fortunately, though, unlike lettuce and some other truck crops, most varieties of melons had a relatively long shelf life. It was not unusual to have cars attached to regularly scheduled north-bound passenger trains. In the mid-1930s Dens Kirk, the pen name of George Kirkland, Jr., a popular columnist for the *Swainsboro Forest-Blade,* had this to say about G&F watermelon business:

> When the writer was a small boy, there were no Watermelon trains such as we see today, from the middle of June till the middle of July, every day in the week, Sundays as well. . . .
>
> Today, Sunday, June 24, 1934, the writer was on a passenger train of the Georgia & Florida, riding for rest and recreation, Swainsboro to Hazlehurst and return. In the make-up of the passenger train, Southbound, was a long string of empty freight cars being hauled down into South Georgia to be loaded with watermelons for up-country markets. Going down we sidetracked at Alston, a station in Montgomery county, in order that a solid watermelon train of fifty-six loaded cars might not be delayed in its onward rush to Northern markets. This was on Sunday, . . . and in spite of the fact that before daylight on the same day, at the same place, in the same sort of a big hurry, a similar solid train had rushed by going also North; and on the return trip in the afternoon of the same day, the passenger train was hauling some ten or fifteen more cars of nothing but watermelons. This is one railroad who beats all the watermelons hauled out of South Georgia by all the railroads having tracks down there. . . . This is a great industry and we are for it, teeth and toenail.[35]

As with the hauling of timber products, cotton, and tobacco, watermelons remained important to the G&F until its corporate demise. In late spring of 1955, for example, Philip James, the railroad's agricultural agent, provided watermelon farmers with information on marketing conditions, car-loading tips and, of course, production advice. "It will be to every melon grower's advantage to remove from vines all ill shaped melons or anything that will make a good melon." Yet as with other agricultural commodities, an erosion of business occurred. In 1940 the *Douglas Enterprise*, for example, noted that "many watermelons were hauled out of this section by trucks during the early part of the season."[36]

SWEET POTATOES, TOMATOES, CUCUMBERS, AND ONIONS

In its ongoing quest to bring about agricultural diversification and enhance car loadings, the G&F encouraged farmers to grow a variety of other fruits and vegetables. The message for raising alternative crops was simple and direct. "The losses resulting from crop damage may be reduced by the farmers themselves. By diversifying he can carry his own insurance," asserted the company. "A single crop farmer risks the loss of his entire crop by one storm or unusual weather conditions. If he plants different crops, he is in a position if he makes a failure on one, to realize on another. When the farmer has different commodities to sell, he is in a position to nearly always make a profit on some of the commodities he produces."[37]

In the 1920s G&F agents pushed farmers hard to try Big Stem Jersey Yellow Sweet Potatoes, especially in north Florida. Some successes occurred, and in Madison County production exceeded several hundred acres with yields averaging from sixty to seventy bushels per acre. In July 1926 the Madison *Enterprise-Recorder* commented: "It looks as if a new industry has been born among us, with a quickly maturing crop at highly profitable returns." Production continued, although the widespread agricultural depression of the 1930s reduced cultivation.[38]

Tomatoes also attracted the attention of the G&F. Although the territory served by the railroad did not become the center of either Georgia or Florida tomato production, some accomplishments occurred during the 1920s and later. In 1932, for instance, W. E. French worked out an arrangement with a south Georgia packing firm, A. J. Hend Produce Company, whereby farmers in Berrien County would raise 235 acres of contracted tomatoes, with about 200 farmers participating and no one individual producing less than one-half acre or more than two acres. The produce firm would furnish crates and do the packing and grading, and the G&F would transport the cars of tomatoes to various northern markets.[39]

Cucumbers, too, caught the eye of the G&F. After World War I cucumbers became part of commonly tended truck-farm plantings. As with some other vegetables, both a spring and fall crop could be raised. Several communities, including Broxton, Douglas, and Valdosta, saw production increase, spurred by profitability. An average of 480 hampers of cucumbers per boxcar generated about $1,500 in income for the producer. For the G&F it meant a good haul, receiving cucumber cars from south Georgia stations for destinations in the North and especially Canada. In time processors appeared at trackside. Shortly after World War II the Nashville Packing Company, for example, began to produce dill-mixed pickles in jars and barrels and these foodstuffs also traveled over G&F rails.[40]

If there is a single food product associated in the contemporary mind with a community along the G&F, it would be the Vidalia onion. Yet commercial production of this sweet onion variety dates from only about 1940, even though it was in 1931 when a Toombs County farmer noticed that some of his onions lacked their usual pungency. It was out of this experience that the famous place-identified product emerged. Perhaps not surprisingly, early on G&F representatives recognized the potential of this cash crop, and by 1942, they promoted cultivation and marketing. It would not be until the 1970s, however, after the G&F lost its corporate identity, that the Vidalia sweet onion would become a national sensation. By that time movement of the crop to climate-controlled warehouses and markets was mostly by truck, although the railroad industry developed special bulk onion cars.[41]

Throughout its life the G&F promoted other truck crops. The Spanish peanut was an example. In May 1929 the G&F's Agricultural and Industrial Department encouraged Emanuel County cotton growers, whose crop had been seriously damaged or destroyed by recent rainstorms, to plant peanuts rather than replant cotton. "There is money to be made growing spanish peanuts and there is yet plenty of time to grow them and these farmers will stand a much better chance of making money on this crop than if they will undertake to make a crop of cotton." The railroad assisted farmers in acquiring seed and in selling the peanuts that were used for both confectionery and oil. Then there were these additional options: asparagus, beets, bell peppers, cabbage, cantaloupes, carrots, Irish (white) potatoes, okra, squash, strawberries, sweet corn, and turnips. "The truthful story is,—The average energetic farmer should be able to come to this section and make a much greater profit by growing and raising the same products he grows on his Northern farm," claimed W. E. French, general industrial agent, in the mid-1920s. "Lower priced land, our two and three crop seasons, our non-freezing winters and our early marketing seasons are our greatest advantages." In fact, the railroad repeated the latter point again and again: "Early spring shipments exploit the best prices in northern produce markets."[42]

And, too, there was the recurring theme of the need to move away from heavy dependence on cotton. "Cotton is gone or going [because of the boll weevil], as a money crop, and there is nothing left for our farmers but truck," editorialized the *Douglas Enterprise* in June 1923. "And when this class of farming is analyzed it will be found that there is more money, and a great deal more satisfaction, in trucking, than in any other line of farming."[43]

LIVESTOCK AND POULTRY

Part of the overall strategy for agricultural diversification and enhanced profitability involved livestock, including cattle, sheep, and hogs, and poultry, mostly chickens. As the G&F did with efforts to promote a variety of crops, particularly bright-leaf tobacco, its agricultural and development arm encouraged more and better livestock production. Special trains with appropriately equipped rolling stock, usually one or two baggage cars and passenger coaches, traveled along the main line and major branches showing farmers practical aspects of beef-cattle raising, dairy farming, and sheep, goat, and swine production. These "Beef Cattle Specials," "Dairy Sire Trains," and "Better Pork Specials" became frequent occurrences, largely between the two world wars. To highlight static displays, company, college, and federal agricultural personnel offered practical demonstrations indicating how, for example, feed grinding machines might be effectively used to yield "great savings" for livestock raisers. Seizing upon the technology of motion pictures, the company also utilized films to educate and to promote. By way of illustration, in November 1928, G&F representatives at Madison showed to a large, attentive crowd of farmers and high school boys several reels that reviewed "the dairy cow, milking machine, separators, etc.," and depicted "the advancement made on the farm, from the old back-breaking, hand-power, drudgery days of the farm to the electrified days of the present, with power machinery, lights, telephone, radio and other modern improvements."[44]

The G&F did not always operate its livestock demonstration specials in a solo fashion. When the company worked with public officials, the railroad might handle a train that traveled over the rails of several carriers. Since extension personnel wished to use these cooperative movements, the G&F agreed. In 1937, for instance, the G&F joined with the Atlantic Coast Line to send a livestock-raising train through large sections of the Peach state.[45]

The railroad also expressed interest in the dairy industry. As early as 1909 John Skelton Williams had told his business associate, Colonel J. M. Wilkinson of Valdosta, that "It has always impressed me as being wrong that we should have to bring nearly all of the butter used in our towns in south Georgia from a distance." And so asked the Colonel, "Do you not think it would be a good idea to try to start a first-class, up-to-date creamery in the vicinity of Valdosta to show what can be done?" Although this creamery proposal came to naught, in the late 1920s G&F management began to stress dairying operations. Company agricultural and development people held a series of public meetings to inform farmers about the benefits of such endeavors. Their work paid dividends. In 1930 Hugh Purvis, receiver and general manager, reported that "as result of our efforts a cheese plant and creamery has been established at Greenwood, S.C. . . . [and] now a thriving creamery has also been established at Douglas, Ga., through our activities."[46]

The G&F and competing railroads adopted a similar approach with poultry culture. In 1929 the company dispatched a highly publicized "Poultry Demonstration Car Train" that operated between Greenwood and Madison. Working closely with federal and state agricultural authorities, experts explained displays and showed interested observers how to manage large flocks of chickens, both for eggs and meat. There was also a strong economic message:

> We have said that the dairy business is the easiest and quickest business for
> a farmer to get started in. He can buy a cow today, feed her tonight and carry
> his cream to market tomorrow. The poultry business is a similar business. You
> can buy two thousand day old chicks in September or October, raise them by
> the wholesale system and have one thousand hens laying early in the spring. If
> the cotton crop fails, you can start in the chicken business . . . and begin mar-
> keting your poultry crop before time to plant cotton again.[47]

Unlike the promotion of truck crops and domestic animals, the G&F was
somewhat unusual in that for years it operated a "Pick-up Poultry Car." This
piece of standard rolling stock was not for exhibits, but rather for sales.
Beginning in Spring 1924 the railroad, working with commercial poultry
dealers, seasonally sent a special car attached to a freight or passenger train
northward from Madison. (Later the company briefly offered this service on
the Stillmore-Summit-Graymont-Garfield branch.) At prearranged stations,
poultry sales occurred. "Anyone that has chickens, ducks, turkeys, etc., for
sale will secure the highest possible market price by bringing them to the
Georgia & Florida Railway Depot on the above date," ran a typical
announcement. "It will be the purpose of the Georgia & Florida Railway to
operate these cars from time to time in order that the farmers along the line
of road may have the opportunity for a cash market for their poultry." These
buying events also allowed railroad agents to promote poultry production,
for they frequently were "mixing and talking with the poultry raisers and
encouraging them in the industry."[48]

The initial year was highly successful for this promotional outreach. "The
poultry cars being operated by the Georgia & Florida Railway have proven
very much of a success in this section, not only to the farmers but to the
buyers," editorialized the *Swainsboro Forest-Blade* in May 1924. "They have
brought about sale for more chickens here than was at first predicted,
because of the high prices they have been paying." Added the editor, "It is
hoped that the G. & F. will see fit to run these cars regularly through this section, and we do not think that they will be disappointed in the results." This
the railroad did, absorbing the costs for this public service, but sensing that
this was money well invested. "The chicken industry is fast becoming one
of the big industries of this section." Moreover, G&F management took considerable satisfaction that these railroad-sponsored trackside sales pumped
money into the farm economy, noting in 1929, for example, that "buyers
paid around $65,000 to the people in our territory for the value of the con-
tents of these cars."[49]

By the late 1920s as chicken production increased, the G&F handled special
movements. The company encouraged farmers to fatten broilers and to arrange
for poultry cars for transporting these birds to northern destinations. By way of
example, in June 1928 the railroad received several poultry cars at Vidalia billed
to New York City. The attention paid to the poultry reaped direct traffic benefits.

Still, the percentage of revenue freight tonnage for all types of "products of ani-mals" was never great, and in the several years before the Great Depression of the 1930s represented only about one percent.[50]

OTHER DEVELOPMENT EFFORTS

While products of forest and farm were vital to the financial health of the G&F, the company always thought in ways to stimulate general economic growth, including the promoting of new towns and energizing existing communities. Although by 1890 the frontier in America had allegedly closed, in reality for several decades frontier-like areas remained. Early in the twentieth century most Americans realized that the settlement process contin-ued; however, they likely associated development, principally town-building, with localities in the trans-Mississippi West, and most of all on the Great Plains. Here major carriers like the Atchison, Topeka & Santa Fe; Great Northern and Soo Line and much smaller roads like the Fort Smith & Western, Midland Continental, and Quanah, Acme & Pacific facilitated the launching of scores of raw prairie towns, either through railroad-owned or independent townsite com-panies. Although the G&F was hardly building in advance of settlement, its coming did stimulate urban growth. Several towns sprang up at trackside, including a vigorous Denton, located in newly created Jeff Davis County about twelve miles south of the county-seat community of Hazlehurst.[51]

In the latter part of 1908 the G&F helped to give birth to Denton. A group of area businessmen, attracted by the presence of the new rails, launched the Denton Land & Investment Company. Its ranks included the well-to-do Colonel J. M. Denton of Hazlehurst, who served as vice-president. The firm quickly platted a townsite on property owned by company member J. D. Pittman, who served as general manager. By early 1909 the village began to take shape, prompting the *Douglas Enterprise* to predict "much success for this little city," adding "it has a splendid location, a large territory surround-ing it, and a model little city will be built right there as the people behind it are determined, which is a great factor in the race for success."[52]

The "go-getter" spirit of the men of the Denton Land & Investment Company led to the customary promotional brochures and repeated news-paper advertisements. Using the theme of "A GREAT OPPORTUNITY" the firm had this to say about this newest town on the G&F:

> This town for beauty and symmetry of design hasn't an equal. With a large and beautiful public square, in center, spacious lots for both business and residences and every lot accessible from the rear by means of a ten foot alley, all streets one hundred feet wide, and with the lots laid out on a perfect square. Grounds com-paratively level but sufficient rolling to afford good drainage. This town is over twelve miles from the nearest town and none other nearer than 15 to 20 miles. It is situated in as fertile section as is within the borders of this great state.[53]

The Denton Land & Investment Company got off to a good start. Both timing and location worked in favor of quick development; the economy boomed after the brief, albeit severe banker's panic of 1907, and competing communities did not overwhelm the Denton site. Scores of lots were sold, thus avoiding the often used ploy of holding a public auction. Indeed, Cook & Fountain Company, which worked with the G&F to develop another new community along its rails, Wesley, located eight miles south of Swainsboro in Emanuel County, felt the necessity of conducting an auction there of 200 lots on February 22, 1911, that featured a barbecue, music and other attractions. As with Wesley two years later, Denton became more than a "paper" town. Soon the place sported a hotel, church, several brick business buildings, and more than a score of residences. The G&F cooperated, quickly erecting cotton-loading sheds and a combination wooden depot that stood within easy walking distance of the commercial center. The railroad also built three modest houses for use by trackmen and their families. Although Denton reached a population of only 215 by 1930, the village became the second largest incorporated community in the county. The G&F station billed substantial quantities of inbound and outbound LCL and carload freight. Town-building appeared to be a winning proposition for both the real-estate company and railroad.[54]

This phenomenon of town-building promoted widespread commentary, encouraged, of course, by railroad officials. In promotional publications the G&F told prospective residents that opportunities existed on the ground floor of every new community. It would be a wonderful chance for a general merchant, hardware dealer, blacksmith, and professional man. Furthermore, the presence of conveniently located trade centers meant that farmers, with their slow-moving animal-drawn wagons that traveled along primitive public roads, would be able to visit commercial establishments with ease, making for more pleasant and profitable lives. "But the thing we appreciate most about this new enterprise [G&F] is the fact that it has put new life into the country thru which it runs," glowed the editor of the *Nashville Herald* in October 1910, who happily took notice of what was unfolding in the region. "While the panic [of 1907] has clogged the wheels of progress in most localities, yet it's a fact that every town along the line of the Georgia & Florida Railway has grown and prospered as never before. Besides, new towns have sprung up all along the line. Look at Ray's Mill [later Ray City], Denton, and Ellenton, the latter on the branch to Moultrie." In the case of Ellenton, located twelve miles east of Moultrie, "Of this town it is said a saw mill of 60,000 feet per day capacity, a brick store, a large two-story hotel and a number of handsome residences have been constructed during the past few months." Concluded the enthusiastic journalist: "As a developer, the Georgia & Florida ranks first in Georgia."[55]

As the *Nashville Herald* observed, the presence of the G&F contributed to the development of existing communities. For example, Midville, a town in

Jenkins County (originally Burke County) located seventeen miles north of Swainsboro, profited from the coming of the Williams road. The G&F did not create Midville; the community appeared decades before the arrival of G&F rails, a result of its location on the pioneer Central of Georgia (CofG) line between Savannah and Macon. (Midville got its name by being ninety-six miles distant from both cities.) For several years after G&F made Midville a strategic rail junction, the place exhibited sustained growth. Population increased from 275 in 1900 to 603 in 1910 (after creation of the G&F), peaking at nearly 1,000 a decade later. "While in the little city of Midville Monday morning it was our pleasure to note the boom of building going on and to be done there soon," observed the *Swainsboro Forest-Blade* in May 1913. "The Farmers and Merchants Bank will soon begin the erection of a fine two-story brick structure. . . . Mrs. Emma Harris will soon have a store building erected . . . and will add much to the looks of the town." Apparently, the only disappointment that Midville residents had was the unwillingness of the G&F and CofG to build a union depot for its portal to the world. "It would be a great convenience to have both depots in one—a new brick building." Although the G&F never entered into a union depot arrangement, the company boomed Midville in its promotional literature, hoping that the town might dominate the immediate trade area, and took pride in expansion of local cottonseed, fertilizer, and other agribusiness enterprises.[56]

Although the G&F did not create a town-site affiliate staffed by its employees, the railroad had on its payroll "industrial representatives" years before it employed agricultural agents. In fact, almost as soon as the G&F unfurled its corporate banner, the company hired men to work aggressively on all aspects of development. In 1911 John Skelton Williams took pride in hiring Colonel T. T. Wright, a former industrial agent for the Plant System, as "Special Representative of the Industrial Department" at a handsome monthly salary of $175 and expenses. In Williams's comments to Vice President E. L. Bemiss, Wright was considered a valuable new asset. "Col. Wright has a very agreeable address and a great fund of experience and information in regard to our territory, which bore fruits while he was with the Plant System some years ago."[57]

Wright and his associates not only sought to attract and to expand businesses, but also these men did what they could to increase online population. One approach was to attract new farmers. In the summer of 1912, for example, the railroad operated an extensively promoted "Home seekers' Excursion" from Augusta to Madison "Through the Land of Opportunity," an undertaking that the Madison newspaper believed would be "the means of bringing a number of settlers to the country." And in the 1920s the company concentrated on recruiting specific groups of farmers. In June 1922 a G&F representative, A. W. Winberg, officially its immigration agent and based in Goshen, Indiana, made the railroad's territory and services known to participants at the annual conference of German Baptist Brethren Church

("Dunkards") held at Winona Lake, Indiana. This contact sought "to exploit a country amongst some of America's most thrifty farmers." Although farm tenancy was high in the Wiregrass Region, the railroad assumed that the Dunkards would become landowners. A few years later the G&F worked briefly with Robbins, Ltd., a Toronto, Ontario, real-estate development firm, to secure agriculturalists from Scotland. "Heretofore the greater proportion of these immigrants have been settling in Canada, but at this time the general desire among them is to locate in a milder climate." It is not known if any Scots found their way to G&F territory.[58]

As part of the overall strategy to attract settlers, the G&F briefly operated a model farm in Coffee County. While this was an unusual practice, a few other railroad-sponsored farms appeared about the same time in the South, notably ones operated by the Norfolk Southern Railway outside Wenona, North Carolina, and the St. Louis Southwestern (Cotton Belt) Railway near Alto, Texas. On July 12, 1912, the Board of Directors approved an expenditure of $4,000 to purchase fifty acres of cut-over land and to provide the appropriate equipment. Funds were quickly spent for a manager's house, dwellings for farm laborers, a barn, outbuildings, fencing, and the required tools and animals. The Board also agreed to provide "the necessary funds for conducting farming operations, estimated at about $2,500 per year." This "Demonstration Farm," located near Garrant (later renamed West Green) and in view of "all passing trains," immediately sought to show how "farming methods might be applied and enlargement occur in the cultivation of diversified crops, especially of Perishable Products, for which the Railway's entire territory is well adopted." Following bankruptcy in 1915, the company announced that the farm "having served a beneficial educational purpose for three seasons, at a considerable expense in experimental work, was leased for the season 1915–16 at a satisfactory rental." And subsequently the railroad sold the facility.[59]

Although the G&F never again sought to attract agrarians by means of a demonstration farm, in 1924 the company took another step in expanding agricultural population. The railroad opened its own real estate arm, the Georgia and Florida Company, headquartered in Valdosta and with an office in Madison, to handle sales of farmlands in south Georgia and north Florida. Later reorganized as the Georgia and Florida Land and Improvement Company, the firm focused on finding and developing properties for would-be tobacco farmers. But as the great Florida land boom, which affected parts of the Wiregrass Region, collapsed by the mid-1920s and the national economy faltered following the stock market crash of October 1929, G&F successes in promoting farm expansion, especially small agricultural operations, mostly disappeared.[60]

The coming of a deadly national depression in the early 1930s, which devastated the rural South, did not cause G&F development personnel to abandon hope. In early 1933 W. E. French, whose title had become general agricultural and immigration agent, announced that he wanted the railroad, local businesses, and civic organizations to work for expansion of small farms in the Wiregrass Region. What French had in mind was to encourage the large landowner "who for numerous reasons finds himself overloaded with surplus but first class farming land" to make these acres available to small owner-operator or tenant farmers. Based on French's travels in the North, he believed that there were "hundreds of highly experienced farmers and ex-farmers now in large cities who have limited financial means yet a sufficient amount of cash with which to start him up on a farm providing he is not required to make a too heavy initial or first payment." To follow up the G&F took out advertising space in several large northern dailies and bought radio time, but apparently aroused little interest.[61]

Even though the concept espoused by French and the G&F held some merit, timing for the near-term was awful. The depression deepened and the passage of the Agricultural Adjustment Act in June 1933 lead to drastic reductions in crop and livestock production. Although often helping landowners, this New Deal relief and recovery response injured tenant farmers, the most common agrarians in the Wiregrass Region. Aid for these landless farmers finally came in 1937 with the Bankhead-Jones Act, a measure that allowed white tenants to borrow sufficient funds at low rates of interest to purchase land. About the same time the Farm Security Administration, another federal relief and recovery agency and attached to the U.S. Department of Agriculture, began to make short-term cash advances to permit small producers to acquire seed, fertilizer, livestock, farming equipment, and the like. Unquestionably, assistance from Washington aided the white landowners and farmers along the G&F.[62]

Surely grasping the ramifications of the farm situation, W. E. French made mid-decade adjustments. In July 1935 he proposed that 1,000 to 1,200 World War I veterans and their families colonize lands in Madison County, Florida. "The veterans are United States pensioners, and the plan is to buy the land and build the homes, allowing the government to deduct from their pensions the monthly installments on the place." While proposals were made to government officials, nothing materialized.[63]

Federal participation, however, could make a difference. It would be funding from the Federal Emergency Relief Administration (FERA), a New Deal relief and recovery agency, that created the Cherry Lake Farms settlement near Madison. French played a pivotal role; "the idea was born in the mind of the land agent [French] of the Georgia and Florida railroad serving that area," noted the *Miami Herald*. French boomed this subsistence farm project, which in a few years evolved into the fourth largest in the nation. At Cherry Lake Farms, begun in 1935, families on relief received thirty acres "of some of the most beautiful farm land in Florida" to raise bright tobacco and various truck crops. The community grew rapidly, ultimately numbering 132 families, and enjoyed the comforts and resources of federally built and reconditioned houses and facilities. What direct benefits the G&F received are unknown, although likely some tobacco, watermelons, and other farm projects traveled to market by rail.[64]

By the late 1930s the federal safety net stimulated a modest private-sector version of the French development plans. In the summer of 1937 the Augusta-based Blanchard & Calhoun Realty Company advertised the availability of small farms near Brooker and Goldsmith, G&F stations south of Hazlehurst. The firm had acquired 3,400 acres and then subdivided this land into units of 100 to 125 acres. "This is the highest grade farm for growing tobacco, cotton, corn and other farm products," boomed Blanchard & Calhoun. And the company indicated that "these most desirable small farms will be sold on terms as low as 25 percent cash and the balance payable over a period of five years at low interest rates." Perhaps these promoters met with some success, although the trend in Wiregrass agriculture was toward larger rather than smaller farming units. Furthermore, a poor white or African-American tenant farmer could hardly afford to participate in the Blanchard & Calhoun scheme.[65]

Commitment by the G&F to the agricultural well-being of its service territory never flagged. Just as the railroad continued to operate an agricultural and industrial development arm, in later years it took a keen interest in promoting irrigation projects. In the early 1950s a severe drought struck the Southeast, the worst in recorded history for south Georgia. Initially, the G&F responded to appeals from local American Farm Bureau Federation organizations with a Band-Aid solution; namely, the company during the fall of 1954 transported water from wells in the Augusta area to the driest communities. By daily filling five 10,000-gallon tank cars, the road supplied for several weeks at its own expense some of this precious fluid to farmers for their most-pressing livestock needs. When the train crew spotted the tank car (or cars), a section man assisted recipients with loading water into their containers: tanks, drums, and barrels. "The railroad's efforts were very much appreciated by the people," remembered a one-time G&F employee, and rightly so.[66]

But the G&F realized that farmers needed more than tank cars of water. Since every locale experiences periods of wet and dry weather, the company thought that a practical solution was needed. The following year the railroad dispatched what it called the "Better Farm Special," a train in the tradition of earlier demonstration operations. Chief Operating Officer Pete Belvin worked with Agricultural Agent Philip James and Industrial Development Agent William Beebe to develop what became commonly known as the "Irrigation Train," which in the summer of 1955 made ten stops during a five-day trip. Belvin knew about such trains since his days as an agricultural agent, particularly his work with the livestock and tobacco specials. Moreover, "he loved these demonstration trains and knew how to entertain." The railroad received assistance from the University of Georgia, the Southeastern Sprinkler Irrigation Association (a trade group) and several banks and agribusiness concerns. A diesel locomotive pulled two flat cars that carried displays and served as a speaker's platform, a tank car to supply water for the demonstration of a portable aluminum sprinkler system supplied by the Aluminum Company of America, and the office car. The onboard equipment allowed demonstrators to show farmers, mostly tobacco producers, various types of equipment in operation, and the businessmen explained purchase and finance arrangements. In some ways this was an historic happening. Observed agricultural historian Roy V. Scott, the Irrigation Train was "one of the last education trains of the traditional type."[67]

During the heyday of farm demonstration trains in the 1920s and 1930s, the G&F also made a contribution to the overall health of its online Georgia communities. For two weeks in May 1931 the railroad operated a health special in conjunction with the Georgia State Board of Health. In a rural region where residents often lacked a proper knowledge of modern diets, medicine, and sanitation, the specially fitted exhibit car contained several displays that a health department physician explained at station stops. Because of the high rate of infant mortality, a popular exhibit focused on health care for babies. The *Swainsboro Forest-Blade* reported that this "most attractive display," loaned by the Children's Bureau of the U.S. Department of Labor, included promotion of "sun baths." To stimulate interest in the train, the health department took a clue from railroad promotional work, announcing two months before the train left Augusta a prize of $10.00 to the child who could best name this special. "The contest is open to all children, white and black, of the 17 counties through which the train will travel." The name, "The Hygienian," was picked from more than 125 entries and was submitted by Curtis Lane, a lad from Statesboro. When the special steamed into the Statesboro station, onboard personnel welcomed the twelve-year-old winner as the guest of honor.[68]

Whether the G&F operated the "The Hygienian," "Blue Mold Special," or a poultry-buying car, the railroad repeatedly showed a commitment to bettering the Wiregrass Region. No company employee would ever deny that self-interest was involved. Even though the successive administrations of John Skelton Williams, Hugh Purvis, and Pete Belvin consistently saw value in such developmental efforts, there is no indication that individuals, groups, or communities objected to what the G&F did or sought to do. In the controversial book *Bad Land,* Jonathan Raban argues that the promotional work conducted early in the twentieth century by the Chicago, Milwaukee & St. Paul Railroad in eastern Montana conned thousands of settlers into believing that they could transform a semi-arid environment into lush farmland. In contrast, the G&F can hardly be accused of any misdeeds. Whether developing the Wiregrass Region succeeded is debatable; nevertheless, this long-impoverished road honestly did its best to create prosperity and happiness for all.[69]

CHAPTER SIX

Depression, War, and Continued Challenges, 1931–1948

HUGH W. PURVIS

When John Skelton Williams died, Hugh W. Purvis emerged as leader of the Georgia & Florida Railway and later of the reorganized Georgia & Florida Railroad. It would be Purvis who would guide the company during the Great Depression, World War II, and the immediate postwar period. Just as Williams was the indisputable personification of the early G&F, Purvis came to personify the railroad until 1948.

Like Williams, Purvis claimed Virginia as his native state. Born on November 10, 1878, in Montreal, a village in Nelson County, the future railroad executive received only a common school education. Although he longed to be a lawyer, the financial troubles in his fatherless family, with "a flock of younger children," forced him to abandon his schooling for a wage-earning job. As with so many other lads of his generation, Purvis went "railroadin'." Perhaps this decision stemmed from his late father being "a railroad man" before a fatal work-related accident. In June 1895 the teenager joined the office staff of the Southern Railway (the former Richmond & Danville Railroad) in Charlottesville, Virginia. This experience enabled Purvis to master the cryptic Morse code. Two years later he was working as an agent-operator for the Norfolk & Western Railway, but after about three years he signed up with the Seaboard Air Line Railway (SAL). Purvis rose rapidly, becoming a division superintendent in Hamlet, North Carolina, the carrier's operating nerve center. But, in 1918, he accepted the challenge of managing the busy Jacksonville Terminal Company in Florida, a property that the SAL partially owned. Purvis held that position for only a year before returning to the SAL to become general superintendent. It was through Purvis's ties to the SAL that John Skelton Williams and his associates discovered Purvis's managerial talents.[1]

When John Skelton Williams returned to the G&F in 1921 as sole receiver, he soon needed a general manager. The incumbent official, D. F. Kirkland, had demonstrated some bad judgement. "I will cite here a purchase of 4.29 miles of relaying rails which was made by the former General Manager in September and October 1920, about nine months before the receiver took charge," Williams told the bankruptcy court. "These rails were purchased at something over $76 per ton, delivered, although new rails had been offered about that same time to the railway by the U.S. Steel Corp. at less than $53 per ton, delivered. The following autumn the present receiver succeeded in purchasing for the railway relaying rails of excellent quality at a total cost under $18 per ton, delivered." When Williams asked Kirkland to explain his rail-purchasing actions, he received no satisfactory answer. Williams demanded his immediate resignation and a distraught Kirkland then committed suicide.[2]

Receiver Williams quickly tapped Purvis, an experienced SAL operating officer, for the general manager position. On April 15, 1922, Purvis began his twenty-six-year association with the G&F. "It is a matter of great pride to me that I have never lost a month's work during the entire half century I have been in the railroad business," he proudly told fellow workers in 1945, on the fiftieth anniversary of his railroad career. "The rise of Mr. Purvis from an obscure telegraph operator as a boy back in the early nineties to the high position of a general manager of a railroad," observed the *Augusta Chronicle*, "has all the earmarks of a Horatio Alger story."[3]

Hugh Purvis made a strong impression physically and professionally. A big man, standing about 6'2" tall and weighing approximately 250 pounds, he took charge immediately, although he allegedly possessed "a quiet and retiring nature." He reported to Williams, and occasionally to the bankruptcy judge, before becoming the G&F's president when the company emerged from receivership in late 1926. Three years later, when the railroad slipped into its second period of court protection, Purvis joined New York banker and railroad specialist William V. Griffin as co-receiver and held the additional title of general manager. Throughout his tenure with the G&F, Purvis ruled with an iron hand. "Uncle Hugh had his own spy network," reminisced a family member. "He always knew what was happening up and down the line." The autocratic Purvis relished being boss and eventually created what a veteran employee called "his own personal fiefdom."[4]

Although remembered as "a workaholic," Purvis enjoyed diversions. He liked to fish and hunt, especially for quail and squirrel, doing so often in the company of shippers, politicians and other railroad officials. And Purvis was deeply committed to his Methodist church. Throughout his adult life he led Sunday school classes and preached to various congregations, including worshipers at historic St. John's Methodist Episcopal Church, South, in Augusta, which he faithfully attended. A strict teetotaler, Purvis often openly criticized his younger brother, Maurice, another G&F official, for his excessive drinking. "Hugh Purvis was a Christian gentleman," happily recalled a friend, and that was the general perception. Yet Purvis was hardly a saint.

Some fellow Methodists might object to his cigar smoking, and they most assuredly would find his womanizing unacceptable. His wife, Zaidee Howard Purvis, "enjoyed bad health throughout her life. She always claimed to be ill." Observed a nephew tongue-in-cheek: "I am surprised if they had sex more than twice [there were two daughters]." He added, "Uncle Hugh had a lot of lady friends as a result."[5]

THE GREAT DEPRESSION

Irrespective of the strengths and weaknesses of Hugh Purvis, leading the G&F was never easy. When the company slipped back into bankruptcy in 1929, there were new demands. The federal judge needed to be pleased, or at least accommodated, and the property required improvements if the expectation that independence from the court were to be achieved. If the railroad could not be reorganized on an income-producing basis, dismemberment loomed. Under good conditions, being co-receiver and general manager could be trying, but after 1930 the deepening economic depression made Purvis's tasks even more daunting.[6]

In 1929 the G&F claimed its maximum size, 504 route miles, but it would not be long before that figure dropped. Indeed, paring the G&F of its unproductive branches constituted an important response to hard times. As with virtually every railroad, physical contractions occurred, especially after World War I when trucks, buses, and automobiles took a larger share of the local freight and passenger business. In the case of the G&F, as early as 1916 a small segment of the Douglas-Broxton-Barrows Bluff branch was retired. The company removed a mile or so of track between Barrows Bluff and Dickey's Farm and subsequently cut back a few more miles to Relee, site of a large lumber mill.[7]

Not until 1930 would an important instance of "line rationalization" take place when scrappers found work along most of the former Millen & Southwestern Railroad (M&SW). Specifically, the G&F received regulatory permission to abandon the approximately fourteen miles between Millen and Garfield and about twenty-three miles between Graymont and Pendleton, a junction several miles north of Vidalia where the branch met the main line. The remaining segment of the Millen branch between Garfield and Graymont continued to be served by mixed-train locals operating over the leased Statesboro Northern Railway (SN) between Midville and Statesboro. This old M&SW trackage, which was in generally poor condition, lost $49,285 in 1927, $25,370 in 1928, and $51,430 in 1929, red ink that the G&F could ill afford. The lower operating losses for 1928 were due to the unusual amount of freight hauled to Oak Park, near Pendleton, a temporary set-up site for materials used by a highway contractor. Control of the SN allowed three Millen-branch towns, Garfield, Graymont and Summit, to remain in the G&F fold. Commercial interests in Millen, however, "put up

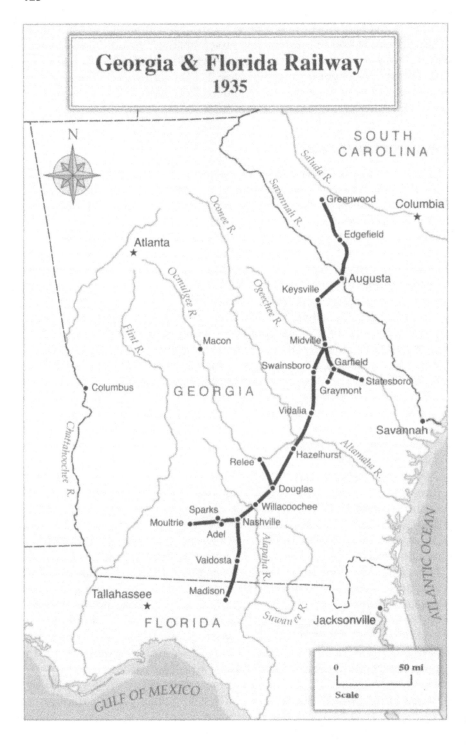

Georgia & Florida Railway
1935

the best fight a town could make to avert the withdrawal of the road by promising a greater volume of business and more diligent guarding of the interests of the Georgia and Florida." Local boosters, who feared having only the single-railroad option of the Central of Georgia, proposed raising money to acquire land for right-of-way and terminal facilities in Millen since the G&F rented space from the town's dominant carrier. Talk, however, was not money in the till.[8]

Evidence of a once active railroad quickly disappeared. "On abandonment of the line, the company salvaged the rails and gave notice that the cross-ties might be had for the hauling," noted an area newspaper. "For miles out of . . . [Millen] every tie has been removed. The road bed is so trodden down by teams used in hauling the ties that no semblance of a railroad ever having traversed the space remains." Even the large wooden trestle over the Ogeechee River nearly vanished, "with only a few timbers from the bed of the river remaining." Much later, men employed by the Works Progress Administration, the massive New Deal relief and recovery agency, converted the old right-of-way southwest of Graymont into a highway, further obliterating the retired branch.[9]

The largest abandonment, though, involved fifty-seven miles of the Tennille branch. This trackage, part of the former Augusta Southern Railroad, ran from the main line at McAdoo (a station [switch] two miles from Keysville that honored William Gibbs McAdoo) westerly and then southerly to Sandersville and Tennille. In August 1934 the G&F sought permission to end service. The reasons paralleled the rationale for lifting much of the Millen branch: poor overall track conditions, necessitating an expenditure of at least $50,000 to cover deferred maintenance, and a sharp decline in tonnage and revenues. In 1929 the Tennille line handled 59,000 revenue tons but in 1932 only 28,893 tons. The financial data reflected this drop: "The decline in revenues from $168,077 in 1929 to $25,947 in the first 5 months of 1934," reported the Interstate Commerce Commission (ICC) examiner, "is conclusive evidence of a downward trend."[10]

Traffic potential on this long G&F appendage seemed dim, indeed. Better roads in the territory led to increased and sustained truck usage. Moreover, much of the commercially valuable timber had been harvested and several textile mills had closed. Interline tonnage generated from Sandersville and Tennille was highly competitive, further hampering revenue development. Although in the Sandersville area there were vast deposits of kaolin clay, "the mines are not operated continuously." The G&F encountered more bad luck. Eventually, though, mining conditions changed dramatically. Arguably if service had remained, in a decade or two kaolin tonnage surely would have soared, justifying operations and perhaps even rebuilding the branch.[11]

Nevertheless, Purvis and other officials could hardly ignore the albatross that the Tennille line had become. The abandonment application made sense. As with reductions on the Millen branch, not only would the G&F benefit from ending operating losses, maintenance costs, and property taxes, but also salvageable materials could be sold or used elsewhere. Real estate, too, could be put up for sale.[12]

Even though the ICC received no objections to the abandonment application, some residents expressed concern. "A business man of Sandersville [gin owner T. I. Harrison] who has been a liberal patron of trucks called at the Progress office last week," reported the *Sandersville Progress* shortly after the abandonment process began, "and suggested that the business men of Sandersville get together in a patriotic spirit and give the Georgia & Florida . . . all the business possible." Concluded the newspaper, "He now realizes that he made a mistake in having his freight hauled by trucks instead of furnishing this railroad with the patronage." About the same time a delegation from Sandersville talked with Purvis about "saving" the branch. Although interested in the possibility of new business, he demanded approximately eight additional carloads daily. Likelihood of an annual increase of 2,000–2,500 cars, though, was an impossibility and so efforts to retain G&F service stopped.[13]

Immediately after the ICC approved abandonment, operations ended. On the afternoon of October 15, 1934, the final revenue freight arrived in Tennille. The following day a clean-up train left for Augusta. "Everything in each depot was loaded into box cars including office supplies, station records, section motor cars, waiting room seats, scales, safes, etc," noted the *Sandersville Progress*. "Engineer John Rheney operated the last train. He stated that he had been running an engine between Augusta and Tennille since 1890 . . . and would retire from service next April." Most employees, if they were willing to relocate, found jobs elsewhere on the G&F. D. D. Hitt, for one, agent at Tennille, replaced Mrs. E. J. Harris as agent in Madison, Florida.[14]

About a month after the final run, lifting the Tennille branch began. The removal process took about two months, although crews did not take up every rail. The G&F sold sidings in Tennille to the Central of Georgia, and in Sandersville the Sandersville Railroad bought industrial and interchange trackage "beginning at T. I. Harrison's mill and ending in front of the Santon Hotel."[15]

With the Millen and Tennille line retirements, the G&F had become much more stem than branch, and in the process the company realized substantial savings of at least $100,000 annually. Until the early 1950s the G&F remained a 408-mile railroad. Yet during the Great Depression the G&F won approval from the ICC to extend the Moultrie branch by building 1.65 miles of track between Kingwood and Moultrie, thus ending a $9,000 annual rental payment with the Atlanta, Birmingham & Coast (AB&C) Railroad for access into Moultrie. Although the estimated construction costs would have run only about $45,000—the railroad planned to use salvaged materials and its own workers—the addition never occurred. The likely explanation was that the AB&C reduced the rent.[16]

Another response to hard times involved reducing passenger train losses. Although the G&F operated only mixed trains on its branch lines, usually attaching a vintage "Jim Crow" combination coach-baggage car, with its racially segregated seating sections, to the local freight, there were two daily main line runs. Not long after the company entered receivership, its name-train, the *Bon-Air Special*, fell to the faltering economy.[17]

Toward the end of its life, the *Bon-Air Special*, pride of G&F employees and communities, experienced difficulties. The extensive flooding that struck the Wiregrass Region during the latter part of 1929 forced a temporary suspension. Then in April 1930 Purvis announced that the *Bon-Air Special* would be canceled. "Due to lack of patronage, resulting in heavy loss in operating cost of these trains," he explained, "notice is hereby given that the Georgia & Florida Railroad will discontinue operations of Trains 9 and 10 (The Bon Air Special) operating between Augusta and Valdosta, with through Pullman car to and from Jacksonville." Part of the financial problem stemmed from an inadequate U.S. mail contract. The trains handled only unsorted or "pouched" mail between Augusta and Hazlehurst (and a connection with the SR), although the railroad had requested a Railway Post Office (RPO) between Augusta and Valdosta that would have added significantly to "head-end" revenues.[18]

Although the *Bon-Air Special* stopped running on April 21–April 22, 1930, its death announcement was premature. On December 14, 1930, the G&F reintroduced these "BETTER THAN EVER BEFORE" trains due primarily to pressures from online civic groups, especially in Augusta, and the expectation of a more remunerative mail contract. The new service cut approximately thirty-five minutes from previous running times between Augusta and Valdosta and offered a triweekly Pullman sleeper between Augusta and Miami via the Florida East Coast Railway at Jacksonville. The G&F, however, permitted Nos. 9 and 10 to make flag stops at all stations, likely resulting in some trips being considerably slower than the advertised schedule. Perhaps this unreliability reinforced a popular expression: "to lie like a timetable."[19]

Business did not justify the G&F continuing the reincarnated *Bon-Air Special*, and it died after the 1930–1931 winter season. On March 31, 1931, the final southbound train left Augusta Union Station. And disappointing to some patrons, there were no more personally conducted tours to Florida and Cuba. Still, pressure mounted for another rebirth of the *Bon-Air Special*, and in early 1934 speculation developed that the company would again provide this overnight Pullman operation. "I am heartily in sympathy with the movement to have this train service established and will do anything I can to help," remarked Thomas Barrett, mayor of Augusta, to the *Augusta Chronicle*. "We have the [newly established] Masters Invitation golf tournament to be played in March over the Augusta National course, and, naturally, we expect hundreds of people to come here from Florida for the event." Further noted the mayor: "In addition to that, people who spend

In this 1935 photograph the somnolent railroad corridor at Ray City, Georgia, is seen, showing a typical small Wiregrass community. The large water tank is a homemade structure fabricated from native cypress lumber. (From the John W. Barriger III National Railroad Library, University of Missouri—St. Louis)

their winters in Florida, do not like to rush back to the severe cold of the North when it begins to get extremely warm in Florida. They like to break their jump at a climate that might be said to come between that of Florida and the North." He, of course, believed that "Augusta is the ideal place to break that jump and the establishment of overnight Pullman service will get hundreds of those people."[20]

While G&F officials might agree with assessments made by Mayor Barrett, a reintroduced *Bon-Air Special* required a lucrative mail contract. But that effort failed. "We have carefully looked into this matter," explained Harllee Branch, second assistant postmaster general, to Joe Lawrence, editor of the *Nashville Herald*, "and find that the amount of mail handled over this line on the trains now operated is very small and that the quantity which might be handled on the night trains, if restored, would not be sufficient to warrant the expense of placing service thereon." Now it was time to write the obituary of the *Bon-Air Special*.[21]

Although discontinuance of the *Bon-Air Special* reduced operating expenses, the G&F was not about to exit the passenger business altogether. Day trains Nos. 4 and 5 carried coaches with a reasonable volume of riders, predominantly the poor and elderly who were unable to own or operate automobiles. Even if an individual possessed a car, the network of public roads remained inadequately developed. "In my early days [1930s]," recalled a life-long Georgia resident, "you had to go around through Waycross or went through McRae to reach Valdosta from Augusta, often spending the night." Nos. 4 and 5 also included a RPO car, baggage car for express and less-than-carload freight (LCL) shipments, and frequently a string of freight cars that at times contained north-bound perishables. The common practice of adding freight cars to passenger trains may explain why the G&F, unlike dozens of other Class 1 carriers and shortlines, never acquired for its passenger operations a gasoline or diesel railcar or "doodlebug." This type of economical passenger equipment, which operated for about half the cost of a train powered by steam, could not handle more than a few loaded freight cars.[22]

The G&F repeatedly promoted these day trains, hoping to fill every revenue-generating seat. During most of the 1930s online newspapers contained advertisements that urged the public to patronize the service. There were financial incentives, for as the depression deepened, the Georgia Public Service Commission slashed intrastate fares from 3.6 cents to two cents per mile and subsequently permitted further reductions. During the summer of 1931 the company announced special bargain "Round Trip Tickets from All Agency Stations at One Cent Per Mile." Not only did patrons feel good about passenger train costs but there were added inducements to travel by rail: "HELP RAILROADS PAY YOUR SCHOOL AND HIGHWAY TAXES. TRAINS RUN RAIN OR SHINE. LOCK UP YOUR AUTOMOBILE, GIVE YOUR NERVES A REST, AND ENJOY YOUR TRIP."[23]

Then there were the ubiquitous excursion specials in the Wiregrass Region. The G&F boomed the "Special Prosperity Train Excursion" that on September 11, 1932, ran round-trip between Valdosta and Augusta. "Conditions Are Getting Better, Cotton Keeps Jumping—Prosperity Is Coming." The ticket price: "$1 Round Trip for Everybody." While the hyperbole was dead wrong, this extra turned out to be a smashing success; 1,300 passengers crowded coaches "in the grand old excursion style." The event prompted popular feature writer Dens Kirk to take note. "In addition to the fifteen passenger coaches, the train carried an extra service car, placed in the train so as to be immediately between the white and colored sections. In this service car was everything one needed to eat or drink, hot or cold. Great quarters of Lowndes county cows, and fat South Georgia hogs, barbecued tender and brown, with plenty of hot coffee, with milk and sugar to go into it. One could eat and drink at the long service table in the car, or take the food and drink into the coaches—the colored people being served at one end of the car, and the white, at the other." Kirk believed that the special held the largest crowd "we had seen on a passenger train since 1911," and he concluded incorrectly that "railroads are coming back."[24]

Perhaps inspired by the public response, the G&F organized more excursions. In spring 1932, for example, perhaps 1,000 persons rode the "Augusta Easter Sunday Special" from Valdosta. The dollar round-trip fare allowed passengers to attend church services, see a movie, and dine cheaply at the centrally located Hotel Richmond, "so you can't go hungry if you have 20 cents to spend."[25]

By the latter part of the decade, however, the G&F operated fewer and fewer extra trains. Increased highway competition, especially from local and regional bus operators, explained this decline. Apparently the last special train before troop movements during World War II was one that pulled out of the Douglas station on Sunday, June 4, 1939, filled with seniors from Douglas High School and given a rousing sendoff by the school band. The destination was Augusta so that these youngsters and their chaperones could continue their rail journey to the immensely popular World's Fair in New York City.[26]

During the Great Depression statistics for the passenger sector were hardly remarkable. Reduction of service, including the *Bon-Air Special* and line abandonments, explains decreasing volume. Passenger train miles plunged from 407,285 in 1928 to 190,289 in 1932 and dropped to only 26,256 in 1939. Passenger revenues remained relatively flat after 1933, having hit lows of $18,840 in 1932 and $19,408 in 1933, but income rebounded to between $21,686 and $33,351 for the years from 1934 to 1940.[27]

Freight traffic, though, was critical for enhancing the bottom line. Unfortunately, the general economic malaise caused downturns in virtually all business activities, ranging from sawmill closings to a commercial glut of watermelons. As might be expected, there were both encouraging and discouraging results. Total freight tonnage for the depression period was not too dreadful: 990,265 tons in 1930 and 825,972 tons in 1939. Reflecting national economic trends, the worst years were 1932 and 1933 when 468,961 and 594,941 tons were hauled. Much better was the "Roosevelt Recession" year of 1937 when the company handled 971,870 tons. The most disappointing category of classified carload freight was "Products of Mines," mostly coal from the Appalachian fields. That amount fell from 333,010 tons in 1930 to only 161,946 tons in 1939, with a meager 96,325 tons in 1932. "Manufacturers and Miscellaneous," on the other hand, rose from 283,924 tons in 1930 to 317,782 tons in 1939 with the low again being that awful year of 1932, 176,278 tons. Operating income remained generally constant, standing at $1,695,137 in 1930 and $1,194,319 in 1939 with a dismal $818,829 in 1932.[28]

The G&F did its best to bolster freight revenues. Employees—traffic personnel and others—actively solicited carload traffic from online sources and from connections. "REQUEST YOUR SHIPMENTS ROUTED VIA G&F RR FOR PROMPT SERVICE," became the oft-repeated cry. And management instructed the public on "How to Route Traffic Over the G&F." There were also inducements; freight rates dropped significantly on most commodities. In the summer of 1933, the old rate of seventy-five cents per 100 pounds of tobacco dipped to sixty-five cents between south Georgia stations and

Danville, Virginia; fifty-eight cents to Fairmount, North Carolina; and fifty-four cents to Darlington, South Carolina.[29]

Then there was LCL freight. The sharp drop during the Great Depression was troubling: 39,260 tons in 1930 to 17,029 tons in 1939. Here again the railroad took an aggressive position to maintain or hopefully increase business. In early 1936 management announced a "Free Storedoor Pickup and Delivery Service," which became available on February 8. Resembling other carriers, including the Atlantic Coast Line and Chicago & North Western, the G&F assumed the cost of LCL pickup and delivery to and from its agency stations. As an additional incentive, the company offered a discount of five cents per one hundred pounds on LCL bills if customers handled their own shipments to and from the depot. Also the G&F allowed LCL lots to be consigned "C.O.D." for a nominal charge. These were good ideas, but they did not prevent a free fall in business, surely attributable to the rising number of local trucking firms. These were often "mom and pop" concerns that had only a used truck or two, a handful of employees, and not much else. These aggressive competitors, who frequently cut rates to bare out-of-pocket costs, might be unlicensed "wildcat" or "gypsy" carriers, a real annoyance to G&F and other railroads.[30]

Even in hard times the G&F labored to keep its rolling stock and physical plant in the best possible condition. To strengthen train operations, the company acquired from the Florida East Coast Railway eight Pacific-type locomotives (4-6-2s), each with a tractive-effort of 31,400 pounds. The price was rock-bottom, collectively amounting to only $14,400. "They are 10 years old and cost G.& F. less than $2,000 each to put in good condition," observed John W. Barriger III, a federal financial official who during spring 1935 inspected the property. No one questioned the need to augment an aging fleet of ten-wheelers. The shops at Douglas also made major repairs to other pieces of motive power and freight equipment. Track gangs, too, kept busy.[31]

Although battered by depression, the G&F was no transportation slum. "The equipment situation on the line is in good shape. Out of 28 engines owned, 18 are in repair and available for active service. The other 10 are awaiting shopping as and when an increase in traffic requires their use," noted a Reconstruction Finance Corporation Railroad Division report in 1935. "Freight car ownership consists of approximately 600 units, averaging about 9 years old, and, in the main, in present good condition. The present ownership of equipment is entirely adequate for a very large increased volume of traffic, and should suffice for several years to come." Moreover, the assessment observed that "track is in good line . . . and is in substantially good condition for the train loads, speeds and traffic volume handled over it," although emphasizing that "approximately 26 miles of the main track rail is in bad condition and should be renewed as soon as practicable."[32]

Wisely, the G&F did not cut back the number of traffic department representatives. Offline agencies dotted the East, Midwest, and South with strategic offices in Florida. Although the impact on freight revenues is impossible to determine, Commercial Agent E. R. "Mack" McKenney, based in Winter Haven, Florida, may have had an unusual, positive impact. This came not so much from repeated visits, telephone calls, and letters to shippers, but rather from his widely circulated poetry with its often racist overtones. During the 1930s and 1940s "Uncle Mack," the "G&F poet," penned thousands of lines, often promoting service on the time freights Nos. 57 and 58, better known as *The Goose*.[33]

> Cap't. they kids me erbout our rusty rails,
> > But de *SCHEDULE*, Cap't. hit seldom fails,
> Except, and when, and in so far,
> > As de 'nitial line delay de car.
>
> Our watchword, Cap't. is E-X-P-E-D-I-T-E.
> > And our *GOOSE* train *flies* every night
> But whuts de use uv all his haste,
> > Ef *SHIPPERS* gwiner let hit got to waste.
>
> Ef *CITRUS* is on it, when de train go by,
> > De Boss he say: "De Goose Hangs High",
> But ef he complain, hit can only mean,
> > De Citrus Shippers done picked her clean.
>
> Boss' favorite bird, is dis here Goose,
> > And when she's underfed, do he let loose
> Such language, dat even de dumbest man,
> > Kin comprehand and understand.
> He say, based on my results to-date,
> > De name *BUZZARD* would be more appropriate
> An Onless I kin feed de Goose some freight
> > *LIVERWURST* is gwiner be her fate.
>
> Uncle Mack

THE GOOSE: is the nickname of our Perishable Train, which unfortunately, some of the shippers are trying to let perish.[34]

The G&F hoped that moral suasion would enhance revenues. Just as the company told the public that there were numerous benefits to train travel, it also emphasized the positive impact a healthy freight-based railroad had on the Wiregrass Region. "Railroad men are known the country over as liberal spenders. They buy food, fuel, and actual necessities as liberally as incomes permit. They buy good and stylish clothes, automobiles, radios, furniture, and indulge themselves in luxuries wherever possible." The message implied that railroaders spent while farmers and others saved. Dispatching freight, carload and LCL, via the G&F would be a powerful force in stimulating local economies. It is difficult to measure success or failure of such arguments, but as one official recalled, "You had to do what you could during those bad times and we tried mightily to fill up our trains."[35]

RECONSTRUCTION FINANCE CORPORATION

Even though the G&F had gained financial protection through the court and won permission to issue a modest amount of receivers' certificates, as depression deepened the company desperately needed additional money. Fortunately, the federal government offered hope for a cash infusion. In early 1932 a somewhat reluctant President Herbert Hoover approved a congressional measure that created the Reconstruction Finance Corporation (RFC), designed to loan money to industrial corporations, insurance companies, railroads, and other major businesses in need of liquidity. For down-and-out concerns, the RFC, with its pool of several billion dollars, emerged as banker of last resort. When Franklin Roosevelt and the New Dealers took over the reins of national government in March 1933, the RFC increased its assistance to a financially strapped business sector. Railroads were especially needy; by this time more than 40,000 miles of lines had fallen into bankruptcy. The Roosevelt administration proclaimed that preservation of the railroads was vital to the national interest, not only for essential transportation but also for maintaining a vast labor force and bolstering consumption of a multitude of products and services. The G&F's management heartily agreed.[36]

The co-receivers were not about to ignore such a "God-send." Almost as soon as the RFC opened its doors, the company applied for financial assistance under Section 5 of the act; the process also required approval from the ICC. On March 7, 1932, the G&F officially requested $1 million to pay various obligations, mostly outstanding receivers' certificates and local property taxes, and to buy track materials and assorted supplies.[37]

Results surely disappointed the G&F, however, as on May 5, 1932, the RFC approved a loan for considerably less than $1 million, agreeing to extend only $271,221. These funds would be earmarked largely to redeem receivers' certificates held by struggling local banks and to pay down taxes owed principally to counties and municipalities, "which are greatly in need of these funds for important governmental purposes." This response met the intent of the act, allowing for a "trickle down" impact on the economies affected by the carrier.[38]

But the federal government would help only so much. Both the RFC and the ICC believed that the G&F was extremely shaky, concluding that evidence "justified doubt as to whether the road can survive." Not only were revenues collapsing, but the company also had an unpaid balance of $792,000 that the federal government had made under the Transportation Act of 1920. Still the RFC inspection report contained positive comments: "there is nothing . . . to indicate that the property, with a few exceptions, is in other than reasonably good condition for the traffic it is called upon to handle, or that its operations are being conducted on other than an economical basis."[39]

Since the G&F had nothing to lose and much to gain, on May 31, 1932, a "Petition for Reconsideration" went to the ICC. This appeal led to a modest victory. Shortly thereafter the ICC and RFC agreed to an additional loan of $83,500 "for the purpose of paying interest due June 1, 1932, on receivers' certificates in the amount of $21,000 and interest and maturing principal on outstanding equipment-trust certificates due September 15, 1932, in the amount of $62,500." As with the earlier obligation, the G&F pledged receivers' certificates equal to the loan.[40]

The G&F appreciated every dollar of federal assistance but wanted additional funding. In 1935 the railroad sought another loan, but the RFC would not approve any further request. "In 1932 this Corporation loaned the Receiver [sic] sufficient money to clear up . . . tax and voucher accruals and now, less than three years later, these accruals are back to where they were before the loan was made," wrote Hilton M. Moore, an examiner for the Railroad Division, in a memorandum to the RFC Board of Directors. "It is the recommendation of the Railroad Division [that the] . . . Corporation take no further steps at this time." Again, the RFC questioned whether the G&F had a future, repeating arguments that others had made earlier. "At present it would seem that there is no hope for the continued operation of this Company as an independent property, but matters have not yet advanced sufficiently to determine whether its ultimate disposition should be scrapping, or sale to one of its trunk line competitors, such as the Atlantic Coast Line." Moore, in fact, thought that the G&F had little value. "Incidentally, if the road is scrapped, practically all of the towns would be left with trunk line service, and the very few that are not now reached by trunk line competitors could easily be served by maintaining short stretches of the present road as trunk line spurs." And Moore gave the same message to Purvis: "We pointed out to them [RFC Board of Directors] that the Georgia & Florida was so completely devoid of earning power that it would be quite impossible for the Examining Division to recommend to the Board a further loan of any kind, and it would not be possible to find that this Corporation [RFC] would be adequately secured."[41]

Although rebuked by the RFC in 1935, the G&F subsequently sought money for equipment trust payments. In 1939 the company asked the RFC to take over $120,000 of equipment trust certificates with a face value of

$219,000 that the Fidelity-Philadelphia Trust Company owned. That large financial institution was unwilling to extend the maturity date, but agreed to sell the paper for $120,000. Even though no additional funds would be forthcoming from the RFC, the railroad discovered that the worst years of depression had mercifully passed and that it could better juggle such obligations. In this case a mutually satisfactory agreement was struck with the trust company.[42]

The G&F tried mightily to honor its outstanding obligations. In the case of the RFC loans, the company could not redeem the debt, but during the Great Depression and into the era of World War II it managed to pay the full interest rate of four percent per annum. Similarly, the railroad could not redeem the receivers' certificates, although some or all of the semiannual interest was covered. Stronger operating revenues, which reached $2,056,770 in 1943, allowed for these payments.[43]

THE G&F FAMILY FACES HARD TIMES

While line abandonments, train discontinuances and loan applications captured the attention of journalists, little, if any, newspaper coverage discussed individual experiences during the Great Depression. Although John Skelton Williams and contemporaries sincerely believed that the Wiregrass Region would boom in the twentieth century, hard times in the 1930s shattered personal dreams and made coping difficult. Notwithstanding a variety of New Deal relief and recovery programs, which ranged from the Civilian Conservation Corps for young men to the Works Progress Administration for older unemployed adults, the service territory suffered, forcing a host of responses. Keysville voters, for example, decided that they could reduce out-of-pocket expenses by "disincorporating" their municipal government. Retrenchments in both the public and private sectors were common.[44]

The G&F cut back on all aspects of operations and maintenance. Management slashed employment by approximately ten percent and repeatedly closed the shops at Douglas for "indefinite" periods of time, often several weeks and sometimes longer. As conditions improved, shutdowns were of shorter duration. The company padlocked the Douglas facility from December 23, 1936, to January 4, 1937, for example, giving workers an extended, unpaid holiday vacation. Wages were adjusted downward and cuts to the work week occurred, the standard for shop and office employees being thirty rather than the traditional forty-eight hours. "An increase in business for the road," happily commented the *Douglas Enterprise* in late 1936, "has kept the force at work all the fall on longer hours which means an increase in pay over former years."[45]

Employees of the G&F did what they could to survive economically. Whether black or white, being a "railroad man" meant that these individuals could usually get extended credit from local merchants, including operators of those ubiquitous country stores. For scores of G&F workers, mostly section-men, housing was free, and everyone benefited from the low cost of living in the Deep South. Moreover, a self-help and barter economy flourished throughout the Wiregrass Region. "Lots of railroad people raised chickens, planted big gardens and helped others out as best they could."[46]

Occasionally, though, G&F men broke the law, perhaps in response to stressful times. In early 1936 a widely reported case took place. Three train-men, who worked on time-freights Nos. 57 and 58, *The Goose,* the compa-ny's "Big Train," over an eighteen-month period repeatedly broke into box-cars and stole merchandise, mostly cigarettes, beer and whiskey, and sold this high-demand contraband to "fences" in the Augusta and Douglas areas. A lengthy investigation, coordinated by Lieutenant J. G. Murphy of the G&F Police, led to their arrests. The G&F family was shocked to learn that a vet-eran conductor, G. E. Ellison, a former Douglas resident who then lived in Augusta, admitted guilt. Only one month from retirement, Ellison was well liked and "his wife and mother and two of the daughters were consistent church people [in Douglas] and were a great help in the work of the church." After their convictions, prison time followed for the three men.[47]

While merchandise thefts from *The Goose* made the pages of regional newspapers, other illegal activities perpetuated by G&F men went largely unrecorded. Indeed, local journalists consistently wrote about the high civic standards of employees, individuals who worked for their churches, donat-ed time to community activities, and showed other acts of kindness. While there were law-abiding, God-fearing G&F men, an untold number either produced or dispensed illegal "hooch." By the Great Depression the G&F had an image of being a carrier where alcohol was tolerated. Although the company's book of rules contained "Rule G," which made drinking on the job grounds for dismissal, officers usually ignored this provision, "largely because nearly everybody drank." Enforcement, when it occurred, generally involved locomotive engineers and "those men who blew their paychecks on drink and left their families to suffer."[48]

At a time when money was tight, some G&F personnel made and sold large quantities of "moonshine" or "white lightning." Specifically, there were two types, the cheaper "scrap iron" and the more expensive "charred red whiskey," although both had high alcohol content. Occasionally these products were offered "uncut," further enhancing potency. The whiskey might be made on G&F property, and often on payday gallons of scrap iron were distributed directly to fellow employees from the drained water barrels carried on maintenance-of-way motor cars. Or the liquor might be sold to ever-present bootleggers. Profits went to both makers and distributors, who probably had to pay off local law enforcement officers. No matter the operational costs, illegal alcohol helped to tide over many a G&F family during both bad and good times. Unquestionably there was a strong, established culture of alcohol on the G&F and throughout the South.

In a practical and somewhat paternalistic fashion the G&F traditionally provided some workers, usually those assigned to the maintenance-of-way department, with free housing. Labeled "Laborers' Houses, Midville, Ga." by John W. Barriger III of the Reconstruction Finance Corporation, this 1935 photograph shows the homes of track laborers. These seemingly well-maintained structures were painted yellow, trimmed in green. Barriger faced his camera north from the crossover diamond of the Central of Georgia Railroad. (From the John W. Barriger III National Railroad Library, University of Missouri—St. Louis)

After all, many a southerner showed "a Saturday night and a Sunday morning side," and the Women's Christian Temperance Union (WCTU)," an organization that thrived throughout the Wiregrass Region before World War II, had a real purpose.[49]

While rank-and-file employees struggled, those men who led the company hardly lived extravagantly. The Augusta homes of top executives, including President Purvis, were strikingly modest, although these individuals lived in the better Summerville neighborhood. Lower-level white-collar and blue-collar employees, on the other hand, commonly owned or rented houses in the downtown Augusta area known as the "Pinch Gut" section.[50]

Hugh Purvis and some associates also had incomes from activities other than their formal railroad jobs. Although details are obscure, Purvis, his younger brother Maurice, who served as the road's purchasing agent, and James M. Hull, Jr., partner in the Augusta law firm of Hull, Barrett, Willingham & Towill and general counsel to the G&F, were ringleaders in two highly unethical and arguably illegal side activities that thrived during the Great Depression. The smaller operation involved an Augusta-based finance company. Railroad management "encouraged" employees to buy items on credit from several local merchants, and then a steep finance charge was added to the bill. The G&F deducted these charges directly from workers' twice-monthly paychecks. Profits went to the Purvises, Hull, and perhaps others; the company, on the other hand, received nothing. A veteran employee remembered being pressured to buy, "on time," a suit of clothes at an Augusta store that involved a hefty finance charge. "I could have gotten that suit for a lot less money," he recalled, adding "I learned my lesson. That was the last time I got involved with that sleazy scheme."[51]

The larger and likely more enduring moneymaker for select executives came from profits generated by a commissary located in Douglas. Surely inspired by company stores that were historically part of operations of the larger sawmills, textile plants, and turpentine camps, the G&F version, housed in the Douglas depot, offered employees various groceries, including cigarettes and candy. Employees could receive these goods on credit, and again the railroad acted as the collection agency. Not only did items have high mark-ups, but there were also handling fees. As with the finance firm, the railroad made *nothing* from the commissary, even though it furnished space, had employees make deliveries, and provided bookkeeping services. Admittedly, the ability to charge necessities of life and a few luxuries was welcomed during hard times and after, but consumer costs were considerable. "The commissary had high prices and had big finance charges," related a former official. "Some employees were so poor that they would then sell cigarettes at half the price they paid for them in order to get some quick cash."[52]

Both the finance firm and the commissary were unusual in modern railroad history. The fact that the G&F was being operated by receivers, under supervision of a federal bankruptcy judge, meant that the company differed from those carriers led by executives sensitive to a board of directors and shareholders. As long as the judge paid little or no attention and the co-receiver-general manager was deeply involved, these exploitative, private ad hoc concerns could flourish. Workers could have complained to the court about the finance company and the commissary, but such objections would likely have prompted their dismissal. During hard times no one wanted to queue up in an employment line or join a relief agency; employees wished to remain railroaders and stay in their home communities. "There really was nothing that they could do about Purvis's outside activities. The best they could hope for was to stay out of debt and keep their kids from being naked."[53]

WORLD WAR II

By the end of the 1930s the federal judge, the co-receivers, and others associated with the G&F believed that the future would be better. A successful reorganization might occur, although there is no evidence that anyone in a leadership position publicly expressed that expectation. Yet individuals who watched the company were encouraged. With the upturn in business in 1939, journalists lauded the introduction of a new freight train between Greenwood and Vidalia. Employees, familiar with *The Goose,* appropriately dubbed the additional operation *The Gander.*[54]

Even before the United States officially entered World War II on December 8, 1941, military expansion in the region led to further growth of business on the G&F. In October 1941 the company added two new traffic agents for its Valdosta territory to manage increasing tonnage stimulated by the construction of bases for the Army Air Corps (Army Air Forces after June 1941) near Moultrie (Spence Field) and Ray City (Moody Field) and the building of a flying school in Douglas. Here the railroad benefited directly by federal policies that created or enlarged military installations in the South, mainly due to favorable climate, ample space, and political clout.[55]

America's active participation in the war had a profound impact on the G&F. As with every carrier, the all-absorbing task was to strengthen the nation's defenses and to bolster the successful prosecution of the war effort. The railroad industry responded admirably. During the conflict, trains handled a whopping ninety-one percent of all military freight and a staggering ninety-eight percent of military personnel movements. This "magnificent performance" occurred without the need to re-create the United States Railroad Administration of the World War I era.[56]

Unlike some smaller Class 1 and larger shortline carriers, the G&F handled considerable troop movements, mostly soldiers for Moody Field and Camp Gordon, located near Augusta. Nearly always these were solid trains of servicemen. Although dining cars might be part of consists received from connecting roads, the G&F never owned such pieces of rolling stock. If food services were required and a diner was unavailable, the railroad regularly encouraged servicemen to leave their cars at the Douglas depot on West Ward Street and walk a few steps to the privately owned G. & F. Café, which catered around the clock to employees and travelers alike and where "troop trains found the cafe menu to their liking."[57]

To handle a rising freight volume, which included war-related shipments of aviation fuel, pine pulpwood, and refractory materials, and to manage troop extras and increased riders on passenger trains Nos. 4 and 5, shop forces in Douglas scrambled to meet the pressing needs for suitable equipment. In November 1942, the editor of the *Coffee County Progress* inspected the shops and chatted with foreman W. V. "Bill" Waters. The facility hummed with activities: "Now during the depression several cars were taken out of traffic, as they were in bad shape and unsafe to use. Now it is a different story. All cars are needed and more, so now Mr. Waters is pulling these old cars out, some of them thirty-eight years old and reworking them from the rails up." Continued this visitor, "But the marvel was an old coach that had been on the siding for years and looked like it was only fit for the junkman. Well, Mr. Waters just put that coach in the work house, took the wheels from under it and put the workmen to rebuilding it, and when it came out it looked fit to run on the fast specials. Nine coats of the best paint available had been put on the outside. The inside had been cleaned of all old paint and varnished with the best of varnishes." And there was more. "The seats had all been rebuilt and electric lights installed and there you were ready to carry you to Augusta or Madison, Fla." Motive power likewise received attention. "Another interesting thing was to see the number 500 engines [4-6-2s] with their high wheels being cut down to smaller wheels. This gives them more power and about the same speed but they take less fuel." And these altered passenger locomotives would receive assignments on main line freight movements.[58]

The G&F also upgraded its physical plant as best it could. Even though there were steel and other material shortages, the company was able to make some needed betterments. These included a Red Devil Locomotive Coaler that a Chicago construction firm installed for the Augusta yards in 1942 and a 50,000 gallon water tank for the Douglas shops in 1945, replacing a worn-out tank erected in 1910.[59]

The railroad corridor itself changed during the war years. Repeated scrap drives produced a tidy right-of-way, especially around shop and engine facilities. The company junked at least three locomotives and in 1942 patriotically sold an elderly 2-8-0 engine to the U.S. Army. And the annoyance of depression-era hoboes disappeared. No longer were there newspaper reports of "Many Arrested for Bumming Rides on the Railroad." As a Douglas newspaper reported in 1944, "Time was when Mr. [B. L.] China [G&F special agent] and his force peeked under the trains every time one came in and pulled off men whom they called hoboes by the hundreds, but that day has passed."[60]

Because former hoboes and other unemployed men had rallied to the colors or had taken work in war-related industries or other readily available positions, the G&F resembled other transportation companies by encountering a loss of workers. The railroad responded by encouraging veteran employees not to retire, pressing hard for overtime work and negotiating with local draft boards for deferments. At times exemptions were difficult to obtain, although the Georgia Selective Service System Board of Appeals routinely granted deferments to locomotive firemen. "The railroad really needed workers," remarked a former G&F employee, "and somehow it managed to keep the trains rolling." And he added, "During the war the G&F was badly short of office help. Many claims were not settled because of a lack of help and there were many that had not been processed when I returned from the army in 1946."[61]

During the war years labor unrest exacerbated the chronic shortage of workers. In the fall of 1944 more than 300 shopmen, maintenance of way personnel, and telegraphers threatened to walk out due to low wages and increased costs of living, but a federal mediation board prevented a strike. Less than a year later approximately 125 operating employees, who were

The territory served by the G&F was hardly flat as a floor. In order to leave the Savannah River valley, train crews faced Hephzibah Hill, frequently requiring a "double-header." In 1947 two former Florida East Coast 4-6-2's blast their way up the grade on a southbound freight from Augusta. (Truman Blasingame photograph, Robert H. Hanson Coll.)

engaged in engine, train, and yard service, demanded that by April 30, 1945, their wage rates be raised to levels comparable to those of other trainmen in the Southeast. The brotherhoods charged that their paychecks ranged from sixty-four to seventy-six percent of "standard" income. Management argued, though disingenuously, that it could not afford any pay hikes and questioned whether "any advances in existing wages to employees would not directly result in disturbing the [wartime] stabilization program of the National Government."[62]

It appeared that labor would gain a slight victory. On July 7, 1945, a federal emergency board, after a careful investigation, recommended that the G&F increase pay by four cents per hour and that workers accept this increase "as a fair and reasonable settlement of their demands." Management reluctantly agreed, but union representatives wanted the higher standard. The company balked, arguing that "its earnings did not permit payment of the standard rates established for large-earning trunk lines."[63]

Although the federal government had entered the fray as a mediator, a strike erupted on August 7, 1945. Not until August 24, 1945, did the operating personnel agree to a settlement. The labor action, however, produced only modest gains for workers. Strikers received an additional penny per hour and a guaranteed minimum rate of seventy-five percent of the regional wage. A few days later normal operations finally resumed, although the walkout had forced shippers to seek transportation alternatives and prompted soldiers "with railroad experience" at Moody Field to use a G&F switch engine to bring aviation fuel and perishable foods to the base from connections in nearby Valdosta.[64]

Despite the vagaries of wartime, as with virtually every American railroad, operating revenues increased markedly between 1941 and 1945. In the case of the G&F the figure for 1941 stood at $1,644,759 and four years later at $2,153,098 with the best results during 1944 when the total reached $2,364,380. These statistics include both freight and passenger income; again, 1944 was the banner year for freight ($2,217,993) and passenger ($82,861) revenues on the G&F.[65]

THE WYER REPORT

If the much improved wartime gross incomes held, the G&F thought it might finally end its second receivership. The number of American railroads in bankruptcy had dropped from 109 in 1937 to seventy-five in 1945: could the G&F join the redeemed? The court, management, and financial community initially had reason to be optimistic, but soon the postwar numbers caused concern. Although operating revenues remained stable or increased between 1945 ($2,153,098) and 1948 ($2,831,987), operating expenses climbed every year, moving from $1,917,875 in 1945 to $2,595,000 in 1948. Problems mounted. The ICC delayed freight rate increases, the postwar boom in vehicle manufacturing and highway construction put more automobiles and trucks on the road, and a decline in farm and small-town populations continued. And labor unrest became another concern. Beginning on February 12, 1947, a twenty-one-day strike involving approximately 500 nonoperating employees, including shopmen and maintenance-of-way workers, caused considerable financial havoc and led to higher wage obligations when the company agreed to an 18 1/2 cents hourly pay hike.[66]

It was time to assess the future of the G&F. On April 16, 1948, Frank M. Scarlett who had replaced A. L. Franklin as the federal bankruptcy judge, engaged the small yet widely respected railroad consulting firm of William Wyer & Company, based in East Orange, New Jersey, "to study, analyze and make recommendations to the Court as to the best methods of reorganizing and disposing of receivership of the Georgia & Florida Railroad." In early May the Wyer firm began work and in late December issued a fact-filled seventy-eight-page report.[67]

All aspects of the G&F received critical attention. As the court expected, the Wyer Company made numerous recommendations on saving money and enhancing revenues. The major suggestions included abandonment of the Statesboro Northern–Summit-Graymont branch, most of the Madison line and a section of the Broxton spur; termination of passenger trains Nos. 4 and 5; renegotiation of the agreement with the Southern Railway for rental of the Savannah River Bridge; and replacement of steam engines with diesel-electric locomotives.

Just as the company during the Great Depression scrutinized the value of branch lines, and lifted nearly 100 miles of track, the Wyer report strongly urged that top priority be given to retiring the Statesboro Northern branch, including the attached Summit-Graymont appendage, and sale, if possible, of the 2.1-mile Statesboro Terminal Company facility in Statesboro to the city's other carrier, the Central of Georgia Railway. The principal source of revenues on these forty-five miles of line came from tobacco that during the summer months moved from the Statesboro station. This traffic was declining due to reduced tobacco plantings and "soft overseas markets" as well as "keen truck competition." Not only would abandonment save nearly $38,000 annually, but the railroad would benefit from more than twenty miles of seventy-pound rail that the consultants found to be "in much better condition than some of the rail of equal weight on the main line of the G&F." The Augusta-Valdosta segment could become better as a result.[68]

The Wyer Company also found that traffic generated by the twenty-eight-mile Madison branch added little to the bottom line. In fact, savings through abandonment of nearly all of this deteriorating trackage would exceed $12,000 annually, based on such factors as per diem freight-equipment charges, maintenance costs, and readjustment of train-crew assignments. Nothing really escaped Wyer, who picked up rumors (which would later be confirmed) that a large paper mill might be constructed near Valdosta. Thus by retaining about four miles of the Madison line, "this would permit the serving of industries on the branch near Valdosta and would leave the branch in place far enough to service the location where there has been discussion of a plant for St. Regis Paper Company."[69]

The recommendation for lifting about ten miles of the upper end of the Broxton branch between Broxton and Relee would save additional dollars. If abandonment had occurred in 1947, net savings would have been $2,526. Since the sole shipper, a veneer plant at Relee, now operated only periodically, the future for this line was nil. The mostly rotten ties had little value, and the elderly forty-pound rail had only scrap value, although surprisingly "this light-weight rail sometimes commands higher prices than other [heavier] rail."[70]

Wyer and Company anticipated considerable savings with the end to main line passenger service. Just as the future of most G&F branch lines was dim, there was really no hope of trains Nos. 4 and 5 increasing or even stabilizing earnings. Since World War II passenger revenues had been on a sharp decline, dropping from $59,718 in 1945 to only $26,730 in 1947. "It would seem that with the stationary population and rapidly increasing automobile registration it would be natural to expect further decline in travel on these trains." Even though Nos. 4 and 5 carried a RPO car and handled freight cars, a substantial financial drain occurred, amounting to a loss of $132,706 annually.[71]

Just as Nos. 4 and 5 incurred out-of-pocket losses, the G&F suffered from paying too much for use of the Savannah River Bridge at Augusta for its Greenwood extension trains. Based on a supplemental agreement that dated from 1933, the G&F paid both a yearly fixed rental fee of $15,000 and *half* of the maintenance costs. In 1947 the bill totaled $18,981. But the G&F had not challenged the arrangement; Purvis and his associates accepted the logic that had been employed long ago, namely that the base rental rate was predicated on the cost of the G&F constructing its own span. This thinking, however, had proven wasteful. "We . . . recommend that negotiations be opened with the Southern Railway looking to the establishment of the rent on a fair basis," urged the Wyer report. "If these negotiations fail, we would be inclined to disaffirm the contract, making a tender to the Southern Railway of what is considered to be a fair rental and expressing a willingness, in case the Southern Railway is not agreeable to accepting the G&F tender, to having the amount . . . determined by the Interstate Commerce Commission." Added Wyer: "We believe that such a course of action will result in a reduction of annual payments by the G&F of at least $5,000 and perhaps substantially more."[72]

Of all of Wyer's recommendations, the best short-term as well as long-range change involved dieselization. The age of steam on American railroads was nearing an end. The monumental diesel-electric locomotive revolution was at hand, being spearheaded by such smaller carriers as the Chicago Great Western; Gulf, Mobile & Ohio; and New York, Susquehanna & Western. "One of the greatest opportunities for economies in modern railroading is the substitution of diesel-electric locomotives for steam locomotives," argued the Wyer report. "The economies of such substitution are particularly large where, as in the case of the Georgia & Florida, locomotive coal does not originate on line but originates on connecting lines to whom freight must be paid." Although the Wyer Company calculated expenditures of $1,050,000 for six 1,500 horsepower and three 600 horsepower diesel units and additional expenditures for servicing and maintenance facilities, savings of nearly $250,000 could be expected in annual operating expenses, a prediction that ultimately proved overly conservative.[73]

Another improvement, albeit much less remunerative than dieselization, involved purchase of additional freight equipment. The examination led to the conclusion that the G&F needed to reduce the high expense of "car hire" and to make a reasonable contribution to the national freight car pool. An important step in meeting these needs involved acquisition of at least 100 box cars and fifty pulpwood cars, augmenting significantly an aging fleet of 305 box cars and thirty gondola and hopper cars. "A road the size of the G&F cannot reasonably be expected to provide itself with specialized equipment such as stock cars," and so Wyer recommended acquisition of basic new rolling stock.[74]

These railroad consultants did not ignore matters of internal operations. A considerable portion of their report focused on activities of the Freight Traffic Department. Criticism centered on the solicitation of Florida perishables. Although for decades the G&F had encouraged movement of northbound fruits and vegetables from the Sunshine state, the Wyer Company concluded that perishable traffic received from the ACL at Willachoochee and the SAL at Vidalia actually hurt the balance sheet, largely attributable to a freight imbalance. "The operation of these perishable trains almost invariably involves a southbound move which would otherwise be unnecessary in order to provide crew and power for the northbound move." When Wyer crunched the numbers, the yearly out-of-pocket savings would be at least $7,500.[75]

The consultants recommended more than simply that the G&F discontinue solicitation of the perishable traffic through the Willachoochee and Vidalia interchanges; they considered changes in the overall activities of the Freight Traffic Department. This aspect of railroad operations lacked real sophistication; in fact, personnel wasted considerable funds on travel, entertainment, and general overhead. Moreover, there was no controlling hand providing adequate direction to the functions of the department. "The lack of guidance in policy matters or the making of a concerted effort to correct many deficiencies which have existed in the department for some time naturally leads to ineffective sales results." Even though the report made no mention of the corrupt commissary system, the problems caused by cronyism and "good ol' boy" policies unquestionably damaged earnings. A variety of suggestions followed on how amateurish practices might be made more professional and hence more profitable.[76]

THE FUTURE

The Wyer Company fervently believed that action on its findings must be forthcoming. "We see no prospect that the Georgia & Florida as its operations have been conducted can ever be financially successful, and a continuance of present conditions will only result in a gradual dissipation of all remaining equity now held by the holders of Receivers' Certificates." Yet the consultants expressed guarded optimism. "We do believe, however, that with the cooperation of all of those interested in the continuation of this property's operation a way can be found to restore the earning power of the G&F and at the same time give the creditors some hope of eventually recovering their investment." The final words of the report gave a straightforward message: "If a plan as outlined cannot be worked out, we recommend complete abandonment of the Georgia & Florida Railroad." This conclusion became a twist to the dictum made in the 1920s by the consulting firm of Coverdale & Colpitts: "Expand or die." Fortunately, the G&F did not ignore the recommendations of Wyer and Company.[77]

CHAPTER SEVEN

The Final Years, 1949–1963

A FRESH START

The post–World War II economic resurgence that swept much of America seemingly eluded the Georgia & Florida (G&F). The company faced a combined debt of more than $1.8 million to the Reconstruction Finance Corporation (RFC), local units of government, and private investors, and red ink continued to flow. On January 27, 1948, Frank M. Scarlett, the federal bankruptcy judge from Brunswick, Georgia, wisely conducted a hearing in Augusta to explore the possibilities of ending these ongoing losses. "The court cannot be unmindful of the obligations incurred by its receivers," he told the news media. Recalled a long-time employee, "The judge decided it was time for a fresh start."[1]

The well-attended public session accomplished Judge Scarlett's goals. He indicated that several likely options existed for the G&F, including reorganization under "a sounder financial plan in the hands of more efficient administrators," sale to another carrier, sale by pieces and junking the remainder, or outright abandonment. Rather than deciding on a specific course of action, the judge named a special commissioner to study the financial prospects and shortly accepted the resignations of the receivers. Moreover, he sought a professional assessment of how to protect debt holders and to determine if service could be maintained along the main stem and principal branches.[2]

Judge Scarlett tapped a capable commissioner, Alfred W. Jones, Jr., a friend from Sea Island, Georgia. In January 1948 when Jones assumed his duties, he served as president of the Brunswick Pulp and Paper Company and headed the Sea Island Company. A native of Dayton, Ohio, and a 1923 graduate of the University of Pennsylvania, Jones soon moved to coastal Georgia to become manager of Sapeloe Plantation, and in 1928 he took charge of the Sea Island Company, turning the bankrupt resort into a profitable concern. As a prominent businessman, Jones served on numerous local and national corporate boards and public and private commissions and also headed Keewaydin Camp, Ltd., an Ontario, Canada, canoe trip camp that developed leadership skills for teenage boys.[3]

Immediately Jones took up his assignments and began to change the course of the G&F. "He was a hands-on receiver, but he had no real knowledge of railroading." Even with that limitation, Jones correctly concluded that new leadership was imperative. Hugh Purvis, long-time co-receiver, general manager and president, according to observers had "stayed too long with the railroad," and perhaps he had become "somewhat senile" as he neared seventy years of age. (He would die on March 16, 1949.) William V. Griffin, the other veteran co-receiver, who had never been heavily involved, lacked much interest in the property. In fact, on January 17, 1947, Judge Scarlett had appointed Augusta businessman Victor Markwalter as a third co-receiver. Markwalter, "a cultured and nice person," headed a prominent accounting firm and lent his expertise to the railroad. The judge appreciated Jones's initial efforts, forcing the resignations of the three co-receivers and naming Jones as sole receiver, effective June 1, 1948. Apparently, James Hull, legal counsel for the G&F and "a close friend of the judge," had suggested other possible receivers, but Jones was a talented businessman and "well connected," and he relished the challenges of solving problems. In addition to the Jones appointment, Charles McDiarmid, a graduate of the Johns Hopkins University, chief engineer, and son-in-law of Maurice Purvis, became the road's chief operating officer.[4]

As William Wyer and his associates carefully scrutinized the G&F, Jones, McDiarmid and others attempted to solve ongoing and nagging problems with organized labor. Even though the railroad had encouraged the "G&F family" concept and workers had remained loyal because of nepotism—"if you worked for the railroad, we will employ your sons"—the general unwillingness of management to enforce "Rule G" on drinking for operating and maintenance employees, free housing for some track workers and other considerations, nasty conflicts repeatedly erupted.[5]

In mid-1948 labor-management relations worsened. This time problems centered on nonoperating workers, namely maintenance, shop craft, and station employees, who four years earlier had threatened to strike over their poor pay. Operating personnel, however, who had walked out in 1945, did not now threaten a job action. Even though a presidential emergency board had recommended a modest wage increase to nonoperating personnel on eighteen shortlines, including the G&F, the matter remained unsolved. Realizing that there would be no real softening by G&F officials, the affected unions sought an increase of just seven cents per hour. Management, though, countered with 2 1/2 cents per hour, although agreeing to award workers "half of any available profits and 50 per cent of any rate increase imposed [by the ICC] on shippers." Ideally this arrangement over time would bring workers up to the standard level of pay in the Southeast.[6]

When an impasse resulted, on September 27, 1948, 440 nonoperating employees struck. As had been the tradition, management played hardball. Even before the walkout began, the judge, in conjunction with the receiver and top-ranking officials, threatened to proceed with liquidation. Moreover, the company continued train service, although admitting that "without the maintenance crews, equipment could only be kept running about ten days to two weeks."[7]

Fortunately for both labor and management, the strike was short-lived. On October 3, the local general chairmen of the Brotherhood of Maintenance of Way Employees, Order of Railroad Telegraphers, and American Federation of Labor System Federation signed a temporary agreement with the receiver and chief operating officer that contained several provisions: the court would not proceed on any plan to close the road; strikers could return to their job "without prejudice" and negotiations would resume.[8]

Lengthy discussions, however, did not ensue. Aided by Wyer and Company and online civic organizations, a formal compromise between the parties came within a few days. The G&F made available $46,000 for an increase in wages and created "standard vacation rules of pay as now used on railroads of comparable size in this section of the country." Moreover, there would be a "revolutionary" profit-sharing scheme designed for a ten-year period. Also, workers received a greater voice in setting policies with management, although decisions would always require approval of the receiver and the judge. Based on a sense of mutual need, the agreement called for creation of a booster organization that would have labor, management and shippers "encourage patronage for the Georgia and Florida Railroad."[9]

Seemingly, a positive, new chapter was being written. "The Georgia and Florida was given a new lease on life [by the settlement]," editorialized the *Moultrie Observer*. "It is in operation now and the union officials and the company officials are putting their problems on the table and seem more disposed to listen to reason. We trust that it means that the Georgia and Florida will come through with new plans of reorganization, a new program for making the operation of the road profitable and a new and brighter future."[10]

EXITING PASSENGER SERVICE

Even before the bankruptcy court received a copy of the Wyer & Company evaluation, G&F management sought to enhance earnings by ending the financial drain caused by main line passenger service. Although railroads often encountered regulatory difficulties in removing money-losing passenger trains before passage of the Transportation Act of 1958, the surge in automobile usage following World War II promoted most passenger-carrying roads to assess their local and branch-line train operations, resulting in scores of abandonment applications.[11]

In late 1947 the G&F announced its intention to discontinue passenger service between Augusta and Valdosta. These trains, Nos. 4 and 5, were big money losers. In October 1947 operating revenues, for example, stood at $4,918 but operating costs amounted to $14,564. Officials estimated that

It was in the twilight of passenger service on the main line when this photograph was taken of train No. 4 standing in the station at Nashville, Georgia. A few years later, 1951, locomotive No. 503 also disappeared, becoming so much scrap metal. (Hugh Comer photograph, Robert H. Hanson Coll.)

termination could save $115,746 annually, a substantial sum for the company. Soon the legal department filed the necessary petition with the Georgia Public Service Commission (GPSC), and that regulatory body scheduled public hearings in Atlanta for January 14 and 15, 1948.[12]

After the discontinuance announcements, howls of protest erupted in most of the affected communities, centering in Douglas, Hazlehurst, Nashville, Swainsboro, and Vidalia. Indeed, it was Mayor B. Morris of Nashville who spearheaded efforts to save the trains. "We need this service," he argued. "It ought to be improved instead of discontinued." The proposed loss of U.S. mail and express service especially troubled Morris and his supporters, which they considered to be "even more serious" than the end of personal travel options. Even though every important community along the route had either intercity rail and bus connections or at least a bus outlet, no direct, parallel Railway Post Office (RPO) and Railway Express Agency service existed between Augusta and Valdosta. The petition, circulated by the Morris group, argued in part: "The excuse or alleged reason for the discontinuance of the two trains is not believed to be grounded in fact in that it is not believed that the alleged income and the alleged expenditures . . . are properly given or stated." The document added: "The vested rights of the property owners . . . along the right-of-way of the road, which have been built up on the faith of the continuance of the road in all its departments, would be greatly impaired and many totally destroyed upon the discontinuance of any one branch or department."[13]

The vigorous complaints impressed the GSPC. On May 14, 1948, regulators by a three to two vote agreed that the Nos. 4 and 5 should continue to operate. Even though the G&F remained mired in bankruptcy and main line passenger operations hemorrhaged red ink, the GSPC felt that the official "takeoff" request lacked proper consideration of freight income generated from the practice of adding freight cars. And the GSPC reached an astonishing conclusion: "The G&F has, with the exception of the war years, operated consistently at a deficit, and there appears little reason to be optimistic about its continued operation. While the abandonment of the passenger trains might forestall for a short period what now appears inevitable, the service of the railroad to its patrons would be so diminished as to make the prolongation of doubtful value."[14]

The GSPC decision proved to be only a temporary setback. Later in 1948 when the railroad again petitioned the regulatory body for discontinuance, public anger failed to materialize. At hearings held on December 22, 1948, the G&F argued its case, and no one spoke in opposition. Likely concern for the future viability of the railroad itself, announced measures by the company to handle express on scheduled freight trains (which the company offered until 1958), and the plan by the U.S. Post Office to use trucks along adjoining highways for mail delivery quelled opposition. In fact, the G&F had lobbied its case with Morris, chambers of commerce, and others who earlier had fought discontinuance.[15]

In mid-January 1949 passenger travel on the main line ended. Collectors cherished the last-day cancellation of envelopes and postcards that contained a "Last Day Passenger on G&F Railroad, January 15, 1949, Augusta & Valdosta RPO" banner and a prominent RPO cancellation mark. The G&F, however, had not technically exited the passenger business. Although the company no longer issued a public timetable, passengers could buy a ticket for daily mixed trains Nos. 25 and 26 between Nashville, Sparks, Adel, and Moultrie. But the GPSC granted permission to discontinue this service at "12 o'clock Midnight, November 25, 1950." For a few years some heroic passengers could ride mixed trains Nos. 17 and 18 between Valdosta and Madison, although few did.[16]

LINE ABANDONMENTS

The Wyer report, filed with the court in late 1948, had considered carefully the matter of line rationalization, and it did not take long for the G&F to seek regulatory authority to make several cutbacks. On June 27, 1949, the railroad officially asked the Interstate Commerce Commission (ICC) for permission to abandon nearly 100 miles of appendages. Specifically, the G&F wanted to scrap the Broxton and Madison branches and to retire the surviv-

In 1950 Ten-Wheeler No. 207 handles a mixed train near Garfield, Georgia, shortly before the G&F retired this piece of branchline trackage. The elderly Jim Crow combination car or "combine" on the rear, with its open central baggage-express-LCL door, transported white riders in the front section and black patrons in the rear. (C. K. Marsh, Jr. Coll.)

ing section of the old Millen extension and all of the former Statesboro Northern Railroad. The G&F also sought to end its affiliation with the tiny Statesboro Terminal Company through either abandonment or sale to the Central of Georgia (CofG).[17]

The ICC took nearly a year to render a decision, but the G&F got mostly what it wanted. The Statesboro Northern and related trackage could be junked and the Statesboro Terminal dissolved. On August 31, 1950, the last train, a mixed consist, rattled over the line. The ICC would permit only partial abandonment of the Broxton branch, however, approving the lifting of four miles between Sapp's Still and Relee. The Commission told the railroad to maintain service on the remaining fourteen miles, arguing that the Wells Lumber Company at Sapp's Still "provides sufficient traffic to warrant continued operation." Ultimately, the ICC allowed the G&F to retire the branch when the lumber operation closed. In August 1958 the last revenue train made its way over the rickety line. As for the Madison trackage, earlier the G&F had asked the ICC not to consider the abandonment request "for the time being" and the ICC agreed.[18]

Although the G&F needed to make extensive improvements, prospects for a major rail shipper along the Madison branch, the original southern portion of the main line, had altered the disposal strategy. Not long after the abandonment case reached the ICC, the National Container Corporation announced plans to build a $25 million kraft pulpboard and paper plant near Clyattville, Georgia, ten miles south of Valdosta. The G&F did not intend to retain the trackage and sought to negotiate a sale to the Valdosta Southern Railroad (VSR), the newly formed railroad subsidiary of National Container, that would serve the facility. In fact, National Container did more than create VSR, building a temporary six-mile spur to connect with the Southern Railway (SR) southeast of Valdosta prior to the plant's construction. The G&F wanted $190,000 for the Madison property; therefore, on September 11, 1952, the railroad filed an application with the ICC to permit the transaction.[19]

A few months later regulators disappointed the G&F. Although the sale could be executed, the ICC allowed National Container to "tender a 10-year option to the roads connecting with the Valdosta Southern under which any, or any combination, of the connecting carriers, [Atlantic Coast Line, Seaboard Air Line (SAL), and SR] could acquire control of the properties of Valdosta Southern on reasonable terms subject to Interstate Commerce Commission approval." Because of its poor financial health, the G&F rightfully worried that it could never exercise the option provision, thus shutting it out of a potential traffic bonanza.[20]

Eventually National Container Corporation and the G&F came to terms. VSR made its debut, providing the new shortline with four interchange partners, including the G&F in Valdosta. (The VSR in the early 1970s abandoned the eighteen miles between Clyattville and Madison.) Moreover, by creating three additional railroad options, National Container (which became Owens-Illinois in October 1956) no longer worried about the fate of the admittedly shaky G&F. The G&F, however, got both cash for the line and after October 1952 a share of the mill traffic that included pulpwood, chemicals and other materials used in papermaking. Part of the agreement with National Container involved the G&F acquiring a fleet of wood-rack cars. The RFC, though a $717,000 loan, made possible purchase of 150 of the 100,000-pound capacity units from the Bethlehem Steel Company. In time, this equipment proved to be wanting: "these cars were light duty and cracked," although the rolling stock met requirements set by the shipper.[21]

DIESELIZATION

Even though the G&F could not claim to be the first fully dieselized Class 1 carrier in the nation or the South (the Texas-Mexican Railway likely deserves that honor), the company embraced this technological replacement as it swept the industry. In 1938 the country's railroads owned 45,210 steam locomotives and only 403 diesel-electric units. A decade later the numbers stood at 34,581 and 8,981, and the trend toward diesel-electric usage rapidly accelerated. In 1951 diesels at last outnumbered steamers.[22]

By 1950 the G&F's fleet of twenty-eight steam locomotives was mostly obsolete and in worn condition. No one questioned the need for new power. After attempts to acquire diesels from at least two manufacturers failed because of credit problems, in 1947 the G&F purchased at a bargain-basement price three former New Orleans Great Northern Railroad (Gulf, Mobile & Ohio) small or "light" Mountain-type (4-8-2) steamers that the American Locomotive Company had built in 1927. Because of their excessive weight for much of the main-line track structure, especially through soft and spongy sections of south Georgia, management relegated these engines to the Greenwood extension. Yet acquisition of these newer, larger, and more sophisticated 4-8-2s, with their 45,700 pounds of tractive effort, hardly solved the road's motive needs, and so the G&F was ripe for diesel-electric locomotives.[23]

The case for dieselization was strong and the Wyer report had urged the end to steam. But how could the G&F afford more than $1 million of state-of-the-art motive power? The Wyer study suggested that the down payment might be raised through the sale of salvageable materials gleaned from branch-line abandonments. But that would take time, and management wanted to dieselize as quickly as possible. "Rolling up its [sic] sleeves," recalled Homer Walker, editor of the *Georgia & Florida Magazine,* "the Road's Officials went to work on selling surplus property and in the space of a few months, the down payment on the Diesel[s] was realized." Moreover, the railroad arranged a ten-year loan of $950,000 from the RFC for the balance.[24]

With financing no longer a roadblock, management considered what major diesel-electric locomotive makers could offer. The nation's foremost manufacturer, Electro-Motive Division of General Motors (EMD), won out, agreeing to supply nine 1,500 horsepower "General Purpose" (GP7) road units and three 600 horsepower switchers (SW1) at a cost of $1,063,859.11. An unusual aspect of the EMD order involved the G&F opting for friction rather than roller bearings, attempting to keep the price as low as possible. (A few years later EMD replaced the cheaper friction bearings with much superior roller bearings on No. 702, and the SR, once it took control, followed suit with the remaining 700 series units.) Still, the G&F benefited from EMD quality and a simplified parts inventory.[25]

On August 7, 1950, the first diesel locomotives began revenue service. Two SW1s, which arrived before the GP7s, were used on train No. 58 between Augusta and Greenwood. The SW1s received both road and switching assignments until September 14, 1950, when the GP7s entered the power pool. For all practical purposes the G&F now had become "completely dieselized." Yet fearing a possible locomotive shortage due to a national emergency or other crisis and needing lightweight power on the few remaining branch lines, management retained several Ten-wheelers and Pacifics.

The transition between steam and diesel motive power on the G&F is captured in this photograph taken in September 1952 at the Douglas, Georgia, shops complex. No. 703, a 1,500 horsepower GP-7 built two years earlier by EMD, awaits servicing. (Herb Koenig photograph [PN 16797], Railroad Avenue Enterprises)

Finally, on May 28, 1955, workers in the Douglas shops serviced the last steam engine and soon these iron horses, sans bells and whistles, became scrap metal. Of course, employees and residents along the road missed the sights, sounds, and smells of steamers. "I regretted to see them go," mentioned veteran engineer I. W. "Con" Drew when he retired in 1959 after forty years of service, "but I know the diesel is more economical and is easier to handle."[26]

The G&F took enormous pride in its shiny fleet of green and yellow diesel locomotives. So much so that the company decided to operate a special train between Augusta and Valdosta on September 16, 1950, showing off its new motive power and demonstrating in a public way that it had become a modern, freight-carrying railroad worthy of the advertising slogan: FAST DEPENDABLE SERVICE. Local newspapers and radio stations were told of this publicity train that would include GP7 No. 702, a baggage car, a vintage coach, and office car No. 100.[27]

The media also gave extensive follow-up coverage to this diesel-powered trip. At the various stops hundreds of well-wishers inspected the new iron horse and chatted with passengers who included mostly G&F active and retired employees and EMD representatives. In Nashville the station agent arranged for A. W. Starling, editor and publisher of the *Nashville Herald,* to receive a cab ride. The following week Starling wrote a front-page account, saying in part:

Having always wished to ride an engine as it pounded down the rails, Roy Youmans, local agent, made arrangements early Saturday for me to ride the cab from Nashville to Valdosta. Arriving at the depot just prior to the train pulling in, I had to wait a lengthy time before boarding it because of the several hundred persons on hand to inspect the new equipment. At Ray City another large group filed through the cab and had looks at the massive engine.

Once underway, I had a good seat opposite the engineer. Riding also in the cab were C. H. Hudson of Vidalia, retired after forty years as a conductor. Mr. Hudson said he started with the road first on the Nashville-Sparks railroad. . . . A former Nashville man, R. W. Shaw of Vidalia, maintenance department, occupied another seat. . . .

The opportunity I had to ride the engine to Valdosta was appreciated. It proved to me the wise choice of Ga. & Fla. officials in purchasing the new equipment, and indicated they plan to make the road more efficient and a paying proposition in the future.[28]

It did not take long before G&F personnel learned the ins-and-outs of diesel locomotives. Although EMD instructors provided training, employees had long been adept at mechanical innovations, ranging from using a junked White Steamer automobile engine to power a small, home-built maintenance-of-way crane "that worked great," to a clever windmill device installed on cabooses to provide electricity for inside lighting and outside marker lamps.[29]

If there was a G&F employee who became "Mr. Diesel," is was L. J. ("Louie") Waters, General Superintendent. Although lacking much formal education, Waters, who was born in 1908 in the lumber village of Olympia, Georgia, located on the Madison branch, hired out in 1926 as a laborer in the Douglas shops. Because of his considerable mechanical acumen, he rose rapidly in the ranks, serving as traveling road fireman, foreman of engines and superintendent of motive power. Fellow employees considered Waters to be "smart as hell and a wonderful person," even claiming that "he was the smartest railroad man in the country." Since the G&F needed power and not speed with its GP7s, Waters had these locomotives geared down so that they could handle more tonnage. "When we first obtained our Geeps [GP7s]," wrote Waters, "they were equipped with 65.12 gears, however in recent months the gears have been changed to a 62.15 ratio coupled to EMD D-37 traction motors, and there is a story of a great improvement and a great saving to the Railroad." He also had cement blocks placed in the locomotives for enhanced traction.[30]

Not long after Waters had the GP7s modified, he personally benefited from these improvements. The G&F had a wreck that blocked the Greenwood extension, so traffic was rerouted over the neighboring Charleston & Western Carolina (Atlantic Coast Line) between Augusta and Greenwood. The C&WC road foreman told Waters that additional power needed to be lashed to the heavy G&F train. If only the existing locomotives were used, the C&WC employee argued, the train would have to be "doubled" on Clarks Hill near Augusta, a time-consuming process. Waters refused. He then bet the road foreman a month's wages that the GP7s could manage just fine; they did and he won the wager.[31]

Before becoming a "fallen flag" carrier, the G&F expanded its stable of diesel electrics. Rather than purchasing new units, the road went to the much less expensive yet expanding used locomotive market. In September 1954 the company added a former Southern Railway (SR) 750 horsepower railcar that Fairbanks Morse-St. Louis Car Company had constructed in 1939 for SR affiliate, Alabama Great Southern Railroad. This odd piece of motive power, originally part of the *Vulcan*, a passenger motor-train set, worked mostly in the Douglas yards stunting cars and occasionally pulled the office car or wrecking-train equipment. To make this addition more useful, shop workers altered the power from the rear two axles to the front three axles. In April 1955 the company acquired two elderly (1937) Electro Motive Corporation-built former Elgin, Joliet & Eastern switch engines (SW1 and NW1) that often handled switching assignments in Augusta.[32]

Although it is impossible to gauge the overall economic impact of dieselization, the G&F benefited enormously. "Those diesels made a tremendous difference on the balance sheet," remembered a former official. The only alternative would have been to acquire better steam locomotives, which were readily available on the used-market during much of the 1950s. But this would have been money wasted; by 1960 the Age of Steam had virtually ended. Parts and other support services for the iron horse became more difficult, and hence more expensive, after nearly total nationwide dieselization. The only real drawback to abandoning steamers for the G&F was the absence of a source of cinders that track gangs had effectively used for inexpensive ballast.[33]

J. PETE BELVIN

It would be J. Pete Belvin who took command of the renewed G&F. In early 1954 Belvin became chief operating officer and remained in that position (his formal titles varied) long after the SR assumed ownership. Under his guidance the G&F developed into a more modern carrier. "It hasn't been very long since the G&F was about the deadest railroad that was still unburied in America," reflected a building-supply dealer in Douglas. "I believe that the doctor that has done more to save its life has been Dr. Pete Belvin, an honest, intelligent, and hard-working man who has been with the G&F for many, many years, and who knows more about its problems than any other man."[34]

Like his principal predecessors, John Skelton Williams and Hugh W. Purvis, Belvin was a native southerner, born on October 29, 1907, in Doerun, Georgia, northwest of Moultrie. His parents paid homage to the rural South by naming him Sidney Lanier Belvin after the beloved Georgia

Perhaps the true "oddball" piece of motive power owned by the G&F arrived in 1954 from the Southern Railway. Constructed in 1939 by the St. Louis Car Company, No. 81 once powered *The Vulcan,* a passenger train operated by Southern Railway affiliate Alabama Great Southern Railroad. On the G&F No. 81 pulled the company office car, handled trains in wrecker service and shunted cars at Douglas. (Herb Koenig photograph [PN 16806], Railroad Avenue Enterprises)

poet. "It didn't take long to find out that I was not meant to be named after any poet," Belvin later explained. "When I was large enough to go to town with Papa everyone would call me 'Little Pete' so my name was gradually changed to James Pete Belvin, Jr."[35]

Belvin grew up in a large, financially struggling family that moved about south Georgia. In 1917 the seventy-seven year old senior Belvin, a Civil War veteran and sometimes lumber inspector, died, forcing the junior Belvin, a younger sister and their mother (Belvin's other nine siblings had left home) to rely heavily on financial support provided by an older brother, James Wiley Belvin, who worked in a lumber-mill commissary in Ellenton and later for the Atlanta, Birmingham and Atlantic Railroad (AB&A) in Moultrie. It would be through his brother's employment with the AB&A that Belvin entered railroading. "When I was about 12 years old, we lived next to the railroad station. My brother, Wiley, was agent for the railroad so I got a job as office boy and worked for either that railroad [AB&A] or another one in town [Georgia Northern Railroad] after school and during summer vacations." He continued, "At a very early age I made up my mind that I would make railroad work a career and it never occurred to me to do anything else."[36]

After graduating from Moultrie High School in 1926, where he had been a popular student and a star athlete, Belvin became a full-time railroad employee. His first positions were in the Moultrie freight warehouse of the Georgia Northern. Wanting to get ahead and to avoid manual labor, he took correspondence courses from the Chicago-based La Salle Extension University on industrial traffic management "so when a job came open as a rate clerk I would be ready for it." In 1928 Belvin joined the office force of the AB&A in Moultrie and by the early 1930s "I had had experience in just about every phase of agency work." Then in February 1934, the twenty-six-year-old Belvin accepted an offer from the G&F to become a traveling freight agent, based in Moultrie. The gregarious Belvin had found a job that suited his personality and business talents.[37] Belvin proudly related his early accomplishments at the G&F:

> Mr. [D. F.] Kirkpatrick, traffic manager, had explained to me that they [G&F] had an application ready to submit to the Interstate Commerce Commission for abandonment of the Moultrie Branch but had agreed to put a man in the territory for one year and if I could generate enough business to put the line on a paying basis, I would keep the job and they would not file for abandonment. In one year I had the Moultrie Branch on a paying basis and was also seeing that the trains were operating properly and the tracks were maintained. I was promoted to commercial agent and in 1938 to division freight agent.[38]

When World War II erupted Belvin, like so many patriotic Americans, sought to enter the armed forces, wanting to join a U.S. Army transportation unit. But carriers, including the G&F, needed to retain personnel and Belvin was "considered essential to the operation of the railroad." During the conflict, he continued to be assigned to the traffic department, traveling extensively between Florida and New York. "My work took me all over the country and Leila [Belvin's wife] had to sit many a night with the [two small] children alone while I was out trying to make another dollar!" He added, "Sometimes the railroad paid off on time—but most times it didn't!"[39]

The crisis of 1948 that might have led to sale, dismemberment, or junking of the G&F understandably caused Belvin to assess his future with the company. "So what did I do? I talked it over with Leila and she said she would abide by my decision. I decided to go for broke! I moved to Valdosta, Ga., as assistant traffic manager and in a few months to Augusta, Ga. as traffic manager."[40]

Even though Belvin had received "better paying" offers from other carriers, he made a good decision. Once he arrived at the headquarters building in downtown Augusta, Belvin became a major player. For one thing, he became close to Charles McDiarmid, the top operating officer. "He was my good friend so I assisted him whenever necessary. In this way I became familiar with all the operations in addition to traffic work." And Belvin learned about the roles played by Judge Scarlett, Receiver Jones, and other men of importance.[41]

Belvin possessed considerable skills; he was a driven individual, ambitious to get ahead for himself and to better the G&F. Although his formal education lacked bona fide college-level instruction, he was an avid reader, especially of works of history. Significantly, Belvin understood how to court shippers. "Daddy knew how to entertain people," recalled his son. This was a gift that he honed well during his professional career. When serving as livestock development agent in Moultrie in the 1930s, Belvin wrote a short pamphlet that he called "Pointers on Showmanship at Fat Cattle Shows." He closed his narrative with these self-revealing comments:

> Now as to the conduct of a calf owner: Be alert, look pleasant and be courteous, not only to the judge but also to your competitors. Then when the competition is close between two good calves, and yours is placed second, be the first to congratulate your competitor. It is all a part of the game, and perhaps you will win next time. But when you win, modesty is the only acceptable form of conduct.[42]

Belvin had other qualities. As was common among white-collar employees of the G&F, especially those who worked in the traffic department, he became a heavy drinker. When he lived in Moultrie, he happily joined the local Elks Club, an atmosphere that facilitated social drinking. After Belvin moved to Augusta, he "switched to Scotch," suggesting greater sophistication. Ultimately, however, he "went and stayed on the wagon." Belvin was strong-willed, making a lasting impression on coworkers. "Pete was both feared and liked," recalled a long-time associate. "He was your friend as long as he could run your life." Similarly, another acquaintance remembered Belvin as "a diamond in the rough" but "ruthless." There is no question that he relished his positions with the G&F, especially after he became chief operating officer. This railroader, with his strong personality, never shied away from responsibilities. "Pete was a real hands-on executive." As a true workaholic, Belvin took off only Sunday afternoons, expecting every high-ranking officer to follow similar work habits.[43]

Pete Belvin's rise to power at the G&F became possible because of several personnel changes. On April 11, 1951, Chief Operating Officer McDiarmid, this "polite gentleman," died suddenly from a massive stroke, likely attributable to job stress and heavy drinking. In May Receiver Jones appointed a seasoned, North Carolina State College–trained operating official from the SAL, John H. Gill, to fill this all-important vacancy. The offer did not immediately go to Gill, however. Jones wanted James Laurie, an employee of William Wyer, to take charge permanently, but Laurie already had a good job and did not particularly care for Augusta because he did not know how to drive and his wife, a former Rockette, preferred life in New York City. The selection of Gill was sound, however, but he did not stay long with the G&F, becoming president and general manager of the Jacksonville Terminal Company. "He was a nice fellow," recalled an underling, "but I think that he came to the conclusion that the railroad was likely too big of a mess." Belvin, though, had a differing opinion of Gill: "he simply didn't know enough about the Ga. & Fla. to do the job."[44]

As chief operating officer Belvin generally worked effectively with individuals associated with the G&F. He developed a close, friendly relationship with receiver Alfred Jones who "loved my daddy," recalled Belvin's son. Moreover, Belvin and Jones learned how to deal with the long-time federal bankruptcy judge, Frank Scarlett, this "little old and mean looking man." The problem with Scarlett was that "he could be unpredictable," and that tendency could disrupt plans for managing the railroad. But Belvin and Jones knew that the judge was a womanizer and loved baseball. For years they would take him and allegedly a "female companion" from Savannah to spring professional baseball camps in Florida. "Then after returning they would go to the judge and say that we need thus and so and he would kindly agree." Later in the year the judge might not be so cooperative.[45]

Belvin repeatedly rewarded those employees who loyally supported the company. An example involved Robert Lindsey, a track supervisor who worked long hours, at times more than 100 hours per week. Before the sale of the G&F, Lindsey, who was underpaid and required additional money to care for his ailing wife, received a "promotion" from Belvin. Rather than giving him a needed salary increase, the chief operating officer changed Lindsey's title from track supervisor to roadmaster. The railroad had never called this position a roadmaster, but Lindsey became roadmaster for the maintenance section between Greenwood and Vidalia, although his counterpart for the Vidalia-Valdosta segment retained the track supervisor moniker. As Belvin said, "I am paying him in title" and the hard-working Lindsey seemed genuinely pleased.[46]

HELPING EMPLOYEES

Pete Belvin showed concern for G&F employees, and during his tenure did more than promote company picnics and other gatherings. It did not take long before Belvin decided to launch the *Georgia & Florida Magazine*, the first employee periodical since the Williams era. What emerged was a sixteen-page, slick-paper quarterly that began in spring 1955 and covered major railroad happenings along with pieces about promotions, retirements, and other topics of interest. To make the publication as professional as possible, Belvin initially hired a part-time editor from the *Augusta Chronicle*, but this female journalist "did not understand railroading" and so a G&F

About 1960 G&F personnel, including officials and labor leaders, gather at a hotel in Valdosta, Georgia, for the annual tobacco market meeting. A smiling President Pete Belvin is seated in the middle. (Frank Napier Coll.)

employee took charge. Worker response was positive; "they enjoyed every issue, especially the personal stories." Belvin again revealed his strong suit of promotion and salesmanship.[47]

Belvin enhanced morale in additional ways. The two-story, downtown Augusta general office building, which the company had long rented "at a fair rate" from the Alonzo P. Boardman Estate, lacked air conditioning, making seasonal heat brutal for G&F personnel. An employee, whose office was directly under the flat, metal roof, recalled: "On a hot summer day, the glass on my desktop would be too hot to touch." He managed the stifling temperatures by "drinking lots of Coke from the office machine." When Belvin ordered Carrier Corporation cooling units in 1955, the staff was appreciative, indeed, "and our work output probably was much better." Subsequently, by mid-1956, the G&F added air conditioning at other sites, including depots in Douglas, Moultrie, and Valdosta, the Augusta freight agency and yard building, and offices at the Douglas shops. The G&F was in the mainstream for this much appreciated technological improvement. What had been largely a curiosity in the pre–World War II South became an essential part of life in the postwar era.[48]

Belvin found still another way to please employees. In the early 1950s the U.S. Army Corps of Engineers completed a major dam on the Savannah River north of Augusta. This massive public works endeavor created what became Clarks Hill Lake, today's J. Strom Thurmond Dam and Lake. The federal government considered the project a flood-control, hydroelectric power, and navigation scheme, although quickly the reservoir became a popular fishing and boating area for neighboring sections of Georgia and South Carolina, especially greater Augusta.[49]

In the late 1950s Belvin took advantage of the $79 million government betterment. He and ten other G&F officers arranged with the Corps to lease twenty-six acres for a lodge building, double set of sleeping cabins and boat and fishing dock on the South Carolina shore. Although the "official" name for this facility became the "G&F Railroad Lodge," Belvin and Stuart B. Austin, the company's chief engineer, came up with their favorite: "G&F Boosters, Bottling and Boating Club." Although technically separate from the railroad, it used company materials and labor. The principal structure, the lodge, which included a main room that measured 30x60 feet and featured a huge stone fireplace with a mantle made from an old piece of bridge timber, a back kitchen, and restrooms, was well built—"it could survive a hurricane." The walls consisted of a double course of bricks salvaged from the Broxton depot, and the roof trusses were forty-pound steel rail also from the abandoned Broxton branch. A south Georgia mill donated lumber; "had we not removed these pieces they would have been burned." A flagpole, made of old boiler tube, graced the entrance.[50]

The G&F lodge site included a small, almost hidden primitive cabin for the caretaker. Belvin hired veteran employee Frank Harris, an African-American from Alston, Georgia, "who had a bad arm after years of being a bridge foreman," to maintain the facility. "He was a fine cook, kept the boats gassed, buried the garbage and did all types of odd jobs."[51]

Lodge membership was available to most G&F personnel; individuals needed to pay annual dues of one dollar and be "deserving." Also, a member-in-good-standing could reserve the lodge for special activities, including those of a church or fraternal group. Apparently, only white workers used the facility; "blacks didn't come." Although some employees considered the Clarks Hill complex to be "a waste of money," the facility particularly pleased the Augusta office force and friends of the railroad.[52]

Whether black or white, nearly everyone associated with the G&F heartily applauded chartering of a credit union in January 1955. It was Belvin's idea for this new financial organization. "He wanted no more of the commissary." Belvin wisely placed the capable Frank Napier, freight claim agent, in charge, and Napier became president of the independent Georgia & Florida Federal Credit Union. Another G&F employee, Frank Griffin, who received a small additional salary as the credit union's secretary-treasurer, ran day-to-day operations. The concept was simple: collect voluntary deposits from employees and use these funds to make low-interest loans. "Most loans were small," remembered Napier, "only $50 to $100 and were frequently used by members for groceries, rent and bills." Later, the credit union encouraged automobile financing and added an automobile insurance plan.[53]

The credit union quickly flourished. By the end of 1957 membership reached about 350 out of nearly 500 eligible employees. "There was very good patronage" and the operation was "well rounded." And as Napier wrote in the credit union's third annual report: "We have been able to help many families in time of need. . . . We have certainly increased thrift on the part of all of our people."[54]

Belvin worked to improve labor relations, which had been reasonably good since the late 1940s. Even though he "hated unions," Belvin and his associates in September 1957 hammered out a "liberal, profit-sharing contract" with the eight craft and maintenance units. Unlike the documents signed nearly a decade earlier, this agreement, which went into effect on October 1, 1957, called for a forty-hour work week and health and welfare benefits for employees and their dependents. The previous arrangements featured a forty-eight hour week and lacked hospital coverage. "Both contracts, the old and the new, contain a clause unique in the entire railroad industry," reported the *Augusta Chronicle*. "Wages are paid from 50 per cent of G&F gross [sic] [net] receipts, with adjustments made every three months. Under this arrangement employees are subject to the ups and downs of railroading—if profits increase wages rise, if profits are off, the paychecks reflect it." The proviso mostly worked in favor of the company. Still, management bragged that the G&F enjoyed "the best Labor-Management relations in the Country."[55]

A BETTER RAILROAD

Just as Belvin moved to adopt the mid-twentieth century technology of air conditioning, he endorsed other technological advancements, notably teletype machines and two-way radios. In the past the G&F relied on traditional forms of railway communications, initially the telegraph, but after World War I also long-distance telephones. Station agents, as on most carriers, continued to use their keys and sounders, however. A problem that long plagued the G&F was often a shortage of "lightning slingers." For decades the company responded by hiring "boomer" telegraphers, a breed of workers who moved from railroad to railroad. And, if they had a problem with alcohol, the G&F appeared to be a promising place to ply their professional trade. Also, the G&F employed at least one husband and wife team of agent-operators, who for years worked in nearby stations.[56]

In 1956 and 1957 a communication revolution swept the G&F. The railroad was hardly a trend setter like the Chicago Great Western, Erie and

Kansas City Southern, but it became a player. In collaboration with Southern Bell Telephone & Telegraph Company, the G&F installed an up-to-date teletype system that appeared in major offices and stations. A variety of messages, including train orders and reports, could be quickly and reliably sent over Southern Bell's land lines. "These machines are proving to be of great value in that the General Offices in Augusta are in 24 hour contact with the various Sub-Offices," reported *The Georgia & Florida Magazine*. "Who knows, perhaps the day will come when the Off-line Offices, such as Jacksonville, New York, Atlanta, etc., may also have teletypes tied in with the On-Line System." That expansion, though, never happened.[57]

Next came a radio network on the G&F. Having received permission from the Federal Communications Commission, employees in the Engineering Department, with assistance from Motorola, Inc., erected a network of base radio stations, placing these units in Augusta, Douglas, Midville, Moultrie, Nashville, Swainsboro, Valdosta, and Vidalia. Later Adel and Greenwood were added. Also, the Mechanical Department installed radios in the diesel locomotives. Officially, on May 28, 1957, the G&F took to the airways. It now became possible for dispatchers, agents, and track supervisors to maintain contact with trains at all times. Somewhat later cabooses received portable radio telephones, known as "Handy Talkies," allowing conductors and other trainmen to communicate directly with locomotive crews and through them with dispatchers. Yard crews, too, received this equipment.[58]

At first not all train personnel cared for radio technology. "Some have ventured the thought that the Radios were installed to enable Management to spy on the trainmen." Understandably, officials made it clear that that notion was nonsense. "By moving our trains over the System with greater dispatch the savings in more efficient operations will enable the Railroad to better serve its patrons which will result in more business and all will reap the benefits."[59]

It did not take long before G&F employees fully utilized radio communications. "The Radios have proven far more successful than anticipated." This allowed the company to dispose of all of its telegraph lines, the last being the thirty-four mile stretch between Augusta and Torbit, Georgia. No one really questioned the radio contribution to enhanced operating efficiency and safety. Trains moving over the tracks of the Augusta & Summerville Railroad in downtown Augusta, for example, no longer had to stop at DeLaigle Avenue and have a trainman call the dispatcher from a public telephone to receive authority to use the "block," thus saving ten to fifteen minutes.[60]

In the mid-1950s American companies started to acquire state-of-the-art data-processing machines. If ever there was an industry that could profit from this rapidly developing office technology, it was railroads. Mountains of paperwork presented a constant burden. Although not a pioneer, the

In the early 1960s members of the Accounting Department assembled for a group photograph in the G&F general office building in Augusta. Typically railroads in the twentieth century, including the G&F, hired a substantial female workforce for clerical assignments. It was common for marriages to occur between railroad employees. (Frank Napier Coll.)

G&F was hardly far behind other carriers. Less than a year after introduction of the radio communications network, the railroad signed a contract with the International Business Machine Company (IBM) for the lease of electronic accounting equipment. After remodeling and rewiring and followed by final installations in the general office building and extensive employee training, on January 21, 1959, IBM "sorters," "collators," "calculating punches," and other machines began to work their magic. It did not take long before the G&F managed more efficiently a host of accounting functions, including freight waybills, per diem car reports, and payroll records. "One of the best labor-saving uses," remembered an office worker, "was for interline revenue distribution."[61]

As the Wyer report had recommended, the G&F sought to increase its fleet of freight equipment. Although a few years earlier the company had acquired 150 wood-rack cars and built twenty-six all-steel hopper cars for online shipments of chicken feed, there was great need for modern boxcars. Management decided in 1958 that 100 fifty-foot all-steel boxcars with wide doors would help meet its needs in the national freight car pool as well as handle paper shipments from the busy Clyattville mill of Owens-Illinois. Indeed, the G&F had signed a traffic agreement "based on the railroad's ability to furnish suitable cars for loading the paper products of the plant."

Unfortunately, the company's existing fleet of forty-foot cars had small doors, but "transportation of this traffic requires Class A cars, 40 and 50 feet long, with doors 9 feet wide."[62]

As always cost became a grave concern; the price tag for 100 boxcars would total nearly $1 million. Fortunately, there was hope that the recently passed Transportation Act of 1958 might facilitate the purchase, but the application ran into difficulty at the ICC. Luckily the railroad managed to win regulatory approval because of the effective intervention of J. Strom Thurmond, the politically savvy U.S. Senator from South Carolina.[63]

The G&F had strong connections to South Carolina. The company operated more than fifty miles of track in the Palmetto state and Senator Thurmond knew the road well. The Greenwood extension passed through his hometown of Edgefield; in fact, thirty years earlier the future senator had participated in the formal opening of the line. Yet the reason for the senator's helpful involvement most likely stemmed from a recent incident. A powerful thunderstorm had caused minor damage to the property of the senator's sister, who lived along the G&F right-of-way in Edgefield. Section men cleaned up the tree damage, but they did not repair an ancient and long-dilapidated fence that stretched along the railroad. Soon Thurmond, using his official U. S. Senate stationery, demanded that the G&F pay $700 in damages. The claims agent, however, refused, believing that Thurmond was "ripping off the company to help his sister who clearly needed the money." Legal counsel, though, thought it wise to settle. The agent then drove from Augusta to the senator's office in nearby Aiken, South Carolina, and handed over the check. A delighted Thurmond presented the G&F representative with an autographed photograph and commented, "if I can help you in the future, please let me know." This conversation was remembered; the senator was contacted and the ICC, influenced by some clever wire pulling by Thurmond, quickly guaranteed the loan, the first awarded under the legislation. This action permitted the railroad to receive funding of $934,960 from the First National Bank of Atlanta in the form of equipment trust certificates. "Not bad for a $700 investment," recalled the G&F official.[64]

It the latter part of 1959, the G&F took possession of the rolling stock. Manufactured by the Pullman-Standard Company in Michigan City, Indiana, the 100 fifty-foot, six-inch "PS-1 type" all-steel cars were painted green with white striping and lettering. And each contained the road's familiar round logo: FAST DEPENDABLE SERVICE wrapped with GEORGIA & FLORIDA RAILROAD and were numbered in the 400 series. Most of the company's other 199 boxcars, which were considerably older, had only steel under frames.[65]

The Belvin administration did not ignore the continuing need for track betterments. In 1955 and 1956 the company made efforts to improve conditions; the needs were considerable. "Because these tracks had been maintained on ballast consisting of sand, [cinders,] or native soil they were not capable, under increased tonnages and wheel loads, of providing the stability and economy of maintenance required today," explained Chief Engineer Austin. At the end of two years of track work, about ninety miles of the main line had been ballasted, retied, and realigned. But funds for additional work were unavailable, and so once again the company turned to the federal government. Using provisions of the Transportation Act of 1958, the G&F received a $1 million loan guarantee to upgrade an additional 182 miles of line. "The rehabilitation of railroad track with borrowed funds is a rarity," commented Austin. "But, to do such work with the proceeds of loan guaranteed by the federal government is unprecedented in the U.S.A." Once more the First National Bank of Atlanta supplied the money.[66]

In February 1960 crews descended on the track and within two years completed this major rehabilitation. Rock ballast, replacement ties, and ties plates became a part of the widely publicized activities. "With its track rehabilitation program under way and with other impressive improvements being made in the physical properties," boasted Austin in *Railway Age*, "it is anticipated on the G&F that the road will soon be in a better position to attract new business and new industries." Austin was correct, but Belvin and his associates wanted to improve the G&F for possible sale. "The only way out of receivership was to sell out" became the unpublicized view of management insiders.[67]

The much-needed track improvements did not create a main-line speedway, however, as the inherent weakness in the rehabilitation plan involved the rail itself. The G&F could not afford replacement steel, and that meant retaining "ancient" seventy-pound jointed rail, some of which dated back to the time of construction. "This steel had crystallized because of age and became brittle and broke," recalled an employee. The more solid track base, which rock ballast and good ties created, actually caused the vintage rail to become less safe, no longer flexing readily under the weight of a passing train. Section-gang laborers in places loosened the rail joint bars, providing greater play. But by the early 1960s the railroad experienced numerous derailments, including a major wreck north of Midville. The G&F's growing reliance on low-revenue, albeit heavy shipments of pulpwood and rock "broke our track all to pieces." Employees worked extended hours to maintain operations. Commented a trackman, "I've been on call for three straight months."[68]

Not only did the G&F need tons of replacement rails, but also the overall quality of maintenance-of-way equipment remained poor. "Maintenance workers put up with a lot." The company, for example, owned only two Racine power rail saws, one for each maintenance district, but when this equipment broke, trackmen had to use a hacksaw for cutting rail. When crews realigned track, they followed long-established, labor-intensive ways. These mostly black laborers selected a fellow worker who would "call track," and the established cadence of "tap, tap, quit, tap, tap, and pull" emanated from the work site.[69]

Matters other than track occupied the Belvin regime. The company made additional improvements, although hardly unusual or unexpected. The final remanents of the age of steam mostly disappeared, whether coal docks or water tanks. Similarly, changes resulted because of dieselization, including alterations to the locomotive and car repair facilities in Douglas and installation of longer passing sidings. As more sophisticated communications developed and LCL and express service ended, most small-town depots became obsolete. In summer 1958, for example, workers dismantled the badly faded yellow with green trim structure in Denton. "The depot, once the focal point in the town of Denton, became just another place when the passenger trains were discontinuèd some years back," observed the *Douglas Enterprise.* "And last year the railroad decided they needed no agent here. Since that time the Hazlehurst agent has handled all transactions at Denton, and now the depot building itself is no more." Bridges, too, received attention. In March 1955, for example, the Altamaha River trestle rebuilding project was completed, allowing trains to move faster than the long-time restriction of only five miles per hour. Some wooden structures, with their standard 7x14 foot stringers, "required much work, especially as train weights increased."[70]

Even though the G&F needed considerable physical improvements, Belvin and his colleagues continued to work hard to attract long-distance interchange movements. For the season of 1958–1959, traffic personnel spent considerable time focusing on promoting "Perishable Freight From Florida to Central West via SAL-G&F-C&WC-CC&O-C&O and Connections." G&F train crews picked up the interchange cars from the SAL in Vidalia and delivered them at Augusta to the C&WC. Yet most of this northbound perishable traffic continued to move from the SR at Valdosta to the G&F and then to the Piedmont & Northern at Greenwood. "This [perishable] business did help and we tried to get as much of this lucrative traffic as we could." The G&F, like other carriers in the South, had long benefited from the rate divisions on these interterritorial north-south movements. Unfortunately, a less desirable business dominated the freight mix: "Our bread and butter seemed always to be pine pulpwood." The company, however, could not exist on transporting what was admittedly a low-profit commodity. Again, something drastic seemed mandatory, and rumors of a sale spread.[71]

THE SALE

By 1960 the G&F had been in receivership for more than three decades. Since the end of the Purvis regime the railroad, without question, had become a better property. By the mid-1950s the Wyer company agreed that the road "has experienced a good turn around," but still the carrier was barely surviving. Net railway operating income rose from a paltry $10,416 in 1956 to $83,060 a year later, but dropped to $64,814 for 1958. Then the negative impact of a national recession, wet weather, and other problems led to a net railway operating deficit of $29,028 for 1959. That figure then soared to a negative $524,113 for 1960, in part because of frequent, costly train derailments. But the company remained optimistic; for one thing, the overall growth rate of Georgia and other states in the Southeast outpaced the national average. The G&F would surely benefit from a vibrant "New, New South," and there was the expectation, at least the hope, that the G&F would find a merger partner.[72]

By the 1950s most American railroads were hardly money machines. Companies faced various problems, some of which management thought unsolvable. At the forefront of their concerns was growing modal competition. The impact of the Federal-Aid Highway Act of 1956, better known as the "Interstate Highway Act," meant that trucks could compete more effectively with trains by traveling on a rapidly expanding network of high-speed, divided, and limited-access roads. Although the G&F did not encounter construction of a closely parallel interstate highway, long-distance "bridge" traffic, especially perishable and tobacco shipments, became vulnerable to motor-carrier competition. Moreover, by the end of this decade most railroads, including the G&F, had already realized the considerable savings that came from dieselization. Likely the best means for responding to enhanced earnings involved corporate unifications. Acquisitions and mergers had long been part of the industry and explained the very makeup of much of the G&F.[73]

The corporate marriages of the post–World War II period knew no geographical bounds. By 1960 the South had already seen some of the most important railroad unions. As early as 1946 the ACL absorbed the Atlanta, Birmingham & Coast (nee Atlanta, Birmingham & Atlantic), both interchange partners of the G&F; a year later the Gulf, Mobile & Ohio acquired the Chicago & Alton, and in 1951, the CofG took control of the Savannah & Atlanta, again connecting roads for the G&F. Then in 1957, the large-scale wave of unifications began when the Nashville, Chattanooga & St. Louis joined the Louisville & Nashville (L&N). "Merger madness" was now in the immediate offing, and shortly would intensify and persist, ultimately by the 1990s producing two colossal companies in the East and two giants in the West. In 1960 the ACL and SAL agreed to merge, and the Southern Railway planned to acquire the CofG; both proposed consolidations would have enormous import to the G&F. Moreover, rumors circulated of other corporate marriages in the region. What would little G&F do? Of course, Belvin and his associates wanted to find a home for their road, hopefully a suitor that would protect investors, customers, and themselves.[74]

The possibilities were limited, however, as the G&F would need to join a large, connecting railroad, probably the ACL, SAL, or SR. In the 1920s the ICC, responding to the dictates of the Transportation Act of 1920, contemplated a limited number of systems. In the tentative plan of consolidation released on August 3, 1921, the ICC placed the G&F with the ACL-L&N, creating "System No. 11—Atlantic Coast Line-Louisville & Nashville." The pairing involved not only the principal roads but also a number of smaller, albeit similar-sized carriers, including the Atlanta, Birmingham & Atlantic; Gulf, Mobile & Northern; Norfolk Southern and Mississippi Central. The second plan, triggered by complaints and additional thinking and made public on December 9, 1929, arranged the G&F in "System No. 9—Southern." This alignment revolved around the mighty SR together with a host of mostly insignificant shortlines, ranging from the Augusta Northern to the Ware Shoals railroads. Only the Florida East Coast, Norfolk Southern, and Tennessee Central were comparable to the G&F. Because of continued corporate wrangling, the Great Depression, and World War II, few mergers occurred until after 1945.[75]

It is not known when G&F officials began to think seriously about finding a corporate partner, although Belvin realized that if the 314-mile G&F could modernize, a suitable suitor might be found. The alternative involved selling off viable parts either to Class I roads or possibly to existing or new shortline operators and junking the rest. Also, some of the rolling stock, notably the diesel-locomotives and modern freight cars, had considerable value on the used-equipment market. The company, however, really did not have major physical assets other than track and rolling stock. It owned limited property, having earlier sold off the best parcels to raise capital for dieselization. In Augusta the G&F rented the general office building; moreover, its small local yards were in a "rough section of town."[76]

As merger activities accelerated, Belvin "sweated blood and tears" to get the G&F sold. In the summer of 1960 efforts began in earnest. Belvin preferred the ACL or SAL, whose leaders he trusted, especially W. Thomas "Tom" Rice of the ACL. The other real possibility was the SR. This 8,200-mile rail system, which in recent years had been an annoyance to the G&F, partly because of a long, contentious fight about rental fees for the Savannah River bridge, was led by the brilliant Dennis William "Bill" Brosnan (executive vice-president, 1952–1962, and president, 1962–1967). Belvin and his associates knew that Brosnan had worked wonders, making the SR into a highly profitable carrier by cutting operating costs through mechanization and centralization. Yet Brosnan was an "extremely difficult" individual. "Bill was never constrained by the niceties of humanity," commented a long-time colleague. "He used whatever means were needed that were legal. People below him feared him and tried to avoid him." A junior officer at the SR remembered Brosnan as being totally in charge and independent. "Brosnan would listen to the lawyers and then he would announce that the company would go the opposite way." Another Brosnan observer wrote that "he disdained mindless government bureaucracy, micromanaged his company to a fault, infuriated his rank-and-file employees, and controlled his managers alternatively with fear and greed."[77]

As the decade began, Belvin met with officials of the three potential buyers. The SAL indicated no interest; the ACL and SR, however, were willing to negotiate. "The G&F fit logically into both the ACL and Southern," recalled a high-ranking SR legal officer, "but nobody needed the G&F." Likely involved at the heart of the explanation were matters of strategy and self-protection, specifically the trackage rights agreement that SR had won in 1902 to operate over the ACL between Hardeeville, South Carolina, and Jacksonville, Florida. If somehow the status quo were to change, perhaps the result of the highly contested merger between ACL and SAL, the SR would suffer. Ownership of the G&F, however, would allow SR to move Atlanta-Macon traffic through Hazlehurst to Valdosta over G&F rails and then use affiliate Georgia Southern & Florida to Jacksonville. The G&F held value for the SR and arguably for ACL *if* that carrier wished to cause mischief. For years there was clearly no love lost between the two roads, especially from the SR perspective. "The Southern Railway had such disdain for the Coast Line management and Coast Line operations," recalled Jervis Langdon, Jr., a prominent railroad executive who once headed the Association of Southeastern Railroads. Still, for either the ACL or SR, the G&F would not be a costly acquisition; its estimated value ranged from $6.5 to $7.5 million.[78]

Fortunately, both the ACL and SR made bids. Initially, Belvin discussed the sale with the SR. Brosnan reportedly told Belvin that "$6.8 million is as high as I am going to go." Belvin then talked with Rice and he agreed to $7 million. Belvin was satisfied, believing that this was going to be the final offer and one that the receiver and judge would gladly sanction. Alfred Jones, the consummate businessman, however, told Belvin to go back to Brosnan and see if the SR would raise the ACL bid. Belvin agreed but he responded, "I'll be damn surprised if Brosnan says yes." In the meeting that followed Belvin explained that the ACL would pay somewhat more. Brosnan then told Belvin: "I don't want or need your railroad," even though the SR had become interested in shortline acquisitions, including the decrepit "Pidcock Kingdom" of roads in south Georgia. Assuming that a deal was dead, Belvin started to leave the room. "Sit down!" shouted Brosnan. "I will be God-damned if Tom Rice is going to have it!" Belvin walked away with an offer of $7.5 million. Related Belvin, "The deal was made in anger." Of course, Belvin was pleased as were Jones and Judge Scarlett.[79]

Action on the sale proceeded steadily, and on June 27, 1961, both parties confirmed the financial arrangement. Then on December 11, 1961, in the lobby of the Augusta-Richmond County Municipal Building, the assets of the G&F were sold in a public auction with the SR being the sole bidder. While technically the G&F had not yet become a "fallen flag" road, the sale needed only approval by the federal court and the ICC. A joint statement, made by Jones and Brosnan at the brief ceremony, said that "due to impending and vital necessary developments in the railroad industry, the prospects at this time are such that the future of G. & F. and its employees must be considered in grave doubt unless Southern's offer is approved and consummated." Their communique added that "Southern's acquisition of the line would serve to stabilize employment of the G. & F. and its continuation as a common carrier, serving the many communities located along its line and assisting in their future development."[80]

Although Judge Scarlett took less than two weeks to bestow the court's blessing, the ICC was another matter. It was not until early January 1963 that an ICC examiner recommended sale and on March 29, 1963, the full commission sanctioned the purchase. The ICC agreed to formation of a "new" G&F, namely the Georgia and Florida *Railway*, controlled by SR subsidiaries Carolina & Northwestern Railway; Live Oak, Perry & Gulf Railroad and South Georgia Railroad. The delay was hardly exceptional; the ICC bureaucracy rarely moved with dispatch.[81]

The hearings, however, were not wholly perfunctory. As with all merger proceedings, objections developed. Both the ACL and Piedmont & Northern worried about the loss of interchange traffic and sought guarantees for this business. Moreover, the Railway Labor Executives' Association, which represented G&F brotherhoods, demanded protection arrangements.[82]

The concerned parties received modest considerations. In its final report the ICC stipulated that "the present traffic and operating relationships existing between the Georgia & Florida Railroad, on the one hand, and all lines connecting with its tracks, on the other, shall be continued insofar as such matters are within the control of the applicants." And the ICC concluded that "we must provide as a minimum the protection to employees required by [statute]." This meant adherence to the so-called New Orleans agreements, allowing employees who lost their jobs to receive pay for a four-year period. The ICC commissioners, though, rejected the examiner's recommendation that the body add provisions for arbitration of labor disputes, contending that "although consummation will result in some losing their jobs, failure of the transaction may cause a loss of employment by all, without separation pay or other benefits." No one seemed surprised by the ICC's positions or by its approval of the sale.[83]

If G&F leaders anticipated a smooth transition to SR control, their expectations did not materialize. The explanation involved Bill Brosnan. When the SR executive learned of the labor-protection provisions, he became enraged. "When I reported to Mr. Brosnan that the ICC had approved the purchase and added, as a sort of minor footnote, that they had attached the usual New Orleans labor conditions," remembered company attorney William McLean, "he went through the ceiling." Bronsan despised organized labor, especially the "featherbedding firemen's union," considering the brotherhoods roadblocks to progress and prosperity.[84]

G&F leaders realized that Brosnan's displeasure might derail their agreement. The SR executive made it clear that he would not accept labor protection, no matter what the ICC said. But Belvin, Jones, and Scarlett were not

After 1963 the influence of the new owner, the Southern Railway, became apparent in the motive power. Although No. 71, an SW acquired from EMD by the G&F in 1950, had served the railroad for more than a decade, a new paint and lettering scheme had been added and mechanical improvements made. In August 1964 No. 71 stands with a short train of company pulpwood cars in Sparks, Georgia. (O.W. Kimsey, Jr. photograph, Robert H. Hanson Coll.)

about to accept possible defeat. And their collective response proved clever and successful, although resolving the labor issue delayed Brosnan's acceptance until June 29, 1963.[85]

Prior to the formal decision of the ICC made in late March, Belvin and Elton Cartrett, G&F personal director, met with employees to urge them to sign a petition sanctioning the sale, wishing to strengthen the case of the company before the regulators. The initial stumbling block occurred in Douglas where shop workers were reluctant to endorse any document. Shopmen worried that they might be discharged prior to the formal sale, thus losing wage protections. "We want it in writing that we'll be employees at the date of consummation of sale," explained F. W. McCarty, a union spokesman. Belvin refused.[86]

The labor situation deteriorated following final ICC approval. The 123 members of the Brotherhood of Maintenance-of-Way Employees balked at the labor proposal. They demanded meaningful protection, fearing (correctly) that their positions would be eliminated with "internal improvements and mechanization" of the G&F by the SR. And shop workers continued to object. The G&F responded by laying off twenty-two clerks, twenty-two mechanical department employees, and sixty-six maintenance-of-way workers, arguing that business declined appreciably because of uncertainty about the road's fate and hinting that a total shutdown of operations would soon take place. Simultaneously the SR blasted the ICC for recommending "costly labor protective conditions which would largely nullify the advantage of buying the G&F."[87]

Labor made known its feelings. In a statement, distributed to the news media on April 30, 1963, by a spokesman for the craft unions, the issues were outlined.

> It is with great regret that the representatives of the employees of the Georgia and Florida Railroad are compelled to announce that the Southern Railway Company has refused to abide by the condition imposed by the Interstate Commerce Commission in its order approving the sale of the Georgia and Florida to the Southern, condition which the Southern in its application to the Commission informed that agency it would accept.
>
> The provisions regarding employees offered by the Southern are less than the minimum required by the Interstate Commerce Act and the Commission would not and could not have approved the sale of the Georgia & Florida to the Southern on that basis.
>
> The Southern has also refused to abide by the provisions of all agreements in effect since 1940 on that railroad and since 1954 on the Georgia & Florida which relates to the protection of employees involved in transfer of work and coordination of facilities.
>
> For these reasons and because the Southern adamantly refuses any protection whatever to more than one-third of the employees of the Georgia & Florida, it does not presently appear that an agreement can be reached.[88]

A full-blown crisis had developed. As Belvin told his son, "The unions are getting in the damn way of this sale." On April 23, at the request of Belvin and Jones, Judge Scarlett sanctioned a traffic embargo that led to a nearly complete shutdown of the Greenwood extension and more limited business on the remainder of the road. Explained the press, "that means that the railroad cannot accept freight for transfer to other railroads without express orders from the G&F traffic department." On May 6, 1963, the last through revenue train operated between Greenwood and Valdosta. Soon thereafter the press reported that on May 17, Judge Scarlett, responding to a petition submitted by the receiver, would hold hearings "on liquidation of the railroad and winding up of the receivership." There would then be no sale to the SR.[89]

Newspapers throughout the Wiregrass Region editorialized on the need to save the G&F. "The Georgia and Florida . . . is vastly too important to the overall economy of this area of Georgia and South Carolina to be lost through liquidation," stated the *Augusta Chronicle* in a typical response. "We urge the operating employees of the G&F, as well as officials of the Southern, to consider this as they meet in what could be the last opportunity to preserve the G&F intact."[90]

Judge Scarlett held the widely publicized hearing. He approved closing down permanently the G&F and directed submission of a liquidation plan to the ICC. "It hurts us all to see this road go," he told a courtroom filled with lawyers, union representatives, and other interested persons. Yet the judge left open the possibility of resuming operations should an agreement on labor protection occur.[91]

While the public and possibly labor believed what they heard or read, the events of late April and May had been carefully orchestrated by Belvin, Jones, and Scarlett. It did not take long before Belvin told union leaders that the G&F would be junked. "We can get more money if we liquidate. Let's fold the tent." But there was considerable skepticism. Indeed, the brotherhood representatives told Belvin that "the railroad was junk and that other carriers wouldn't be interested in its rolling stock and the like." Belvin quickly responded that they were wrong. "We can sell equipment in Mexico and other underdeveloped countries. Ours is modern when compared to what they have." And Belvin reiterated the view that if the sale failed, *all* workers would likely become jobless as a result of liquidation. It did not take long before these men relented, saying "Hell, we'll sign the [SR] agreement." The embargo and liquidation threat, then, "was all part of bluff agreed to by Dad, Jones and Scarlett and a well-kept secret," recalled Belvin's son. "My daddy played that so well."[92]

With the brotherhoods on the G&F finally accepting labor-protection terms that were less than what the ICC customarily dictated, the SR moved speedily to take control of the property. Public reaction was universally positive. Shippers were delighted that normal service quickly resumed, especially companies that depended heavily on the railroad. The Albion Kaoline Division of Interchemical Corporation, for one, which operated a kaolin mine near Hephzibah, faced the likelihood of shutting down. Members of local chambers of commerce and related civic promotional efforts like "Blast-Off Boosters of Berrien County" believed that with strong ownership, new industries would come to G&F rails. Although for decades the G&F had engaged in developmental work, the SR operated a large, professional, and successful industrial-development organization. "The prospects for industrial growth along the line will be enhanced by the greater stability provided by Southern's operation," editorialized the *Douglas Enterprise,* "and its proven ability to attract industry." And it was assumed, based on earlier statements by SR, that the new regime would upgrade trackage and provide improved rolling stock, including more powerful diesel-electric locomotives and specialized freight cars.[93]

The leaders of the G&F were relieved and satisfied. Belvin would remain as president of the G&F *Railway,* and he was delighted. Moreover, the court compensated Jones and the Hull legal firm handsomely for their involvement. The SR easily raised $7.5 million by floating a $50 million bond issue, largely designed by the acquisition of the CofG. Holders of receiver certificates were paid off first; any balance went to owners of first-mortgage bonds. In the case of Jones, Hull, and possibly others, these men, anticipating a handsome return on their speculative investments, had purchased at dirt-cheap prices sizeable amounts of the outstanding debts. In July 1957, for example, the Sea Island Company, Jones's firm, acquired $110,000 of G&F first-mortgage bonds (6% 1946 Series A) for $16,500. After the sale, owners received a quarter of the face value for these obligations, yielding in this instance $27,500 for Sea Island. Surely these financial antics smacked of "inside trading."[94]

Communities along the Greenwood to Valdosta main line and the Nashville to Moultrie branch believed that at last the G&F would become a truly modern railroad. Likely the reorganized company, with direct ties to a thriving interregional carrier and "hometown" service, would serve well the needs of shippers for decades to come. That expectation, though, would not prove to be correct.

Epilogue

The pervasive optimism that prevailed when the Southern Railway (SR) officially took control of the Georgia & Florida Railroad (G&F) in 1963 continued for several years. Immediately following the takeover, the "new" Georgia & Florida *Railway* (G&FRy) and parent SR received positive acclaim. In July 1963 the *Coffee County Progress*, for one, featured a front-page photograph of a modern tie-replacement machine with this caption: "Meet Mr. Monster—The Southern Railway machine now in Douglas getting ready for track repairs up and down the 300 mile track of the Georgia and Florida." Subsequently the *Douglas Enterprise*, the town's other newspaper, editorialized happily that the "Southern has a strong record supporting the fact that industry follows its track." And at the end of 1963 SR President D. W. Brosnan told area journalists that "we work toward our goal of making the Georgia & Florida a valuable economic force in the communities it serves." He added, "there is great potential for industrial growth and our Industrial Development people will do everything possible to get new industries to locate along the railway." Somewhat later J. Pete Belvin, who remained in charge of the G&F, informed the press that "since the G&F has been sold to the Southern Railway Company, there has been more inquiries from prospective new industries than in the past 10 years combined." These events encouraged shippers, civic boosters, and others interested in better rail service for the Wiregrass Region. Yet privately, the SR wondered, "what the hell are we going to do with this railroad?"[1]

When the ownership changed, the common consensus among SR personnel was that the G&F was just a "big run-down shortline." Indeed, the belief existed that train movements were exceedingly dangerous, but there was a grudging admiration for what G&F maintenance forces had accomplished. "Southern [Railway] people were amazed with what we could get by with in regards to our 'rotten' physical plant," recalled a former employee. "One Southern official wanted to condemn a major bridge, but it really needed only modest repairs. The old cypress timbers were exceedingly strong and durable." Although there were trouble spots, especially during periods of wet weather, the Belvin regime had made considerable improvements to the track structure. The exception, of course, was the often brittle rail.[2]

In 1978 the remains of the Georgia & Florida, nee Augusta Southern, depot still stood in Mitchell, Georgia. The "Colored Waiting Room" sign hangs over a structure that had been abandoned nearly forty-five years earlier. (Larry Goolsby photograph)

It did not take long before even casual observers noticed physical improvements. By summer 1963 mechanized track crews arrived on the property. These men and their machines started south of Midville, picking up the seventy-pound rail to create a long stretch of continuous welded rail (CWR) or "ribbon rail." The SR temporarily installed heavier, jointed rail that was superior to the steel it replaced and a joy to train and track crews alike. Seeking to keep rail-improvement costs low, however, the SR had workers weld together most of the old rail. This was a rare instance of a railroad creating such lightweight CWR. Yet this ribbon rail produced stronger track and required less maintenance, reducing derailments and allowing for increased train speeds (thirty miles per hour or higher). Construction workers also appeared in the Gwinnett Street neighborhood (south of Laney Walker Boulevard) of Augusta, where the SR spent $600,000 to consolidate and expand yard facilities for its local operations and those of affiliates Central of Georgia Railway and G&FRy. Soon the old Twiggs Street Yard of the G&F largely disappeared, initially being used by the SR for locomotives to lay over in Augusta. Norfolk Southern Corporation (NS), successor to SR, however, never used the G&F complex in any capacity and by 2005 only one track remained.[3]

A section of the former G&F right-of-way received a major upgrade. In 1966 the SR took possession of the Georgia Northern (GN), which connected with the G&FRy at Moultrie, and then used the GN and the G&FRy's Moultrie-Sparks line as part of its vaunted Atlanta-Macon Bypass that allowed faster freight service between Birmingham, Alabama, and Florida points. "High iron" now rested on about twenty miles of G&FRy right-of-way. Years later, however, the NS altered traffic patterns and disposed of portions of this route to shortline operators, including the one-time G&F trackage.[4]

Under SR control, the more than fifty-year-old shops complex in Douglas closed. The SR had no need for this small, outdated facility. By 1965 the equipment was mostly scrapped (or taken home by employees), the old buildings and property sold, and structures eventually razed. Unlike some railroad communities, whether a Bradford, Ohio; Horton, Kansas; or Spencer, North Carolina, the loss of the G&F facilities did not damage seriously the Douglas economy. Soon the local press crowed about the increase in new jobs, nearly 500 between June 1963 and July 1964 alone. Additional employment opportunities had come about, sparked in late 1964 by the arrival of the Biltmore Mobile Homes Company. The community's low labor costs, reasonable taxes, mild winter climate, and growing junior college helped to attract industries.[5]

The fate of former G&F employees, though, varied. Those who had jobs that were unprotected by the labor agreement drifted into the regional workforce. Some found employment on neighboring railroads while others took jobs in expanding communities, particularly Augusta, Douglas, and Valdosta. In the mid-1960s both the national and regional economies were robust. For those ex-G&F workers who were eligible, several score opted for severance payments. In September 1963 the G&FRy distributed checks totaling $240,000 to forty-five former employees, and more payouts followed. The SR retained several G&F officials, but these men may have been disappointed. Stuart Austin, the company's chief engineer, for one, received an assignment to the Spring Street office complex in Atlanta and "was placed in a cubicle with nothing to do." In time Austin resigned "since he enjoyed being out in the field" and entered the railroad contracting business. Those blue-collar workers who remained with the SR generally prospered. In early 1967, they had their pay raised to the "standard rail industry level," something that the G&F had never been able to achieve.[6]

Former G&F employees not only found more in their paychecks, but they benefited also from a better workplace. Modern power track equipment, for example, enhanced productivity and eased physical strain. "Mr. Monster" was but one of many useful machines. Although the G&F's motive power adequately pulled the slow-moving freight trains, the SR added to the fleet. In 1961 the company had sold to the G&F No. 801, an elderly albeit rebuilt Electro-Motive Division "F" [freight] locomotive, and soon after the takeover provided No. 4192, another F unit. All engines received mechanical upgrades and the standard Southern black, white and gold paint treatment.[7]

The altered livery served as an omen of sorts. On June 1, 1971, the formal corporate obituary for the G&F, technically the G&FRy, could at last be written. Earlier in the year the Interstate Commerce Commission (ICC) granted the SR permission to unify several properties it owned. Specifically, the SR had the G&FRy, Central of Georgia *Railway*, Savannah & Atlanta Railway, and Wrightsville & Tennille Railroad placed in the new Central of Georgia *Railroad*. "The proposed consolidation is a part of an overall plan of corporate simplification undertaken by Southern and its subsidiaries," observed the ICC. "The transaction will result in the substitution of a single new carrier corporation for four corporate entities." Added the ICC, "The consolidation will also simplify accounting and financial reporting, eliminate the necessity of separate corporate boards of directors and officers, permit various operating and managerial economies, eliminate certain interchanges, and simplify tariff and routing provisions." The G&F of John Skelton Williams, Hugh W. Purvis, and J. Pete Belvin was no more.[8]

The corporate demise of the G&F understandably attracted attention from area journalists. Lurner Williams, a correspondent for the *Atlanta Journal and Constitution,* contributed a personal essay to the Sunday edition. "June 1, they discontinued the name 'Georgia & Florida,' or 'G&F' for the road, but they cannot erase the memory of the trains, the sounds, the events, of those who grew up along the line, beside the tracks." Reflected Williams, "In fact, for this reporter, it was not pleasing when they brought in the big, shiny diesels to replace the coal-burning engines that puffed and chugged up the hill from Whitehead creek into Denton, and then the laborious puffing and huffing away from the Denton depot after letting off passengers and the mail. Good-bye G&F—but not my memories."[9]

It would not be long before the departed G&F began to disappear physically. In December 1980 the SR and Norfolk & Western Railway asked the ICC for authority to merge. In time their request received the green light, and on June 1, 1982, the 17,000-mile Norfolk Southern Corporation made

A section of a modern steel bridge stands on the abandoned Greenwood extension, a reminder that this piece of G&F trackage had experienced a relatively short life. (Jack Parker photograph)

its official debut. Excess trackage soon drew the attention of management. Of the 2,700 miles of lightly used rail lines, the company ultimately decided that about 1,500 should be abandoned but that the remaining possessed shortline potential. The result was formation of the Thoroughbred Short Line Program in which NS helped buyers, often start-up shortlines, acquire this economically viable trackage.[10]

The policy of retrenchment affected former G&F trackage. The Greenwood extension was retired in pieces, and portions of the Augusta-Valdosta line also changed dramatically. NS kept the track from Augusta to near Hephzibah, but abandoned the remaining portion to Midville. By the 1990s the segment between Midville, Swainsboro and Kirby had become property of the Georgia Department of Transportation (GDOT) and leased to the Heart of Georgia Railroad, a for-profit contract operator. Further south, the NS retained the segment between Vidalia and Hazlehurst, using portions for car storage. This track ultimately became inactive, although GDOT purchased part of the line south of Vidalia. Between Hazlehurst and Valdosta, some trackage disappeared, although public authorities acquired from NS the Willacoochee-Valdosta segment. Ultimately, the Georgia & Florida Railroad Company, Inc., a new corporation, provided service to several

Portions of the former G&F main line remain in place but unused. The inactivity of the track south of the Altamaha River bridge is evident in this photograph made in the spring of 2004. (Author's photograph)

shippers, mostly located in Nashville and near Willacoochee. NS also retired the links between Nashville, Sparks and Adel. (Although unrelated to NS, in 1992 the truncated, ten-mile Valdosta Southern Railroad became the Valdosta Railway, LP.) Appearance of these small shortlines was strongly reminiscent of those independent predecessor companies that nearly a century earlier had become the core of the G&F. A cyclical process had seemingly occurred.[11]

Although it is still possible to see a train rumbling over a few sections of the former G&F rails, other parts also survive. Former depots stand in several communities, including Hephzibah, Douglas, and Modoc, and the old two-story general office building in downtown Augusta has recently undergone an extensive remodeling. Small portions of the right-of-way have become recreational rails-to-trails, six miles in the vicinity of North Augusta and shorter distances in Greenwood and Douglas. And that signature structure, the stately Altamaha River bridge, still stands, albeit badly rusted. It remains a local landmark and a fitting symbol for the "God Forgotten" or as some rail enthusiasts have said: "The Gone & Forgotten."[12]

There is much more to the legacy of the G&F. The company long realized that the prosperity of the Wiregrass Region was in its own self-interest. Whether onions, tobacco, or watermelons, extensive promotion of diversified agriculture left a lasting mark and arguably a better reminder of this railroad than a building, path, or bridge. The railroad and its territory were wholly linked.

Notes

1—BEFORE THE G&F

1. Samuel Melanchthon Derrick, *Centennial History of South Carolina Railroad* (Columbia, SC: The State Company, 1930), 82–127; John F. Stover, *Iron Road to the West: American Railroads in the 1850s* (New York: Columbia University Press, 1978), 90–92; Robert C. Black, III, *The Railroads of the Confederacy* (Chapel Hill, NC: University of North Carolina Press, 1952), 20–21.

2. Peter S. McGuire, "The Railroads of Georgia, 1860–1880," *Georgia Historical Quarterly* 16 (September 1932): 179; *Thirty-Sixth Report of the Railroad Commission of Georgia* (Atlanta, GA: Foote & Davies Company, 1908), 11–14.

3. C. R. Fish, "The Restoration of the Southern Railroads," in *University of Wisconsin Studies in the Social Sciences and History* (Madison, WI: University of Wisconsin, 1919), 5; Howard D. Dozier, *A History of the Atlantic Coast Line Railroad* (Boston, MA: Houghton Mifflin Company, 1920), 139.

4. *Prospectus: The Middle Georgia and Atlantic Railway* (n.p. ca. 1890), 2.

5. Barton C. Shaw, *The Wool-Hat Boys: Georgia's Populist Party* (Baton Rouge, LA: Louisiana State University Press, 1984), 5–77; C. Van Woodward, *Tom Watson: Agrarian Rebel* (New York: Rinehart & Company, 1938), 146–66.

6. Woodward, *Tom Watson*, 370–95; Alton D. Jones, "Progressivism in Georgia, 1898–1918" (Ph.D. diss., Emory University, 1963), 93–99, 105–6.

7. See Wilber W. Caldwell, *The Courthouse and the Depot: The Architecture of Hope in an Age of Despair* (Macon, GA: Mercer University Press, 2001).

8. *Pine Forest* (Swainsboro, GA), July 4, 1901.

9. *First Annual Report of the Georgia and Florida Railway For the Year Ending June 30, 1908* (Richmond, VA: Georgia & Florida Railway Company, 1908), 3.

10. "Corporate History of the Georgia and Florida," Interstate Commerce Commission, National Archives, Record Group 134, Box 560, hereafter cited as "Corporate History of the G&F."

11. *Abstract of the Fourteenth Census of the United States* (Washington, DC: Government Printing Office, 1923), 53; "Plan of the Organization and Development of the Georgia & Florida Railway: Letter from the President to the Syndicate Managers, January 1, 1907," John Skelton Williams Papers, University of Virginia Library, Charlottesville, VA; George Crowder, "Origin and Development of the Georgia and Florida Railroad," *Georgia & Florida Bulletin* 6 (August 1929): 14–16; *First Annual Report of the Georgia and Florida Railway*, 3.

12. *First Annual Report of the Georgia and Florida Railway*, 3; George W. Hilton, *American Narrow Gauge Railroads* (Stanford, CA: Stanford University Press, 1990), 373; *True Citizen* (Waynesboro, GA), July 22, 1893; "Augusta & Florida," *Railway Age* 40 (September 8, 1905): 303.

13. Robert H. Hanson, compiler, "The Railroads of Georgia, 1833–2000," privately printed, n.p.; "Augusta & Florida," *Railway Age* 38 (December 2, 1904): 802; *Forest-Blade*

(Swainsboro, GA), January 12, 1905; February 9, 1905; April 6, 1905; September 14, 1905; Albert M. Hillhouse, *A History of Burke County, Georgia, 1777–1950* (Swainsboro, GA: Magnolia Press, 1985), 208.

14. *Augusta* (GA) *Chronicle,* September 3, 1905.

15. "Georgia & Florida Railroad Roster," Georgia & Florida Railroad Collection, Railway & Locomotive Historical Society, Sacramento, CA; *Official Railway Equipment Register* 22 (July 1906): 176.

16. *Forest-Blade,* September 14, 1905; August 31, 1905; November 30, 1905; February 1, 1906.

17. Hanson, "The Railroads of Georgia," n.p.

Red Bluff, a hamlet in Montgomery County, now part of Treutlen County, Georgia, was located near the Oconee River.

18. Hanson, "The Railroads of Georgia," n.p.; *Forest-Blade,* March 2, 1905; James E. Dorsey, *Footprints Along the Hoopee: A History of Emanuel County, 1812–1900* (Spartanburg, SC: The Reprint Company, 1978), 163.

19. Caldwell, *The Courthouse and the Depot,* 447–48; *Poor's Manual of Railroads, 1894* (New York: H. V. & H. W. Poor, 1894), 1351; Dorsey, *Footprints Along the Hoopee,* 168.

20. Dorsey, *Footprints Along the Hoopee,* 164; *Forest-Blade,* December 15, 1904; *Pine Forest,* March 14, 1901.

Toward the end of its corporate life the MS&RB owned three locomotives and twenty-two cars. *Official Equipment Register* 19 (January 1904): 169.

21. *Forest-Blade,* June 2, 1904; Roland Harper diary, April 4, 1904, Roland Harper Collection, W. S. Hoole Special Collections Library, University of Alabama, Tuscaloosa, hereafter cited as Harper diary.

22. *Forest-Blade,* March 23, 1905.

23. Ibid., August 16, 1906; *Pine Forest,* June 18, 1903.

24. Hanson, "The Railroads of Georgia," n.p; *Poor's Manual of Railroads, 1894,* 177.

25. "Origins of the Georgia and Florida Railroad, and Development," in possession of John E. Parker, Aiken, South Carolina; New York News Bureau news clipping, September 3, 1897, in Pliny Fisk Collection, John W. Barriger III National Railroad Library, University of Missouri-St. Louis; *Pine Forest,* March 21, 1901.

26. *Forest-Blade,* February 18, 1904; February 25, 1904.

27. Ibid., January 26, 1905; October 12, 1905; *Watt's Official Railway Guide of the South,* May 1906, n. p.

About the time the G&F acquired the M&SW, the shortline owned seven locomotives, eighteen forty-foot flatcars, three coaches, and four combination baggage and mail cars. *Official Equipment Register* 19 (January 1904): 94.

28. "Corporate History of the G&F"; Hanson, "The Railroads of Georgia," n.p.

29. "Corporate History of the G&F"; *Douglas* (GA) *Enterprise,* December 15, 1966; *Douglas* (GA) *Weekly Breeze,* July 9, 1902; January 23, 1904; Harper diary, May 14, 1904; *Official Guide of the Railways* (New York: National Railway Publication Co., June 1903), 893; *Waycross* (GA) *Journal,* September 2, 1902; October 28, 1902; *Thirteenth Census of the United States Taken in the Year 1910, Population* (Washington, DC: Government Printing Office, 1913), II: 345.

30. Warren P. Ward, *Ward's History of Coffee County* (Atlanta, GA: Foote & Davis, 1930), 150; *Douglas Breeze,* June 14, 1895; August 13, 1898; July 9, 1902; *Douglas Weekly Breeze,* October 1, 1904; October 8, 1904.

The Douglas & McDonald Railroad reflected the nature of logging tramroads frequently found in the Wiregrass Region. Remembered Albert Lott, a lifelong resident of Coffee County, "The first engine to come in on the tram road was known as the 'Black Bull.' It was an old wood burner and had a cabbage head smoke stack, and its only passenger car was a converted caboose. What a rough ride that was." *Douglas Enterprise,* December 15, 1966.

Douglas also experienced another transportation betterment, a two-mile "bicycle road" between the town and Gaskin Springs, location of a health spa and Methodist religious encampment. The overall poverty of the region undoubtedly explains why a graded path for bicycles was built rather than either an animal-car street railway or an electric trolley, the likely response to a similar transportation need in a more prosperous region. See Thomas Hubert Frier, *Gaskin Springs: A Centennial History of the Famous South Georgia Camp Ground* (Toccoa, GA: Currahee Printing Co., 1995), 7.

31. *Douglas Weekly Breeze,* December 12, 1903; *Waycross Journal,* April 26, 1904; Harper diary, May 14, 1904.

32. *Forest-Blade,* November 3, 1904; *Waycross Journal,* February 26, 1904.

33. "Origins of the Georgia and Florida Railroad, and Development"; Hanson, "The Railroads of Georgia," n.p.; *Nashville* (GA) *Herald,* January 27, 1905; *Forest-Blade,* February 25, 1904; April 6, 1905.

34. Hanson, "The Railroads of Georgia," n.p.

35. Ibid.

36. Ibid., *Nashville Herald,* January 29, 1904.

37. *Douglas Breeze,* February 2, 1896; *Douglas Enterprise,* November 27, 1909; *Nashville Herald,* April 8, 1904; June 3, 1904.

38. *Forest-Blade,* November 3, 1904; *Douglas Weekly Breeze,* August 20, 1904.

39. *Valdosta* (GA) *Times,* June 11, 1904.

40. *Douglas Weekly Breeze,* March 11, 1905; *Nashville Herald,* December 9, 1904.

41. "Douglas, Augusta & Gulf," *Railway Age* 39 (May 26, 1905): 835; *Nashville Herald,* January 20, 1905; May 19, 1905.

42. Hanson, "The Railroads of Georgia," n.p.; *Official Guide of the Railways* (New York: National Railway Publication Company, July 1906), 1011.

43. *Douglas Weekly Breeze,* February 25, 1905.

44. *Nashville Herald,* September 29, 1905; July 27, 1906; August 3, 1906; September 21, 1906.

45. Hanson, "The Railroads of Georgia," n.p.; *Adel* (GA) *News,* March 8, 1901.

46. Ibid.; *Index-Journal* (Greenwood, SC), June 19, 1929; *Poor's Manual of the Railroads of the United States, 1906* (New York: Poor's Railroad Manual Co., 1906), 271; *Nashville Herald,* March 30, 1906; April 7, 1906.

47. *Nashville Herald,* April 15, 1904; April 7, 1906; July 20, 1904.

48. *Thirteenth Census of the United States Taken in the Year 1910,* 342; *Nashville Herald,* August 31, 1906.

49. Hanson, "The Railroads of Georgia," n.p.

50. *Nashville Herald,* April 22, 1904; "Corporate History of the G&F."

51. *Nashville Herald,* January 27, 1905.

52. "Corporate History of the G&F."

53. Hanson, "The Railroads of Georgia," n.p.; "Corporate History of the G&F"; *History of Lowndes County, Georgia, 1825–1941* (Valdosta, GA: General James Jackson Chapter, D.A.R., 1942), 209; Russell Tedder, "A History of the Valdosta Southern Railroad—Including the Development of the Georgia & Florida Railroad in South Georgia and North Florida," privately printed, 2002, 1.

54. Tedder, "A History of the Valdosta Southern Railroad," 1–2; "Corporate History of the G&F."

55. Tedder, "A History of the Valdosta Southern Railroad," 3; *Poor's Manual of Railroads of the United States, 1906,* 275; "Georgia & Florida Railroad Roster"; *New Enterprise* (Madison, FL), August 7, 1902.

56. Clipping from *Valdosta Daily Times,* n.d., Lowndes County Historical Society, Valdosta, GA; Harper diary, September 2, 1902; *New Enterprise,* January 17, 1907.

57. Tedder, "A History of the Valdosta Southern Railroad," 3–4; Harper diary, September 2, 1902; Valdosta Southern R.R. Co., Time Table No. 11, July 21, 1907, Lowndes County Historical Society.

58. *New Enterprise,* May 21, 1903.

59. *Poor's Manual of Railroads of the United States, 1906,* 275; "Plan of the Organization and Development of the Georgia & Florida Railway."

60. J. D. Latimer, "The Greatest Year of New Railroad Enterprises," *Review of Reviews* 34 (October 1906): 447–60.

61. *Coffee County Progress* (Douglas, GA), January 2, 1936.

2–THE G&F EMERGES

1. "John Skelton Williams: The Center of the Latest Cyclone Gathering in Washington," *Current Opinion* 58 (June 1915): 399; Dumas Malone, ed., *Dictionary of American Biography* (New York: Charles Scribner's Sons, 1936), 10:279; "John Skelton Williams," Stock Exchange Historical Society, ca. 1906, John Skelton Williams Papers, University of Virginia Library, Charlottesville, hereafter cited as Williams Papers.

2. Malone, ed., *Dictionary of American Biography,* 279; "In Memoriam," *Georgia and Florida Railway Bulletin* (November 1926); *Macon* (GA) *Telegraph,* November 8, 1926.

As national prosperity returned in the late 1890s Williams told an audience in New York City that he wanted a South modeled upon the industrial North, indicating that he hoped "to see in the South in the not distant future many railroads and business institutions as great as the Pennsylvania Railroad, the Mutual Life Insurance Co., the Carnegie Steel Co. or the Standard Oil Co." And Williams added: "Business is reviving everywhere, capital will soon be seeking new investments, and with the right spirit evinced this capital can be turned southward. But it can also find *other* avenues of employment, and it will do so *unless* the South makes the most of its opportunity. I wish that this could be impressed upon every man interested in the progress of our section, in creating employment for its people, and thus in increasing the sum of its happiness." Richard H. Edmonds, "The Way to Permanent Prosperity," *Manufacturers' Record* 34 (September 9, 1898): 101.

3. Malone, ed., *Dictionary of American Biography,* 279; *Biographical Directory of the Railway Officials of America* (New York: Simmons-Boardman Publishing Co., 1922), 674–75; John Skelton Williams to E. Clarence Jones, November 27, 1906, Williams Papers; Cliff Downey, *Tennessee Central Railway: History, Locomotives and Cars* (Lynchburg, VA: TLC Publishing, 2005), 6–7.

4. Robert Wayne Johnson, *Through the Heart of the South: The Seaboard Air Line Railroad Story* (Erin, ON: Boston Mills Press, 1995), 39.

5. Burke Davis, *The Southern Railway: Road of the Innovators* (Chapel Hill, NC: University of North Carolina Press, 1985), 33–44; Howard D. Dozier, *A History of the Atlantic Coast Line Railroad* (Boston, MA: Houghton Mifflin Company, 1920), 138–56.

6. Johnson, *Through the Heart of the South,* 44–45; Dumas Malone, ed., *Dictionary of American Biography* (New York: Charles Scribner's Sons, 1935), 8:265–66; *Forest-Blade* (Swainsboro, GA), October 21, 1909.

7. *Forest-Blade,* February 4, 1909.

8. *Poor's Manual of the Railroads of the United States, 1906* (New York: Poor's Railroad Manual Company, 1907), C.

The circular edition appeared as "Plan of the Organization and Development of the Georgia & Florida Railway, Letter from the President to the Syndicate Managers, January 1, 1907," copy in Williams Papers.

9. *Florida Times-Union* (Jacksonville, FL), January 13, 1909.

10. John W. Middendorf to John Skelton Williams, July 12, 1907, Williams Papers; New York News Bureau news clipping, July 25, 1907, in Pliny Fisk Collection, John W. Barriger III National Railroad Library, University of Missouri-St. Louis.

11. John Skelton Williams to International Trust Company of Maryland, et al., January 12, 1907, Williams Papers; *Manufacturer's Record,* May 31, 1906.

12. *Poor's Manual of the Railroads of the United States, 1906,* D.

13. "Georgia and Florida Railway," July 7, 1906, Reel 58, Railroad Charters, State of Georgia, Microfilm Division, Georgia Department of State, Atlanta.

14. "Georgia & Florida Railway Financial Plan," January 1907, Williams Papers; Minute Book 1, Georgia & Florida Railway, November 12, 1908, 1, Norfolk Southern Archive, Atlanta, GA; John W. Middendorf to John Skelton Williams, April 22, 1909, Williams Papers.

15. *Douglas* (GA) *Enterprise*, February 27, 1909; "Corporate History of the Georgia and Florida Railway"; Interstate Commerce Commission, National Archives, Record Group 134, Box 560, hereafter cited as "Corporate History of the G&F Railway."

16. "Corporate History of the G&F Railway."

17. Douglas H. Gordon to John Skelton Williams, January 30, 1906, Williams Papers.

It became apparent that the G&F focused on the Augusta-Madison main line before it began to consider seriously other destinations. Yet the local press was full of rumors. In March 1906 the *Savannah Press* reported that "the object is to reach the Gulf of Mexico, and this may be done by building to Tallahassee to connect with the Georgia, Florida and Alabama Railway, which would take it to the port of Carabelle [*sic*], or a direct line south might be chosen. From 50 to 60 miles of new line might be required" (*Forest-Blade*, March 15, 1906). But once the main line opened, the Williams group considered more seriously other options, including a segment between Augusta and Columbia, South Carolina. Since the syndicate owned a position in the Augusta-Aiken Railway and Electric Company, this small Midwestern-like interurban between Augusta and Aiken, South Carolina, might be used, although upgraded, and a connection built between Aiken and Columbia. See James U. Jackson to John Skelton Williams, March 17, 1910, Williams Papers.

18. John Skelton Williams to J. William Middendorf, February 2, 1906, Williams Papers.

19. "Corporate History of the G&F Railway."

20. *New Enterprise* (Douglas, GA), February 28, 1907; *Nashville* (GA) *Herald*, May 26, 1906; June 1, 1906; *Railroad Age Gazette* 45 (August 21, 1908): 788.

21. *First Annual Report of the Georgia and Florida Railway For the Year Ending June 30, 1908* (Richmond, VA: Georgia & Florida Railway Company, 1908), 5.

22. *Douglas Enterprise*, July 11, 1908; October 10, 1908; November 21, 1908; *First Annual Report of the Georgia and Florida Railway*, 5.

23. *First Annual Report of the Georgia and Florida Railway*, 5; Minute Book 2, Georgia & Florida Railway Company, January 27, 1908, 6, Norfolk Southern Archive, Atlanta, GA, hereafter cited as NS Archive; Robert H. Hanson, compiler, "The Railroads of Georgia, 1833–2000," privately printed, n.p.

24. Minute Book 2, Georgia & Florida Railway, January 27, 1908, 6; June 21, 1909, 60–61.

25. *First Annual Report of the Georgia and Florida Railway*, 5; *Douglas Enterprise*, September 5, 1908; October 24, 1908; *Forest-Blade*, February 4, 1909.

26. "Georgia & Florida," *Railroad Age Gazette* 45 (August 28, 1908): 838; Georgia & Florida Railway Papers, Interstate Commerce Commission, National Archives, Record Group 134, Box 560; *First Annual Report of the Georgia and Florida Railway*, 5; *Douglas Enterprise*, August 22, 1908.

27. Minute Book 2, Georgia & Florida Railway, January 27, 1908, 6.

28. *First Annual Report of the Georgia and Florida Railway*, 6; *Fourth Annual Report of the Georgia and Florida Railway For the Year Ending June 30, 1911* (Richmond, VA: Georgia & Florida Railway Company, 1911), 3.

29. *Official Guide of the Railways* (New York: National Railway Publication Company, January 1911), 64; Minute Book 2, Georgia & Florida Railway, May 28, 1909, 41; *New Enterprise* (Madison, FL), October 31, 1907; William D. Edson, compiler, *Railroad Names: A Directory of Common Carrier Railroads Operating in the United States, 1826–1989*, privately printed, 1989, 74.

30. *Douglas Enterprise*, November 28, 1908; Minute Book 2, Georgia & Florida Railway, May 15, 1909, 18.

31. *First Annual Report of the Georgia and Florida Railway,* 6; *Second Annual Report of the Georgia and Florida Railway For the Year Ending June 30, 1909* (Richmond, VA: Georgia & Florida Railway Company, 1909), 4; *Douglas Enterprise,* May 2, 1908; May 23, 1908.

As an indication that railroad promotion remained an active part of the Wiregrass Region, the *Nashville Herald* of April 1, 1910, happily reported that "fifteen new railroads [are] now under consideration in Georgia against a marked decline in railroad construction for the whole country." Added the newspaper, "With their bank accounts swelled from the golden influx which followed the record-breaking crops of last year, farmers, merchants and professional men all over the state, and in South Georgia especially, have welcomed the opportunities presented to invest their new wealth, and at the same time lend to the material development of their various sections."

32. *First Annual Report of the Georgia and Florida Railway,* 7.

33. *Nashville Herald,* May 3, 1907; *Forest-Blade,* January 27, 1910; *Douglas Enterprise,* April 4, 1908; Minute Book 2, Georgia & Florida Railway, 7.

34. Minute Book 2; Georgia & Florida Railway, January 27, 1908, 5.

35. *Second Annual Report of the Georgia and Florida Railway,* 3; Minute Book 2, May 28, 1909, 53–54.

36. *Second Annual Report of the Georgia and Florida Railway,* 3; *Forest-Blade,* January 16, 1908.

The G&F initially did not own the A&GSL, rather controlling the property through majority stock ownership. *Railway Age* 42 (September 28, 1906): 396.

37. Minute Book 2, May 28, 1909, 54; *Forest-Blade,* June 3, 1909; September 23, 1909.

As early as 1906 Swainsboro showed excitement about being on the main stem of the G&F. "Let us have the G&F," demanded the local newspaper editor. "It is time for the people of Swainsboro to make some effort in the direction of getting this trunk line, or at least, it seems that way to us. There will probably not be such another opportunity" (*Forest-Blade,* June 14, 1906).

38. *Forest-Blade,* May 20, 1909.

39. Ibid., March 4, 1909; August 26, 1909; September 2, 1909; September 23, 1909; *Railroad Age Gazette,* November 26, 1909, 1037.

40. *First Annual Report of the Georgia and Florida Railway,* 4; *Second Annual Report of the Georgia and Florida Railway,* 4; *Third Annual Report of the Georgia and Florida Railway For the Year Ending June 30, 1910* (Richmond, VA: Georgia & Florida Railway Company, 1910), 4; *Nashville Herald,* June 25, 1910.

41. Minute Book 2, Georgia & Florida Railway, November 10, 1910, 15.

42. *Third Annual Report of the Georgia and Florida Railway,* 4; Wilber W. Caldwell, *The Courthouse and the Depot: The Architecture of Hope in an Age of Despair* (Macon, GA: Mercer University Press, 2001), 494.

43. *Poor's Manual of Railroads of the United States, 1911* (New York: Poor's Railroad Manual Company, 1912), 505; *Forest-Blade,* October 20, 1904; May 23, 1907; June 27, 1907; Hanson, "The Railroads of Georgia," n.p.

44. *The Biographical Dictionary of the Railway Officials of America* (Chicago, IL: Railway Age Company, 1906), 215; Cecil Gabbett to John William Middendorf, "Sunday," 1908, Williams Papers.

45. Hanson, "The Railroads of Georgia," n.p.; *Electric Railway Journal* 32 (September 19, 1908): 684; ibid. 32 (October 3, 1908): n.p.; *Poor's Manual of Railroads, 1911,* 569.

46. *Valdosta* (GA) *Daily Times,* November 10, 1910; *Fourth Annual Report of the Georgia and Florida Railway,* 3.

47. Minute Book 2, Georgia & Florida Railway, November 11, 1908, 30; September 14, 1910, 115.

48. Ibid., November 10, 1910, 15.

49. Ibid., May 15, 1908, 18; *Times-Union,* November 15, 1908; *Douglas Enterprise,* October 10, 1908; November 11, 1908.

50. H. Roger Grant, *The Corn Belt Route: A History of the Chicago Great Western Railroad Company* (DeKalb, IL: Northern Illinois University Press, 1984), 37.

51. *Douglas Enterprise,* May 16, 1908.

52. Ibid., October 10, 1908; November 21, 1908; February 27, 1909.

53. Ibid., November 21, 1908.

54. Ibid., February 20, 1909; *Second Annual Report of the Georgia and Florida Railway,* 6; Minute Book 2, Georgia & Florida Railway, May 28, 1909, 42, 52; April 21, 1910, 100; *Annual Report of the Georgia and Florida Railway to the Railroad Commission of the State of Georgia For the Year Ending June 30, 1911* (Atlanta, GA: Georgia Railroad Commission, 1911), 91, RCB-54058, Georgia Archives, Morrow, GA.

55. *Augusta Chronicle,* July 29, 1909; *Douglas Enterprise,* May 2, 1908; September 25, 1909; October 9, 1909.

56. Minute Book 2, Georgia & Florida Railway, March 12, 1910, 94; *Third Annual Report of the Georgia and Florida Railway,* 7.

57. Minute Book 2, Georgia & Florida Railway, November 18, 1908, 34; April 21, 1910, 98; "Georgia & Florida Railway—List of Passenger Equipment as of Nov. 1st, 1916," NS Archive.

58. *Fourth Annual Report of the Georgia and Florida Railway,* 14.

59. *New Enterprise,* June 11, 1908.

60. *Douglas Enterprise,* November 13, 1909; Georgia & Florida Railway public timetable, June 15, 1910; *Nashville Herald,* November 19, 1909.

61. *Douglas Enterprise,* March 5, 1910; Georgia & Florida Railway, Passenger Traffic Department, Passenger Circular 370, August 3, 1910, reprinted in *Forest-Blade,* August 11, 1910.

62. *Forest-Blade,* May 26, 1910; August 4, 1910; *Douglas Enterprise,* February 12, 1910; *Nashville Herald,* December 3, 1909.

63. *Douglas Enterprise,* July 2, 1910; *Fourth Annual Report of the Georgia and Florida Railway,* 14; *Forest-Blade,* June 30, 1910.

64. John Skelton Williams to James T. Wright, September 15, 1910, Williams Papers.

Williams not only promoted traffic, but he tried to assist communities along the line. In 1907 when the Ladies Aid Society of the Southern Baptist congregation in Gough, Georgia, sought to raise money for a church building, Williams responded by "handing you herewith check for ten dollars as a personal subscription towards this worthy enterprise." Mrs. A. M. Torbit to John Skelton Williams, March 13, 1907, Williams Papers; John Skelton Williams to Mrs. A. M. Torbit, March 15, 1907, Williams Papers.

65. *Third Annual Report of the Georgia and Florida Railway,* 8

66. *Fourth Annual Report of the Georgia and Florida Railway,* 10.

67. *Douglas Enterprise,* October 15, 1910; *Forest-Blade,* October 14, 1909.

3—ESTABLISHED AT LAST

1. John Skelton Williams to the Robinson-Humphrey Co., February 13, 1911, John Skelton Williams Papers, University of Virginia Library, Charlottesville, hereafter cited as Williams Papers.

2. "Report on Trip over Georgia & Florida Railway—Jan. 22 to 26, 1911," p. 2, Williams Papers.

3. Robert H. Hanson, compiler, "The Railroads of Georgia, 1833–2000," privately printed, n.p.; "Report on Trip over Georgia & Florida Railway—Jan. 22 to 26, 1911," 2–3; *Fifth Annual Report of the Georgia and Florida Railway For the Year Ending June 30, 1912* (Richmond, VA: Georgia & Florida Railway Company, 1912), 5.

4. "Report on Trip over Georgia & Florida Railway—Jan. 22 to 26, 1911," pp. 1–2; *Manufacturer's Record,* April 21, 1910.

5. Williams to the Robinson-Humphrey Co.; John Skelton Williams to E. M. Edgar, August 15, 1911, Williams Papers.

6. *Street Railway Journal* 31 (January 18, 1908): 102; 31 (February 29, 1908): 35; *Electric Railway Journal* 38 (August 12, 1911): 300.

7. *Douglas* (GA) *Enterprise*, November 12, 1912; *Swainsboro Forest-Blade*, February 13, 1913.

8. Max L. McRae to John Skelton Williams, May 4, 1912, Williams Papers; *Nashville* (GA) *Herald*, December 20, 1912.

9. Richard H. Edmonds to John Skelton Williams, May 28, 1912, Williams Papers.

10. *Wall Street Journal*, June 28, 1912.

11. *Nashville Herald*, May 12, 1911, *Fifth Annual Report of the Georgia and Florida Railway For the Year Ending June 30, 1912*, 6; *Official Equipment Register* 28 (September 1912): 407; 32 (January 1917): 5.

12. *Enterprise-Recorder* (Madison, FL), November 22, 1912; April 19, 1912.

13. *Official Guide of the Railways* (New York: National Railway Publication Company, January 1911), 1199; *Douglas Enterprise*, June 24, 1911; February 15, 1913.

14. *Douglas Enterprise*, July 19, 1913; *Nashville Herald*, June 6, 1913; July 23, 1913; *Enterprise-Recorder*, May 23, 1913; *Swainsboro Forest-Blade*, April 22, 1915.

15. *Nashville Herald*, May 29, 1914; *Douglas Enterprise*, August 4, 1917.

16. *Douglas Enterprise*, June 4, 1920; *Sparks* (GA) *Eagle*, June 23, 1916.

17. *Swainsboro Forest-Blade*, April 10, 1913.

18. John Skelton Williams to L. Huffer, May 4, 1911, Williams Papers.

19. "Concerning the Georgia and Florida Railway, 1911," Williams Papers.

20. *Fifth Annual Report of the Georgia and Florida Railway For the Year Ending June 20, 1912*, 4.

21. Ibid.

22. Interview with E. Frank Napier, Augusta, GA, September 9, 2004, hereafter cited as Napier interview; *Douglas Enterprise*, September 30, 1911; *Enterprise-Recorder*, October 6, 1911.

23. Quoted in *Nashville Herald*, October 6, 1911.

24. Ibid.

25. Ibid., October 13, 1911; *Fifth Annual Report of the Georgia and Florida Railway*, 4.

26. *Nashville Herald*, October 6, 1911.

27. *Fifth Annual Report of the Georgia and Florida Railway*, 4; F. Q. Brown to John Skelton Williams, December 12, 1911, Williams Papers; *Wall Street Journal*, March 31, 1915.

28. *Sixth Annual Report of the Georgia and Florida Railway For the Year Ended June 30, 1913* (Richmond, VA: Georgia & Florida Railway, 1913), 5; *Seventh Annual Report of the Georgia and Florida Railway For the Year Ended June 30, 1914* (Richmond, VA: Georgia & Florida Railway, 1914), 8.

29. Roland Harper diary, August 21, 1913, Roland Harper Collection, W. S. Hoole Special Collections Library, University of Alabama, Tuscaloosa.

30. *Nashville Herald*, February 7, 1913; *Seventh Annual Report of the Georgia and Florida Railway*, 30; *Richmond* (VA) *News Leader*, November 5, 1926.

31. Minute Book 1, Georgia & Florida Railway, November 29, 1913, 54, Norfolk Southern Archive, Atlanta, GA; *Financial America*, January 3, 1914.

32. *Swainsboro Forest-Blade*, April 1, 1915; *Eighth Annual Report of the Georgia and Florida Railway For the Year Ended June 30, 1915, Including Also Report of Receivers For the Six Months Ended September 30, 1915* (Richmond, VA: Georgia & Florida Railway, 1915), 5.

In a widely noted effort to increase cotton prices, Captain Charlie Hudson, a popular G&F passenger conductor, who lived in Augusta, developed what he called "The Hudson Plan," whereby everyone would buy a bale of cotton (for future sale) and acquire as many cotton goods as possible. The intent was noble, but the impact was negligible. See *Augusta Chronicle*, October 1, 1914.

33. *New York Times,* March 30, 1915; *Poor's Manual of Railroads 1921* (New York: Poor's Publishing Company, 1921),1926.

34. *Railway Age* 120 (January 5, 1946): 85.

35. *Poor's Manual of Railroads 1921,* 1926; *Biographical Directory of the Railway Officials of America* (New York: Simmons-Boardman Publishing Co., 1922), 674–75.

36. "Augusta Southern Railroad Company with Georgia and Florida Railway Agreement for Joint Use of the Line between Augusta and Keysville, Ga.," January 1, 1910, Virginia Tech Digital Library and Archives, Blacksburg, hereafter cited as AS-G&F Agreement; "Report on the Georgia & Florida Railway," (New York: Coverdale & Colpitts, 1925), 6–7; *Third Annual Report of the Georgia and Florida Railway For the Year Ending June 30, 1910* (Richmond, VA: Georgia & Florida Railway Company, 1910), 4.

37. George W. Hilton, *American Narrow Gauge Railroads* (Stanford, CA: Stanford University Press, 1990), 371–77.

38. Ibid., 373; *Poor's Manual of Railroads 1887* (New York: H. V. and H. W. Poor, 1887), 570–71.

39. Augusta, Gibson & Sandersville Railroad Minute Book, February 3, 1885, 26, Virginia Tech Digital Library and Archives, Blacksburg, hereafter cited as AG&S Minute Book; AG&S Minute Book, August 25, 1884, 3; AG&S Minute Book, May 12, 1886, 82; *Poor's Manual of Railroads 1887,* 570; *Station Directory No. 5* (Washington, DC: Southern Railway Company, July 1, 1912), 218.

40. G. P. Turner, "Railroads in the South in 1887," typed manuscript in Bureau of Railway Economics Collection, John W. Barriger III National Railroad Library, University of Missouri-St. Louis, hereafter cited as BRE Coll.

41. Ibid.

42. AG&S Minute Book, September 23, 1889, 178; AG&S Minute book, 220.

43. Augusta Southern Minute Book 1, May 8, 1894, 32, Virginia Tech Digital Library and Archives, Blacksburg, hereafter cited as AS Minute Book 1; AS Minute Book 1, May 5, 1896, 82.

44. Minutes of Sandersville and Tennille Rail Road, June 23, 1876, 9, Virginia Tech Digital Library and Archives, Blacksburg, VA; Hanson, "The Railroads of Georgia," n.p.; Mary Alice Jordan, ed., *Cotton to Kaolin: A History of Washington County, Georgia, 1784–1989* (Sandersville, GA: Washington County Historical Society, 1989), 49–50; AS Minute Book 1, May 8, 1894, 33.

45. *Poor's Manual of Railroads 1897* (New York: H. V. and H. W. Poor, 1897), 151; AS Minute Book 1, May 8, 1894, 34.

46. *Sandersville* (GA) *Herald,* August 16, 1894; August 23, 1894; AS Minute Book 1, May 8, 1894, 33.

47. *Poor's Manual of Railroads 1901* (New York: H. V. and H. W. Poor, 1901), 394; Burke Davis, *The Southern Railway: Road of the Innovators* (Chapel Hill, NC: University of North Carolina Press, 1985), 100; Augusta Southern Minute Book 2, November 22, 1909, 79, Virginia Tech Digital Library and Archives, Blacksburg, hereafter cited as AS Minute Book 2.

48. *Poor's Manual of Railroads 1915* (New York: Poor's Railroad Manual Company, 1915), 1606; AS Minute Book 2, November 22, 1909, 71–72.

49. Walter A. Clark, *A Lost Arcadia or The Story of My Old Community* (Augusta, GA: Chronicle Job Print, 1909), 193, 195–96.

50. AS Minute Book, 2, November 22, 1909, 82.

51. Ibid., April 19, 1911, 146–47.

52. Ibid., December 18, 1915, 252–53.

53. Ibid., February 13, 1912, 167, 180.

54. Napier interview; *Official Railway Equipment Register* 32 (January 1917): 5.

55. Ibid.

56. K. Austin Kerr, *American Railroad Politics, 1914–1920* (Pittsburgh, PA: University of Pittsburgh Press, 1968), 72–91; John F. Stover, *The Life and Decline of the American Railroad* (New York: Oxford University Press, 1970), 161; Aaron A. Godfrey, *Government Operation of the Railroads, 1918–1920* (Austin, TX: Jenkins, 1974).

57. *Enterprise-Recorder,* January 4, 1918.

58. Ibid., November 22, 1918; "The Short Lines," *Railroad Herald* 22 (May 1918): 125–27.

59. Ibid., 125; *Douglas Enterprise,* August 30, 1918; November 22, 1918.

The G&F was unusual in that at the time of final settlement with the USRA on December 31, 1924, the company owed money to the federal government, $55,256.51. See "U.S. Railroad Administration Final Settlements A to K," copy in BRE Coll.

60. *Nashville Herald,* December 19, 1919.

61. *Enterprise-Recorder,* December 26, 1919.

62. George H. Drury, *The Historical Guide to North American Railroads* (Milwaukee, WI: Kalmbach Publishing Company, 1985), 93–95, 187–89.

63. Quoted in *Enterprise-Recorder,* January 2, 1920.

At the time of proposed sale of the G&F, newspaper reports indicated that the SAL might buy the railroad. "There has not yet been any information given out to this effect, but it is a fact that the Seaboard officials have been going over the lines of the G. &. F., with officials of that road, and have spent considerable time in consultation over the matter." Perhaps the SAL was preparing to make a bid for all or some of the G&F. See *Swainsboro Forest-Blade,* January 15, 1920.

64. *Swainsboro Forest-Blade,* January 15, 1920; *Nashville Herald,* January 16, 1920.

65. *Enterprise-Recorder,* January 23, 1920; February 13, 1920; *Swainsboro Forest-Blade,* January 22, 1920; *Douglas Enterprise,* January 16, 1920; January 30, 1920; March 19, 1920.

66. *Sparks Eagle,* January 23, 1920; "The Georgia & Florida," *Railroad Herald* 24 (November 1920): 11.

67. *Swainsboro Forest-Blade,* November 25, 1920; *Douglas Enterprise,* November 26, 1920.

68. *Sparks Eagle,* April 1, 1921; *Vidalia (GA) Advance,* April 15, 1921; *Swainsboro Forest-Blade,* March 31, 1921; May 5, 1921.

69. "Report on the Georgia & Florida Railway" (New York: Coverdale & Colpitts, 1925), 84; *Augusta (GA) Chronicle,* December 6, 1922.

70. *Augusta (GA) Herald,* July 1, 1922; July 2, 1922; July 5, 1922; *Douglas Enterprise,* August 18, 1922.

71. *Douglas Enterprise* January 14, 1922; February 24, 1922; March 3, 1922; *Vidalia Advance,* March 30, 1922.

72. *Swainsboro Forest-Blade,* December 22, 1921; *Vidalia Advance,* December 1, 1921.

As with other carriers, management spent considerable time complying with the Valuation Act of 1913. The G&F, though, appealed the findings of the Interstate Commerce Commission that placed for rate-making purposes a value of $2,775,000 on the property as of June 30, 1917. The company believed that the valuation of its real estate, especially in Augusta, was too high. See H. W. Purvis to George B. McGinty, June 28, 1923, Interstate Commerce Commission, National Archives, Record Group 134, Box 560, and *Railway Age* 79 (December 5, 1925): 1071.

73. *Enterprise-Recorder,* August 24, 1917; *Sparks Eagle,* July 13, 1917; *Swainsboro Forest-Blade,* July 31, 1919; May 20, 1920.

74. Quoted in *Swainsboro Forest-Blade;* May 27, 1920.

75. *Sparks Eagle,* June 20, 1919; October 14, 1921; *Swainsboro Forest-Blade,* June 22, 1922; November 23, 1922; December 7, 1922; *Enterprise-Recorder,* September 25, 1925.

76. *Douglas Enterprise,* March 26, 1920; *Official Guide of the Railways* (New York: National Railway Publication Company, March 1922), 539; *Official Guide of the Railways* (New York: National Railway Publication Company, December 1922), 551; "Timely Talks, No. 15," Georgia & Florida Railway, December 8, 1924, BRE Coll.

77. Napier interview.

78. Ibid.; *Vidalia Advance*, November 23, 1922.

79. *Official Guide of the Railways* (New York: National Railway Publication Company, January 1923), xxix; *Swainsboro Forest-Blade*, December 14, 1922; *Vidalia Advance*, December 14, 1922; December 21, 1922.

80. Georgia & Florida Railway public timetable, Spring 1923.

81. *Swainsboro Forest-Blade*, March 8, 1923.

82. *Official Guide of the Railways* (New York: National Railway Publication Company, August 1923), xxvii.

83. *Swainsboro Forest-Blade*, December 18, 1924.

84. Ibid., January 31, 1924; January 1, 1925; *Douglas Enterprise*, March 26, 1926; "Seeing Florida and Cuba with Georgia & Florida R. R. Personally Conducted Tour" (Augusta: GA: Georgia & Florida Railroad, 1927).

85. *Swainsboro Forest-Blade*, December 12, 1924; January 15, 1925.

86. *Douglas Enterprise*, October 13, 1922.

87. *Sparks Eagle*, December 14, 1923.

88. *Swainsboro Forest-Blade*, March 31, 1916; "Brinson Railway Company," Harvey Fisk & Sons Papers, John W. Barriger III National Railroad Library, University of Missouri-St. Louis, hereafter cited as Fisk Coll.

89. Hanson, "Railroads of Georgia," n.p.; *Swainsboro Forest-Blade*, April 24, 1913; *Poor's Manual of Railroads* (New York: Poor's Railroad Manual Company, 1910), 390; "Brinson Railway Company (Savannah Northwestern Route)," Fisk Coll.; Brinson Railway clippings in ibid.

90. Hanson, "Railroads of Georgia," n.p.; *Poor's Manual of Railroads* (New York: Poor's Publishing Company, 1923), 2061; Les R. Winn, *Ghost Trains & Depots of Georgia (1833–1933)* (Chambler, GA: Big Shanty Publishing Company, 1995), 359.

91. *Swainsboro Forest-Blade*, November 24, 1921; March 27, 1924; May 11, 1922; *Douglas Enterprise*, April 4, 1924; *Poor's Railroad and Bank Section* (New York: Poor's Publishing Company, 1930), 1073.

92. "Acquisition of Line by Statesboro Northern Ry," Finance Docket No. 4030, *Interstate Commerce Commission Reports*, July 12, 1924.

93. Hanson, "Railroads of Georgia," n.p.; *Poor's Manual of Railroads* (New York: Poor's Publishing Company, 1919), 1415.

94. Ibid.; *Coffee County Progress* (Douglas, GA), April 2, 1931; *Douglas Enterprise*, May 7, 1931; "Savannah & Statesboro Railway Company Abandonment," Finance Docket No. 9771, *Interstate Commerce Commission Reports*, January 21, 1933.

95. *Douglas Enterprise*, December 11, 1925; January 1, 1926; "Timely Talks, No. 24," Georgia & Florida Railway, February 10, 1926, BRE Coll.; *Annual Report of the Georgia and Florida to the Georgia Public Service Commission of the State of Georgia For the Year Ended December 31, 1924*, n.p.

96. "In Memoriam," supplement to *Georgia and Florida Railway Bulletin*, November 1926, 1.

97. *Augusta Chronicle*, November 5, 1926.

4—"EXPAND OR DIE"

1. "Report on the Georgia & Florida Railway" (New York: Coverdale & Colpitts, 1925), 6, 12, 14; hereafter cited as Coverdale & Colpitts Report; R. C. Hicks to E. Williams, May 4, 1926, Charleston & Western Carolina Papers in possession of John E. Parker, Aiken, South Carolina.

2. *Douglas* (GA) *Enterprise*, March 1, 1913; *Augusta* (GA) *Chronicle*, February 23, 1913. For a time G&F board member Franklin Q. Brown served as president of the Augusta-Aiken Railway and Electric Company and its affiliate, the Georgia-Carolina Power Company.

3. *Enterprise-Recorder* (Madison, FL), March 7, 1913.

4. Thomas T. Fetters and Peter W. Swanson, Jr., *Piedmont and Northern: The Great Electric System of the South* (San Marino, CA: Golden West Books, 1974); Coverdale & Coplitts Report, 21; *Index-Journal* (Greenwood, SC), May 10, 1925.

5. Fetters and Swanson, *Piedmont and Northern*, 43, 45–47; *Index-Journal*, October 2, 1924; December 21, 1924; July 13, 1925; *Greenville* (SC) *News*, January 6, 1925; *Douglas Enterprise*, May 8, 1925; Robert F. Durden, *Bold Entrepreneur: A Life of James B. Duke* (Durham, NC: Carolina Academic Press, 2003), 127–28.

6. *Florida Times-Union* (Jacksonville, FL), August 25, 1923; August 30, 1923; *Tampa* (FL) *Tribune*, July 21, 1925; *Index-Journal*, May 20, 1925; *Douglas Enterprise*, April 10, 1925.

7. *Swainsboro* (GA) *Forest-Blade*, March 27, 1924.

8. Coverdale & Colpitts Report; *Douglas Enterprise*, February 11, 1927.

9. Ibid., 12, 23, 26.

10. Ibid., 23–25; *Poor's Manual of Railroads of the United States* (New York: Poor's Railroad Manual, 1913), 1441–42; James Hutton Lemly, *The Gulf, Mobile and Ohio: A Railroad That Had to Expand or Expire* (Homewood, IL: Richard D. Irwin, Inc., 1953), 296–307.

11. *Finance Docket No. 5812, Reorganization and Extension of Georgia & Florida Ry.* (Washington, DC, 1926), 473–89.

12. Ibid., 476–85; *Railway Age* 82 (January 8, 1927): 216.

13. *Finance Docket No. 5812, Reorganization and Extension of Georgia & Florida Ry.* (Washington, DC, 1927), 789.

14. *Finance Docket No. 5812, Reorganization and Extension of Georgia & Florida Ry.* (1926), 487.

15. "Georgia & Florida Railroad," Railroad File No. 180, South Carolina Department of Archives & History, Columbia, South Carolina.

16. *Index-Journal*, January 15, 1925; March 10, 1925; James H. Wade, Jr., *Greenwood County and Its Railroads, 1852–1992* (privately printed, 1993), 197.

Much earlier, part of the route that the G&F selected had been the proposed path of the Edgefield & Augusta Electric Railway, a project that largely Edgefield and Saluda backers unsuccessfully launched in 1908. See *Street Railway Journal* 31 (May 23, 1908): 880.

17. *Index-Journal*, May 15, 1925.

18. H. W. Purvis to F. S. Wynn, January 17, 1925; April 11, 1925; September 25, 1925; November 8, 1926; November 26, 1926; December 9, 1926, in Southern Railway Papers, Box 7, Virginia Tech Digital Library and Archives, Blacksburg, VA, hereafter cited as SR Papers.

19. *Index-Journal*, August 27, 1925.

20. *Douglas Enterprise*, March 12, 1926; *Swainsboro Forest-Blade*, March 10, 1927.

21. H. W. Purvis to F. S. Wynn, March 25, 1927, SR Papers.

22. *Edgefield* (SC) *Advertiser*, February 1, 1928.

23. *Index-Journal*, June 19, 1929; Davenport Steward, "The Georgia and Florida's Augusta-Greenwood Extension," *Railroad Herald* 33 (August 1929): 25.

24. *Edgefield Advertiser*, February 13, 1929; February 27, 1929; May 25, 1929; June 26, 1929; *Fifty-Second Annual Report of the Railroad Commission of South Carolina* (Columbia, SC: 1931), 5.

25. *Index Journal*, June 19, 1929; *Edgefield Advertiser*, October 3, 1928.

26. *Edgefield Advertiser*, November 11, 1928; January 2, 1929; January 9, 1929; February 13, 1929; May 1, 1929.

According to the *Edgefield Advertiser*, May 29, 1929, track laying progressed in the following fashion:

December 15, 1928. . . . . 2.5 miles total
January 12, 1929. . . . . . 10.3 miles total
February 1, 1929. . . . . . 19.7 miles total
February 15, 1929 . . . . . 27.2 miles total
March 1, 1929. . . . . . . .33.4 miles total

March 16, 1929 . . . . 37.6 miles total
April 1, 1929. . . . . .48.7 miles total
April 15, 1929 . . . . 53.1 miles total
May 1, 1929 . . . . .completed

27. Ibid., May 30, 1928; *Douglas Enterprise,* February 22, 1929; interview with J. Pete Belvin, Jr., Augusta, Georgia, August 31, 2004.

28. *Edgefield Advertiser,* February 6, 1929; February 13, 1929; *Swainsboro Forest-Blade,* April 11, 1929.

29. *Enterprise-Recorder,* February 22, 1929; *Index-Journal,* March 12, 1929; *Swainsboro Forest-Blade,* April 18, 1929.

30. *Vidalia* (GA) *Advance,* June 28, 1934; *Edgefield Advertiser,* March 6, 1929.

31. *Index-Journal,* March 31, 1929; May 9, 1929; June 9, 1929; June 18, 1929; *Nashville* (GA) *Herald,* June 6, 1929; *Swainsboro Forest-Blade,* June 6, 1929.

32. *Index-Journal,* May 5, 1909; *Swainsboro Forest-Blade,* April 11, 1929.

The prediction that the Greenwood extension celebration would be the largest such event in South Carolina fell far from the mark. Less than two months later, August 8–10, 1929, between 25,000 and 30,000 well-wishers attended the opening festivities of the Cooper River Bridge over Charleston harbor. As with the Greenwood gala, dedication of the new Charleston Airport was timed to coincide with the bridge opening. See Jason Annan and Pamela Gabriel, *The Great Cooper River Bridge* (Columbia, SC: University of South Carolina Press, 2002).

33. *Index-Journal,* June 2, 1929; June 3, 1929.

34. Ibid., June 14, 1929.

35. *Douglas Enterprise,* June 13, 1929.

36. *Nashville Herald,* June 20, 1929; *Swainsboro Forest-Blade,* June 27, 1929.

37. *Index-Journal,* June 19, 1929; June 19, 1930; *Greenville* (SC) *Piedmont,* June 19, 1929.

38. *Index-Journal,* June 19, 1929.

39. *Edgefield Advertiser,* June 26, 1929.

40. Ibid., June 19, 1929.

41. Ibid., June 5, 1929; June 19, 1929.

The only unhappiness that some residents of Edgefield had with the construction was spoken tongue-in-cheek. The *Edgefield Advertiser* of May 16, 1928, told of the engagement of a popular local woman, Elizabeth Lott, to Richard Minor III of Charlottesville, Virginia. "The fortunate young groom-to-be has deeply and favorably impressed the people of this community from the time he came to become associated with Winston and Company in the building of the Georgia and Florida railroad," noted the editor. "He is a young man of sterling qualities and his rectitude of conduct has been such as becometh a scion of an old and cultured Virginia family. It is thought that possibly in a few short months they will steal away from Edgefield to reside elsewhere. Here's hoping that it will take 40 years to complete the Augusta-Greenwood extension." In a more serious vein the paper editorialized on October 24, 1928, that "the Winston organization brought so many cultured and altogether lovely people to Edgefield who have greatly endeared themselves to many of our townspeople and their going away will be profoundly regretted."

42. *Edgefield Advertiser,* June 26, 1929.

43. *Douglas Enterprise,* June 20, 1929.

44. *Index-Journal,* July 8, 1929; July 23, 1929; *Edgefield Advertiser,* July 17, 1929.

45. *Index-Journal,* May 26, 1929; May 27, 1929; June 23, 1929; July 7, 1929; July 10, 1929; July 23, 1929; *Swainsboro Forest-Blade,* August 8, 1929.

46. Ibid., June 19, 1930; *Douglas Enterprise,* September 25, 1930.

47. *Index-Journal,* October 7, 1929; *Coffee County Progress* (Douglas, GA), October 24, 1929; *Swainsboro Forest-Blade,* July 31, 1930; *Nashville Herald,* October 31, 1929; July 24, 1930; *Georgia & Florida Railroad Report of Operations, 1929* (Augusta, GA: Georgia & Florida Railroad Company, 1930), 2; *Augusta Chronicle,* October 21, 1929.

48. *Nashville Herald,* October 24, 1929; *Railway Age,* 87 (November 2, 1929): 1077; *Edgefield Advertiser,* September 10, 1930.

49. *Augusta Chronicle,* October 21, 1929.

50. *Electric Railway Journal* 71 (April 21, 1928): 671; ibid. 71 (April 28, 1928): 708; *Index-Journal,* February 12, 1925; March 12, 1930; April 17, 1930; Fetters and Swanson, *Piedmont and Northern,* 43–47.

51. Glenn Hoffman, *Building a Great Railroad: A History of the Atlantic Coast Line Railroad Company* (Jacksonville, FL: CSX Corporation, 1998), 145–60; *Index-Journal,* January 15, 1930; February 8, 1930; June 20, 1930; *Coffee County Progress,* July 30, 1930; *Douglas Enterprise,* March 19, 1931; *Vidalia (GA) Advance,* March 19, 1931; William Way, Jr., *The Clinchfield Railroad: The Story of a Trade Route Across the Blue Ridge Mountains* (Chapel Hill, NC: University of North Carolina Press, 1931), 188–91, 214–18.

52. *Index-Journal,* October 17, 1930; *Edgefield Advertiser,* June 24, 1931; October 14, 1931.

53. *Edgefield Advertiser,* September 25, 1929; November 20, 1929; *Index-Journal,* November 18, 1929; December 3, 1929; December 6, 1929.

54. *Index-Journal,* December 7, 1929.

55. *Fifty-Second Annual Report of the Railroad Commission of South Carolina,* 133; *Fifty-Third Annual Report of the Railroad Commission of South Carolina* (Columbia, SC, 1932), 322.

56. *Fifty-Second Annual Report of the Railroad Commission of South Carolina,* 134; *Fifty-Third Annual Report of the Railroad Commission of South Carolina,* 324; *Fifty-Fourth Annual Report of the Railroad Commission of South Carolina* (Columbia, SC, 1933), 3; *Fifty-Fifth Annual Report of the Railroad Commission of South Carolina* (Columbia, SC, 1934), 20.

57. *Edgefield Advertiser,* June 12, 1929.

58. *Swainsboro Forest-Blade,* January 8, 1925; *Index-Journal,* January 23, 1931.

5—DEVELOPING THE WIREGRASS REGION

1. A quality literature exists on railroad land and town promotion activities. Several valuable studies are Paul Wallace Gates, *The Illinois Central Railroad and Its Colonization Work* (Cambridge, MA: Harvard University Press, 1934); John C. Hudson, *Plains Country Towns* (Minneapolis, MN: University of Minnesota Press, 1985); and Richard C. Overton, *Burlington West: A Colonization History of the Burlington Railroad* (Cambridge, MA: Harvard University Press, 1941).

2. Mark V. Wetherington, *The New South Comes to Wiregrass Georgia, 1860–1910* (Knoxville, TN: University of Tennessee Press, 1994), 2–3, 5.

3. Ibid., 3; *Georgia & Florida: The Nation's Garden* (Augusta, GA: Georgia & Florida Railway, ca. 1926), 9.

4. Willard Range, *A Century of Georgia Agriculture, 1850–1950* (Athens, GA: University of Georgia Press, 1954), 6.

5. R. Harold Brown, *The Greening of Georgia: The Improvement of the Environment in the Twentieth Century* (Macon, GA: Mercer University Press, 2002), 20; Clifton Paisley, "Madison County's Sea Island Cotton Industry, 1870–1916," *Florida Historical Quarterly* 54 (January 1976): 285.

6. *Moultrie (GA) Observer* quoted in *Tifton (GA) Gazette,* January 26, 1900; *Douglas (GA) Enterprise,* March 18, 1911; *The Heart of the Empire* (Augusta, GA: Georgia & Florida Railway, 1911).

7. Wetherington, *The New South Comes to Wiregrass Georgia,* 6; *Swainsboro (GA) Forest-Blade,* November 25, 1915.

8. Roy V. Scott, *Railroad Development Programs in the Twentieth Century* (Ames, IA: Iowa State University Press, 1985), 36–57.

9. *Greenwood (SC) Index-Journal,* September 5, 1929; *Enterprise-Recorder* (Madison, FL), August 30, 1929.

10. *Nashville* (GA) *Herald,* October 3, 1929.

11. Robert B. Outland III, *Tapping the Pines: The Naval Store Industry in the American South* (Baton Rouge, LA: Louisiana State University Press, 2004), 160; *Vidalia* (GA) *Advance,* April 6, 1939.

12. Range, *A Century of Georgia Agriculture,* 170–74; *Georgia & Florida Railroad Report of Operations, 1928* (Augusta, GA: Georgia & Florida Railroad Company, 1929), 4.

13. *Swainsboro Forest-Blade,* November 16, 1911.

14. Range, *A Century of Georgia Agriculture,* 172–74; Paisley, "Madison County's Sea Island Cotton Industry, 1870–1916," 301, 303.

15. *Swainsboro Forest-Blade,* February 16, 1917; *Georgia & Florida: The Nation's Garden,* 6–7.

16. Barbara Hahn, "Into the Belly of the Beast: The 2002 North Carolina Flue-Cured Tobacco Tour," *Southern Cultures* 9 (Fall 2003): 25, 32–35.

17. *Georgia & Florida: The Nation's Garden,* 19.

18. *Douglas Enterprise,* July 26, 1918; August 10, 1961; Warren P. Ward, *Ward's History of Coffee County* (Atlanta, GA: Foote & Davis, 1930), 242; *Official Guide of the Railways* (New York: National Railway Publication Company, March 1923), 3.

19. F. L. Spivey to S. B. Thompson, October 6, 1939, J. Pete Belvin, Jr. Papers, Augusta, GA, hereafter cited as Belvin Papers.

20. *Douglas Enterprise,* August 20, 1920.

21. *Enterprise-Recorder,* November 21, 1924.

22. Nannie May Tilley, *The Bright-Tobacco Industry, 1860–1929* (Chapel Hill, NC: University of North Carolina Press, 1948), 152–54.

23. *Coffee County Progress* (Douglas, GA), August 9, 1945; "Report for the Year ended December 31, 1944," Georgia Public Service Commission, 512, Georgia Archives, Morrow; S. B. Thompson to H. W. Purvis, October 1, 1939, Belvin Papers.

24. *Nashville Herald,* August 14, 1930; "Junctions via which Tobacco Shipments Moved, Seasons 1938–1939," October 1, 1939, Belvin Papers.

25. *Nashville Herald,* August 14, 1930.

26. Ibid., July 25, 1935; interview with E. Frank Napier, Augusta, GA, September 9, 2004.

27. *Nashville Herald,* January 6, 1938; January 20, 1938; *Douglas Enterprise,* January 13, 1938; *Vidalia Advance,* January 20, 1938.

28. *Nashville Herald,* January 20, 1938.

29. Range, *A Century of Georgia Agriculture,* 194–95; James L. McCorkle, Jr., "Moving Perishables to Market: Southern Railroads and the Nineteenth-Century Origins of Southern Truck Farming," *Southern Studies* 11 (Fall/Winter 2004): 5–7.

30. *Sparks* (GA) *Eagle,* January 28, 1916; February 11, 1916.

31. Ibid., February 28, 1916; *Swainsboro Forest-Blade,* January 19, 1917, August 25, 1921; Minnie Shaw, compiler, *History of Cook County* (Sparks, GA: Cowart Publications, 1984), 68.

32. "Timely Talks, No. 66," Georgia & Florida Railroad, June 21, 1929, Bureau of Railway Economics Collection, John W. Barriger III National Railroad Library, University of Missouri-St. Louis, hereafter cited as BRE Coll.

33. *Georgia & Florida: The Nation's Garden,* 11; *Enterprise-Recorder,* June 24, 1921; July 1, 1927; July 5, 1929.

34. *Sparks Eagle,* June 17, 1921.

35. *Swainsboro Forest-Blade,* June 28, 1934.

Until his death in 1941 George Kirkland, Jr., known to many as "Dens Kirk," for several decades contributed pieces to the *Swainsboro Forest-Blade.* A booster of Emanuel Country, the Wiregrass Region, and the G&F, Kirkland lived in the Summertown community. "Many of his productions were copied by national periodicals and he was quoted far and wide," observed Charles Rountree, editor of the *Wrightsville* (GA) *Herald,* shortly after Kirkland's passing. "Since coming here we have had the pleasure of carrying his articles from time to time." See *Swainsboro Forest-Blade,* March 13, 1941.

36. *Douglas Enterprise*, July 25, 1940; June 16, 1955.

37. "Timely Talks, No. 25," Georgia & Florida Railway, March 19, 1926, BRE Coll.

38. *Enterprise-Recorder*, December 18, 1925; July 16, 1926; February 15, 1927; *Swainsboro Forest-Blade*, April 17, 1930.

39. *Nashville Herald*, April 21, 1932.

40. *Douglas Enterprise*, May 30, 1924; *Nashville Herald*, April 4, 1946.

41. Thomas Frederick Howard, "The Onion Landscape of Georgia," *Geographical Review* 92 (July 2002): 452–60; *Vidalia Advance*, April 30, 1942; May 14, 1942; January 4, 1944.

42. *Swainsboro Forest-Blade*, May 9, 1929; *Enterprise-Recorder*, August 30, 1929; December 20, 1929; *Georgia and Florida: The Nation's Garden*, 3–4, 11.

43. *Douglas Enterprise*, June 15, 1923.

44. *Douglas Enterprise*, November 30, 1928; January 18, 1940; *Coffee County Progress*, October 13, 1938; January 11, 1940; *Vidalia Advance*, February 21, 1929; January 11, 1940; *Nashville Herald*, January 18, 1940; *Enterprise-Recorder*, November 30, 1928.

45. *Nashville Herald*, October 7, 1937.

46. John Skelton Williams to Col. J. M. Wilkinson, September 18, 1909, John Skelton Williams Papers, Box 21, Manuscripts Department, University of Virginia Library, Charlottesville, hereafter cited as Williams Papers; *Georgia & Florida Railroad Report of Operations 1929* (Augusta, GA: Georgia & Florida Railroad, 1930), 4.

47. *Douglas Enterprise*, June 15, 1923.

48. *Enterprise-Recorder*, April 4, 1924; *Douglas Enterprise*, April 18, 1924; *Swainsboro Forest-Blade*, April 4, 1929; *Nashville Herald*, March 15, 1928.

49. *Swainsboro Forest-Blade*, May [?], 1924; *Douglas Enterprise*, June 6, 1924; *Georgia & Florida Report of Operations, 1928* (Augusta, GA: Georgia & Florida Railroad, 1929), 16.

50. *Vidalia Advance*, June 21, 1928; *Georgia & Florida Report of Operations, 1928*, Exhibit B.

51. For the overall impact of the arrival of the Georgia & Florida Railway, see Wilber W. Caldwell, *The Courthouse and the Depot: The Architecture of Hope in an Age of Despair* (Macon, GA: Mercer University Press, 2001), 524–31.

When the G&F upgraded service on trackage that earlier had served communities likely developed by shortline predecessors, booms of sorts followed. One example was Olympia, Georgia, a station on the Valdosta-Madison line that dated from the days of the Valdosta Southern Railroad. See Albert S. Pendleton, Jr., "Olympia, Georgia and the West Yellow Pine Company," *Lowndes County Historical Society* 10 (January 5, 1981): 1–3.

52. *Douglas Enterprise*, February 20, 1909.

53. Ibid., March 27, 1909.

54. *Swainsboro Forest-Blade*, February 16, 1911; February 23, 1911; *Second Annual Report of the Georgia and Florida Railway for the Year Ending June 30, 1909* (Augusta, GA: Georgia & Florida Railway, 1909), 5; *Fifteenth Census of the United States: 1930: Population* (Washington, DC: U.S. Government Printing Office, 1931), 1:238; *Nashville Herald*, January 24, 1929.

55. *Nashville Herald*, October 14, 1910.

56. *Population by Counties and Minor Civil Divisions, 1910, 1900, 1890* (Washington, DC: U.S. Government Printing Office, 1912), 91; *Fifteenth Census of the United States: 1930: Population*, 231; *Swainsboro Forest-Blade*, September 7, 1905; May 22, 1913.

57. John Skelton Williams to E. L. Bemiss, March 22, 1911, Box 117, Williams Papers.

58. *Enterprise-Recorder*, August 9, 1912; *Douglas Enterprise*, June 9, 1922; *Vidalia Advance*, June 15, 1922; *Official Guide of the Railways* (New York: National Railway Publication Company, December 1922), 551; "Timely Talks No. 31," Georgia & Florida Railway, September 13, 1926, BLE Coll.; *Sparks Eagle*, March 30, 1928.

59. Roy V. Scott, "American Railroads and Agricultural Extension, 1900–1914: A Study in Railway Developmental Techniques," *Business History Review* 39 (Spring 1965): 87; *80 Years of Transportation Progress: A History of the St. Louis Southwestern Railway* (Tyler, TX: St. Louis Southwestern Railway, 1958), 59–61; Minute Book 2, Georgia & Florida Railway Company, July 12, 1912, 171, Norfolk Southern Archive, Atlanta, GA; *Sixth Annual Report of the Georgia and Florida Railway for the Year Ended June 30, 1913* (Augusta, GA: Georgia & Florida Railway, 1913), 7–8; *Ninth Annual Report of the Georgia and Florida Railway for the Year Ended June 30, 1916* (Augusta, GA: Georgia & Florida Railway, 1916), 6.

60. *Enterprise-Recorder,* February 27, 1925; March 27, 1925.

61. *Nashville Herald,* February 9, 1933.

62. See Range, *A Century of Georgia Agriculture.*

63. *Enterprise-Recorder,* July 26, 1935.

64. Ibid., February 15, 1935; June 21, 1935.

65. *Douglas Enterprise,* July 29, 1937.

66. Ibid., November 4, 1954; interview with J. Pete Belvin, Jr., Augusta, GA, October 28, 2004.

67. *Railway Age* 139 (July 4, 1955): 12; interview with J. Pete Belvin, Jr., Augusta, GA, August 31, 2004; *Douglas Enterprise,* March 24, 1955; March 31, 1955; Scott, *Railroad Development Programs in the Twentieth Century,* 108.

68. *Douglas Enterprise,* March 19, 1931; May 7, 1931; *Nashville Herald,* March 19, 1931; *Coffee County Progress,* March 26, 1931; *Bulloch Times* (Statesboro, GA), April 23, 1931.

69. Jonathan Raban, *Bad Land, An American Romance* (New York: Vintage Books, 1997).

6–DEPRESSION, WAR, AND CONTINUED CHALLENGES

1. *Who's Who in Railroading* (New York: Simmons-Boardman Publishing Company, 1930), 424; *Douglas (GA) Enterprise,* July 5, 1945; *Swainsboro (GA) Forest-Blade,* September 14, 1933.

2. *Commercial and Financial Chronicle,* September 13, 1924.

3. *Augusta (GA) Chronicle,* June 16, 1945; *Nashville (GA) Herald,* May 8, 1947.

4. *Who's Who in Railroading* (New York: Simmons-Boardman Publishing Company, 1940), 250; interview with Charles McDiarmid, Jr., Augusta, GA, October 14, 2004, hereafter cited as McDiarmid interview, October 14, 2004; interview with La Forest ("Tree") Meyer, Augusta, GA, October 28, 2004, hereafter cited as Meyer interview; *Augusta Chronicle,* March 3, 1949.

5. Meyer interview; interview with Charles McDiarmid, Jr., Augusta, GA, October 28, 2004; *Vidalia (GA) Advance,* April 26, 1928; *Douglas Enterprise,* April 25, 1935; *Coffee County Progress* (Douglas, GA), April 21, 1938; February 21, 1946.

6. McDiarmid interview, October 14, 2004.
Supporting the "workaholic" description, in August 1933 Hugh Purvis accepted appointment from President Franklin D. Roosevelt to become coordinator of 106 shortlines that operated under provisions of the recently passed National Recovery Act. This assignment was in addition to Purvis's role as co-receiver and general manager of the G&F.

7. *Official Guide of the Railways* (New York: National Railway Publication Company, September 1917), n.p; *Official Guide of the Railways* (New York: National Railway Publication Company, January 1921), 529.

8. *Railway Age* 89 (September 13, 1930): 560; *Interstate Commerce Commission Reports* (Washington, DC: Interstate Commerce Commission, 1930), 166:539–47; *Vidalia Advance,* March 13, 1930; *Index-Journal* (Greenwood, SC), March 26, 1931.

9. *Index-Journal,* March 26, 1931; *Swainsboro Forest-Blade,* February 15, 1940.

10. *Sandersville (GA) Progress,* August 9, 1934; *Interstate Commerce Commission Reports* (Washington, DC: Interstate Commerce Commission, 1934), 202:340.

11. Ibid., 338–39.

12. *Sandersville Progress,* November 15, 1934.

13. Ibid., August 30, 1934.

14. Ibid., October 11, 1934; October 18, 1934; *Enterprise-Recorder* (Madison, FL), November 2, 1934.

15. Ibid., November 22, 1934.

16. *Interstate Commerce Commission Reports* (Washington, DC: Interstate Commerce Commission, 1936), 217:49–52; *Railway Age* 101 (August 8, 1936): 225; "Reconstruction Finance Corporation, Railroad Division, Report [on] Georgia & Florida Railroad (in Receivership)," John W. Barriger III Collection, John W. Barriger III National Railroad Library, University of Missouri-St. Louis, hereafter cited as RFC Report.

17. *Official Guide of the Railways* (New York: National Railway Publication Company, March 1930), 657.

18. *Coffee County Progress,* November 14, 1929; *Vidalia Advance,* April 17, 1930; *Nashville Herald,* December 4, 1930.

19. *Vidalia Advance,* December 18, 1930; February 19, 1931.

20. *Swainsboro Forest-Blade,* March 26, 1931; February 15, 1934; February 22, 1934.

21. *Nashville Herald,* February 22, 1934.

22. Interview with E. Frank Napier, Augusta, GA, September 9, 2004, hereafter cited as Napier interview; E. Frank Napier to author, July 27, 2005; Stanley Berge, "Diesel Motor Trains, Part 1," *Diesel Power and Diesel Transportation* 28 (March 1950): 39. See also Debra Brill, *History of the J. G. Brill Company* (Bloomington, IN: Indiana University Press, 2001), 147–58.

The G&F eventually acquired a railcar from the Southern Railway, a shovel-nosed Fairbanks-Morse product, but this piece of rolling stock never handled regularly scheduled passenger trains. See Chapter 7.

23. *Douglas Enterprise,* June 4, 1931; October 6, 1932; *Swainsboro Forest-Blade,* March 23, 1933.

24. *Douglas Enterprise,* September 8, 1932; *Swainsboro Forest-Blade,* September 22, 1932.

25. *Vidalia Advance,* April 13, 1933.

26. *Coffee County Progress,* June 1, 1939.

27. *Moody's Manual of Investments: Railroad Securities* (New York: Moody's Investors Service, 1934), 625; *Moody's Manual of Investments: Railroad Securities* (New York: Moody's Investors Service, 1940), 1097.

28. Napier interview; *Sparks* (GA) *Eagle,* June 27, 1930; *Moody's Manual of Investments: Railroad Securities,* 1934, 624–26; *Moody's Manual of Investments: Railroad Securities,* 1940, 1093–94.

29. *Swainsboro Forest-Blade,* September 25, 1930; *Vidalia Advance,* August 20, 1931; *Nashville Herald,* July 13, 1933.

30. *Moody's Manual of Investments: Railroad Securities,* 1940, 1094; *Nashville Herald,* May 24, 1934; *Douglas Enterprise,* March 26, 1936; Merrill J. Roberts, "The Motor Transportation Revolution," *Business History Review* 30 (1956): 78–79.

31. Caption in Scrapbook, 7–102, John W. Barriger III Collection, John W. Barriger III National Railroad Library, University of Missouri-St. Louis, hereafter cited as Barriger Coll.

The 144-mile Savannah & Atlanta Railway also acquired two similar Pacifics from the Florida East Coast Railway, but paid somewhat more than the G&F, $2,075 per unit.

32. RFC Report.

33. *Nashville Herald,* May 12, 1932.

34. J. Pete Belvin, Jr. Papers, Augusta, GA, hereafter cited as Belvin Papers.

35. *Coffee County Progress,* August 25, 1932; Napier interview.

36. Roger Biles, *A New Deal for the American People* (DeKalb, IL: Northern Illinois University Press, 1991), 23–24; *Railway Age* 120 (January 5, 1946): 85.

37. *Interstate Commerce Commission Reports* (Washington, DC: Interstate Commerce Commission, 1932), 184:731.

38. Ibid., 332–41.

39. RFC Report.

40. *Railway Age* 93 (July 2, 1932): 32–33.

41. Memorandum to the Board of Directors from Hamilton M. Moore, Examiner, Railroad Division (RFC), June 6, 1935, Barriger Coll.; Memorandum in re Conference on Georgia and Florida Railroad, June 4, 1935, Barriger Coll.

42. *Railway Age* 107 (October 21, 1939): 638; ibid. 108 (June 1, 1940): 992.

43. *Moody's Manual of Investments: Railroad Securities* (New York: Moody's Investors Service, 1945) 92, 94.

44. Interview with Robert Hanson, Loganville, GA, May 18, 2004.

The poverty that plagued the Wiregrass Region occasionally prompted residents to act dangerously. In September 1937 passenger train No. 4, which carried seven loaded tank cars of gasoline, derailed near West Green, GA. Several of the tankers overturned or were tilted so that their contents ran into a large pool. "People in the vicinity brought every available empty vessel and helped themselves to the flowing gasoline. One party is said to have gathered up several hundred gallons of the escaping oil." See *Coffee County Progress*, September 16, 1937.

45. Napier interview; *Douglas Enterprise*, December 24, 1936; June 9, 1938.

46. Napier interview.

47. *Coffee County Progress*, February 25, 1936; *Douglas Enterprise*, February 27, 1936.

Most railroads operated the "Big Train." The flagship freight for the G&F was *The Goose*, and this daily movement helped to create a corporate identity. The passing of *The Goose* reminded employees that whatever other downfalls might occur, the G&F could still deliver goods with efficiency and even a sense of style.

48. Interview with J. Pete Belvin, Jr., Augusta, GA, August 31, 2004, hereafter cited as Belvin interview.

49. Ibid.; Napier interview.

50. McDiarmid interview, October 14, 2004.

51. Napier interview.

52. Ibid.

53. Ibid.; Belvin interview.

54. *Swainsboro Forest-Blade*, January 26, 1939.

55. *Nashville Herald*, August 7, 1941; November 27, 1941.

56. *Historical Statistics of the United States: Colonial Times to 1957* (Washington, DC: U.S. Department of Commerce, 1960), 430–31.

57. Napier interview; *Douglas Enterprise*, December 16, 1965.

58. *Coffee County Progress*, November 12, 1942.

59. *Railway Age* 112 (March 28, 1942): 678; *Douglas Enterprise*, October 25, 1945.

60. Napier interview; Albert J. Langley, Jr., *Georgia & Florida Railroad Album* (North Augusta, SC: Union Station Publishing, 2004), 25; *Douglas Enterprise*, September 24, 1936; July 27, 1944.

61. J. P. Belvin to H. W. Purvis, March 10, 1944, Belvin Papers; Napier interview.

62. *Index-Journal*, October 17, 1944; *Douglas Enterprise*, October 19, 1944; August 9, 1945; *Report to the President by the Emergency Board* (Augusta, GA, July 7, 1945), 3–4; hereafter cited as *Report to the President*.

63. *Report to the President*, 9–10; *Railway Age* 119 (July 28, 1945): 186; ibid. (August 18, 1945): 312.

64. *Coffee County Progress*, August 9, 1945; August 30, 1945; *Valdosta (GA) Daily Times*, August 14, 1945; *Railway Age* 119 (September 1, 1945): 119.

65. *Moody's Manual of Investments: Railroad Securities* (New York: Moody's Investors Service, 1949), 665.

66. *Railway Age* 120 (January 5, 1946): 85; *Moody's Manual of Investments,* 1949, 665; *Douglas Enterprise*, February 13, 1947; February 27, 1947; *Coffee County Progress*, March 6, 1947; D. W. Hertel, *History of the Brotherhood of Maintenance of Way Employes: Its Birth and Growth, 1887–1955* (Washington, DC: Ransdell, Inc., 1955), 210.

67. *Report on Georgia & Florida Railroad* (East Orange, NJ: William Wyer & Company, December 23, 1948), 3, hereafter cited as Wyer Report.

The G&F was fortunate to have engaged the services of William Wyer & Company. This firm, which later became Wyer, Dick & Company, dated from 1940 when William Wyer and Corwin Dick former their partnership. The philosophy of the two men was simple: "You must be able to do what you say." The Wyer organization was "honest, conservative, and well-staffed," and it developed a substantial business, particularly during the railroad merger craze of the 1960s. *Wm. Wyer & Co. Organized in 1940* (n.p., n.d.), 1; interview with Charles J. Meyer, Livingston, NJ, May 25, 1988.

68. Wyer Report, 10–13.

69. Ibid., 14–19.

70. Ibid., 20–21.

71. Ibid., 6.

72. Ibid., 24–25.

73. Ibid., 63–65.

74. Ibid., 65.

75. Ibid., 28–31.

76. Ibid., 31–45.

77. Ibid., 73, 78.

7—THE FINAL YEARS

1. *Nashville* (GA) *Herald,* January 22, 1948; February 5, 1948; interview with E. Frank Napier, Augusta, GA, September 9, 2004, hereafter cited as Napier interview, September 9, 2004.

2. *Douglas* (GA) *Enterprise,* January 29, 1948.

3. "Meet Our Receiver," *The Georgia & Florida Magazine* 4 (April 1958): 4; *Who's Who in America* (Chicago: A. N. Marquis Company, 1965), 36:1038; interview with J. Pete Belvin, Jr., Augusta, GA, August 31, 2004, hereafter cited as Belvin interview, August 31, 2004.

4. *Douglas Enterprise,* June 3, 1948; *Augusta* (GA) *Herald,* June 1, 1948; Napier interview, September 9, 2004; interview with Charles McDiarmid, Jr., Augusta, GA, October 14, 2004, hereafter cited as McDiarmid interview; interview with La Forest ("Tree") Meyer, Augusta, GA, October 28, 2004.

5. Napier interview, September 9, 2004; McDiarmid interview.

6. *Nashville Herald,* February 5, 1948; *Savannah* (GA) *Evening Post,* September 30, 1948.

7. *Coffee County Progress* (Douglas, GA), September 30, 1948.

8. Ibid., October 7, 1948; October 14, 1948.

9. Ibid., October 21, 1948; *Douglas Enterprise,* October 21, 1948; *Nashville Herald,* October 21, 1948.

10. Quoted in *Nashville Herald,* October 14, 1948.

11. Ibid., January 1, 1948.

12. Ibid.; *Douglas Enterprise,* January 8, 1948.

13. *Nashville Herald,* January 1, 1948; *Forest-Blade* (Swainsboro, GA), January 15, 1948; January 22, 1948; *Coffee County Progress,* January 29, 1948.

14. *Nashville Herald,* May 20, 1948.

15. Ibid., December 23, 1948; Napier interview, September 9, 2004.

16. Interview with Robert Hanson, Loganville, GA, July 17, 2004; *Nashville Herald,* November 16, 1950; *Official Guide of the Railways* (New York: National Railway Publication Company, November 1951), 673.

17. *Nashville Herald,* June 30, 1949; *Railway Age* 127 (July 16, 1949): 141.

At a time when the G&F and other carriers in the region began to trim trackage, a Philadelphia, Pennsylvania, entrepreneur, E. T. Mitchell, proposed building a 229–mile high-speed "Straight-Line" railroad between Atlanta and Savannah. By 1950, part of the route included the soon-to-be-abandoned G&F Statesboro Northern and Graymount-Summit lines. "The business people of Twin City [Graymount-Summit] have asked me to build the first portion of our line Swainsboro to Twin City soon as possible to restore railroad service to them. I have agreed to do this and am now extending all my efforts in this direction." The craziness of the concept, plus carrier and regulator opposition, torpedoed the Mitchell scheme.

18. *Augusta* (GA) *Chronicle,* July 13, 1950; *Traffic World* 85 (May 27, 1950): 26–27; *Railway Age* 129 (August 26, 1950): 63; *Douglas Enterprise,* May 25, 1950; E. T. Mitchell, *Proposed Southeastern Rail Road* (n.p., n.d.), 38; *Douglas Enterprise,* August 7, 1958.

19. *Madison* (FL) *Enterprise,* August 31, 1951; Russell Tedder, "Eskay, Georgia," *Yesterday and Today* 31 (March 2002): 3.

20. Napier interview, September 9, 2004.

21. *Madison Enterprise,* July 25, 1952; *Railway Age* 133 (September 22, 1952): 68; *Augusta Chronicle,* March 29, 1953; "Meet Your Patrons," *The Georgia & Florida Magazine* 3 (October 1957): 12–13; Belvin interview, August 31, 2004.

22. George W. Grupp, "Diesels in the Railroad Industry," *Diesel Power and Diesel Transportation* 28 (September 1950): 40–46; Maury Klein, "Replacement Technology: The Diesel as a Case Study," *Railroad History* 162 (Spring 1990): 109–20.

23. Interview with John E. Parker, Aiken, SC, May 13, 2004, hereafter cited as Parker interview; Albert M. Langley, Jr., *Georgia & Florida Railroad Album* (North Augusta, SC: Union Station Publishing, 2004), 23, 25.

24. *Report on Georgia & Florida Railroad* (East Orange, NJ: William Wyer & Company, December 23, 1953), 63–65; "G&F Locomotive Fleet Cleared of Debt," *The Georgia & Florida Magazine* 6 (October 1960): 8; *Railway Age* 127 (October 29, 1949): 782.

25. *Augusta Herald,* July 28, 1950; Parker interview.

26. "G&F Locomotive Fleet Cleared of Debt," 8–9; Langley, *Georgia & Florida Railroad Album,* 25; Belvin interview, August 31, 2004; "Douglas Shops," *The Georgia & Florida Magazine* 1 (July 1955): 9; *Douglas Enterprise,* July 2, 1959.

Belvin used the brass locomotive bells as gifts for corporate and personal friends, often adding inscriptions. The brass whistles mostly became table lamps, given to friends and kept for the Belvin family.

27. Parker interview; *Nashville Herald,* September 14, 1950; *Forest-Blade,* September 14, 1950; *Coffee County Progress,* September 14, 1950.

28. *Nashville Herald,* September 21, 1950.

29. Belvin interview, August 31, 2004; Parker interview.

Unquestionably, wind-electric generators became a distinctive feature of G&F rolling stock. In the early 1950s shopmen installed these inexpensive devices on most of the cabooses. "All G&F trainmen heaped praise upon George K. Rheney of Augusta for developing an electric lighting system for G&F cabooses which is not only economical and dependable—but unique in this section," wrote a company employee. Rheney, however, refused to take credit for the concept. "I got the idea from a Conductor . . . on the P&N. And I don't think the idea was original with him, either. We did make some adaptations to suit our own needs. . . ." Patrick Kelly, "Ever See a Caboose-Borne 'Windmill'?" *The Georgia & Florida Magazine* 4 (October 1958): 12.

30. Belvin interview, August 31, 2004; "Know Your Officials," *The Georgia & Florida Railroad Magazine* 1 (December 1955): 6; "Motive Power," *The Georgia & Florida Railroad Magazine* 3 (April 1957): 12, 15.

31. Belvin interview, August 31, 2004.

Railroad historian Robert Hanson observed that "I've heard similar stories regarding detouring Georgia Railroad trains and Clarks Hill, and similar wagers. Either the C&WC had a deep and abiding respect for the hill, or total disrespect for the neighboring roads' motive power. Or a third possibility, the C&WC had poorly maintained motive power." Robert H. Hanson to author, August 14, 2005.

32. Belvin interview, August 31, 2004; Parker interview; Langley, *Georgia & Florida Railroad Album,* 34, 40.

33. Telephone interview with E. Frank Napier, Augusta, GA, May 28, 2005.

34. *Jeff Davis County Ledger* (Hazlehurst, GA), March 18, 1954; C. L. Lott to J. P. Belvin, May 22, 1964, J. Pete Belvin, Jr. Papers, Augusta, GA, hereafter cited as Belvin Papers.

When Belvin received his promotion from traffic manager to chief operating officer, his salary increased from $6,378.42 to $8,629.55, yet hardly a stellar annual income for this position. He saw his salary, however, reach $15,000 for 1958, and he received a $3,000 bonus in both 1955 and 1956 and a $5,000 bonus the following year.

35. James Pete Belvin, II, *The Story of James Wiley Belvin, His Ancestors and Descendants* (privately printed, 1972), 58.

36. Ibid.; interview with J. Pete Belvin Jr., Augusta, GA, May 25, 2005, hereafter cited as Belvin interview, May 25, 2005.

37. Belvin, *The Story of James Wiley Belvin,* 58; Belvin interview, August 31, 2004; Belvin interview, May 25, 2005.

38. Belvin, *The Story of James Wiley Belvin,* 58–59.

39. Ibid., 59; Belvin interview, August 31, 2004; Belvin interview, May 25, 2005.

40. Belvin, *The Story of James Wiley Belvin,* 60.

41. Ibid.; Belvin interview, August 31, 2004; McDiarmid interview.

42. Belvin interview, August 31, 2004; J. P. Belvin, "Pointers on Showmanship at Fat Cattle Shows," n.d., Belvin Papers.

43. Belvin interview, August 31, 2004; Napier interview, September 9, 2004; McDiarmid interview.

44. Napier interview, September 9, 2004; *Augusta Chronicle,* May 18, 1951; *Who's Who in Railroading in North America* (New York: Simmons-Boardman Publishing Corporation, 1954, 13th ed.), 254; Belvin, *The Story of James Wiley Belvin,* 60.

45. Belvin interview, August 31, 2004.

The role played by the Savannah prostitute may have been "round house talk." E. Frank Napier to author, Augusta, GA, December 20, 2005.

46. Belvin interview, August 31, 2004.

47. *Douglas Enterprise,* May 3, 1956; Napier interview, September 9, 2004.

48. Napier interview, September 9, 2004; "Railroad Building and Facilities," *Georgia & Florida Magazine* 2 (October 1956): 10; Raymond Arsenault, "The End of the Long Hot Summer: The Air Conditioner and Southern Culture," *The Journal of Southern History* 50 (November 1984): 597–628.

49. *Augusta Chronicle,* March 3, 1963.

50. Interview with E. Frank Napier, Augusta, GA, October 26, 2004, hereafter cited as Napier interview, October 26, 2004; interview with J. Pete Belvin, Jr., Augusta, GA, October 28, 2004, hereafter cited as Belvin interview, October 28, 2004; E. Frank Napier to author, June 1, 2005.

G&F officers employed an imaginative, albeit illegal way to meet additional requirements of the new lodge. The main structure needed kitchen appliances and so an official found a carload of stoves and refrigerators in the Augusta yards. He called Belvin and asked which side of the stove and refrigerator would be placed against the wall. With that knowledge and alone in the boxcar, the individual used a hammer to chip out a piece of porcelain on each appliance. A damage claim followed and the railroad took ownership of the needed items.

51. Belvin interview, October 28, 2004.

52. Napier interview, October 26, 2004; McDiarmid interview.

53. Napier interview, September 9, 2004; Napier interview, October 26, 2004; "Georgia & Florida Credit Union," *The Georgia & Florida Magazine* 1 (December 1955): 5; ibid. 3 (December 1957): 13; "Auto Insurance Plan Announced by Credit Union," ibid. 5 (July 1959): 11.

Although not part of the Credit Union program, the G&F, with Belvin's blessing, allowed employees to purchase safety, steel-toed work shoes at J. C. Penney stores through payroll deductions.

54. Napier interview, September 9, 2004; *The Georgia & Florida Magazine,* December 1957, 13.

55. Belvin interview, August 31, 2004; *Augusta Chronicle,* September 26, 1957; "Going & Forward Progress," *The Georgia & Florida Magazine* (December 1958): 5.

56. Napier interview, September 9, 2004.

57. "Communications," *The Georgia & Florida Magazine* 3 (July 1957): 5, 7; Belvin interview, May 25, 2005.

58. Napier interview, October 26, 2004; "Radio Is Here!" *The Georgia & Florida Magazine* 3 (April 1957): 9; "Progress in Communications," ibid. 3 (October 1957): 7, 13.

59. "Communications," 5.

60. "Progress in Communications," 7.

61. "I.B.M. Data Processing Equipment Installed," *The Georgia & Florida Magazine* 5 (July 1959), 10; note from E. Frank Napier, May 31, 2005.

62. Parker interview; *Official Railway Equipment Register* (New York: Official Railway Equipment Register Company, January 1960), 7; Interstate Commerce Commission, *Finance Docket No. 20517* (Washington, DC: Interstate Commerce Commission, May 8, 1959), 6.

63. Napier interview, September 9, 2004. See George W. Hilton, *The Transportation Act of 1958: A Decade of Experience* (Bloomington, IN: Indiana University Press, 1969), 79–96.

64. Ibid.; *Railway Age* 146 (May 18, 1959): 7.

65. "Something New on the G&F," *The Georgia & Florida Magazine* 5 (October 1959): 8.

66. "Rehabilitation of Road Bed," *The Georgia & Florida Magazine* 2 (April 1956): 8–9; Stewart B. Austin, "Georgia & Florida Pushes Its 182–Mile Track Program," *Railway Age* 148 (May 2, 1960): 20.

By the 1950s the G&F experienced the demise of locally produced cypress ties. The treated hardwood alternatives cost considerably more than the durable cypress products. Moreover, tie replacement was often woefully inadequate. The saying went that "we just can't get the spikes to stick in the Bermuda grass!"

67. Austin, "Georgia & Florida Pushes Its 182–Mile Track Program," 22; Belvin interview, August 31, 2004.

68. Belvin interview, October 28, 2004; Belvin interview, May 25, 2005; Parker interview.

69. Interview with J. Pete Belvin, Jr., Augusta, GA, October 7, 2004, hereafter cited as Belvin interview, October 7, 2004.

70. *Douglas Enterprise,* January 9, 1958; July 24, 1958; Belvin interview, August 31, 2004.

71. Georgia & Florida Railroad, "Freight Schedules for Handling Carload Shipments of Fruits and Vegetables from Florida," 1958; Napier interview, October 26, 2004; transcript of Jervis Langdon interview, September 13–14, 1996, Railroad Executive Oral History Program #1, John W. Barriger III National Railroad Library, University of Missouri-St. Louis, hereafter cited as Langdon interview.

72. *Moody's Transport Manual* (New York: Moody's Investors Service, 1963), 9; Napier interview, September 9, 2004.

73. See Richard Saunders, Jr., *Merging Lines: American Railroads, 1900–1970* (DeKalb, IL: Northern Illinois University Press, 2001).

74. See Gus Welty, ed., *Era of the Giants: The New Railroad Merger Movement* (Omaha, NE: Simmons-Boardman, 1982); Saunders, *Merging Lines,* 277–84, 300–301.

75. William Norris Leonard, *Railroad Consolidation Under the Transportation Act of 1920* (New York: Columbia University Press, 1946), 305–6, 323–24.

76. Napier interview, September 9, 2004.

77. Belvin interview, October 7, 2004; interview with James A. Bistline, Kansas City, MO, October 1, 2004, hereafter cited as Bistline interview; *Augusta Chronicle*, May 6, 1963; interview with James Hagen, Harrisburg, PA, September 30, 2005; Bill Schafer, "The Professionals: A Southern Legend, D. W. Brosnan," *Trains* 60 (January 2000): 52–53.

78. Bistline interview; Langdon interview.

For a review of the SR's usage of ACL trackage, see George Eichleberger, "Southern Railway Trackage Rights, Part 2: The Atlantic Coast Line Agreements," *Ties* (November-December 1999): 314.

79. Belvin interview, August 31, 2004.

In September 1962 Brosnan testified before the ICC that "the policy of the Southern in recent years has been to acquire small railroads connecting with its lines in order to provide potential for industrial development which, in turn, will permit them to develop feeder traffic for Southern's main line operations."

80. *Moultrie (GA) Observer*, July 5, 1961; *Atlanta (GA) Journal*, December 12, 1961; *Southern Railway Company Sixty Eighth Annual Report for the Year Ending December 31, 1961* (Washington, DC: Southern Railway Company, 1962), 21.

81. *Interstate Commerce Commission Reports* (Washington, DC: Interstate Commerce Commission, 1963), 317:745, 747.

The intended corporate home for the G&F would be with two shortlines that the Georgia Southern & Florida, a SR subsidiary, had acquired in 1954, Live Oak, Perry & Gulf and the South Georgia.

82. Bistline interview; *Wall Street Journal*, January 7, 1963; *Florida Times-Union* (Jacksonville, FL), March 30, 1963.

83. *Atlanta Journal*, March 30, 1963; *Railway Age* 154 (April 8, 1963): 72.

84. Charles O. Morgret, *Brosnan: The Railroads' Messiah* (New York: Vantage Press, 1996), 1: 607.

85. Belvin interview, August 31, 2004.

86. *Coffee County Progress*, February 21, 1963; Belvin interview, August 31, 2004.

87. *Coffee County Progress*, April 25, 1963; April 30, 1963; *Southern Railway Company Sixty-Ninth Annual Report for the Year Ending December 31, 1962* (Washington, DC: Southern Railway Company, 1963), 28–29; *Albany (GA) Herald*, May 6, 1963.

88. *Coffee County Progress*, April 30, 1963.

89. Belvin interview, August 31, 2004; *Nashville Herald*, May 2, 1963; *Douglas Enterprise*, May 2, 1963; June 6, 1963.

90. *Augusta Chronicle*, April 30, 1963.

91. *Coffee Country Progress*, May 21, 1963.

92. Belvin interview, August 31, 2004.

93. *Athens (GA) Banner Herald*, June 5, 1963; *Coffee County Progress*, June 18, 1963; *Florida Times-Union*, June 14, 1963; *Douglas Enterprise*, July 11, 1963.

William Mahoney, an attorney for the Railway Labor Executive Association, explained the final agreement with the SR. "G&F employees, who are laid off and whose work will be transferred to the Southern, will receive monthly allowances equal to their present salary for four years, or less if they have been with the G&F less than four years. At the end of the four-year period, however, they would lose all seniority rights with the railroad. On the other hand, the employees could take a cash settlement for the allowance and thereby terminate their seniority rights immediately." Perhaps a third of the G&F employees, though, did not receive protection, and they were overwhelmingly maintenance-of-way workers, most of whom where people of color. See *Douglas Enterprise*, June 20, 1963.

94. *Wall Street Journal,* June 17, 1963; Burke Davis, *The Southern Railway: Road of the Innovators* (Chapel Hill, NC: University of North Carolina Press, 1985), 238; District Court of the United States for the Southern District of Georgia, Augusta Division, *Petition of Chemical Bank New York Trust Company, as Trustee, for a Decree Authorizing an Initial Distribution of Funds to Be Paid Over to It by the Receiver* (1963); C. E. Tiller to J. P. Belvin, July 9, 1957, Belvin Papers.

EPILOGUE

1. *Coffee County Progress* (Douglas, GA), July 30, 1963; *Douglas* (GA) *Enterprise,* October 24, 1963; November 19, 1963; interview with James Hagen, Harrisburg, PA, September 30, 2005.

2. Interview with J. Pete Belvin, Jr., Augusta, GA, August 31, 2004, hereafter cited as Belvin interview.

3. Ibid.; *Augusta* (GA) *Chronicle,* October 11, 1963; *Douglas Enterprise,* February 20, 1964; John E. Parker to author, August 25, 2005.

4. Belvin interview; Albert M. Langley, Jr., *Georgia & Florida Railroad Album* (North Augusta, SC: Union Station Publishing, 2004), 9.

5. Belvin interview; *Douglas Enterprise,* June 25, 1964; April 22, 1965; October 28, 1965.

6. *Coffee County Progress,* September 3, 1963; June 18, 1964; interview with E. Frank Napier, Augusta, GA, September 9, 2004; Belvin interview.

7. Belvin interview; Langley, *Georgia & Florida Railroad Album,* 34–35.

8. *Interstate Commerce Commission Reports* (Washington, DC: Interstate Commerce Commission, 1971), 338:353, 356, 358.

9. *Atlanta* (GA) *Journal and Constitution,* June 13, 1971.

10. Richard Saunders, Jr., *Main Lines: Rebirth of the North American Railroad, 1970–2002* (DeKalb: Northern Illinois University Press, 2003), 150–51; 228–31; Edward A. Lewis, *American Shortline Railway Guide* (Waukesha, WI: Kalmbach Books, 4th ed., 1991), 288–89.

11. Lewis, *American Shortline Railway Guide* (5th ed., 1996), 130–31, 321.

12. Langley, *Georgia & Florida Railroad Album,* 9.

Index

9 780875 803654